Understanding Atonement

for the Mission of the Church

JOHN DRIVER

Foreword by C. René Padilla

D0745781

HERALD PRESS
Scottdale, Pennsylvania
Kitchener, Ontario

Library of Congress Cataloging-in-Publication Data

Driver, John, 1924-
  Understanding the atonement for the mission of
the church.

  Bibliography: p.
  Includes index.
  1. Jesus Christ—Person and offices.   2. Atonement.
I. Title.
BT202.D635   1986   232'.3   86-3133
ISBN 0-8361-3403-6 (pbk.)

UNDERSTANDING THE ATONEMENT FOR THE
MISSION OF THE CHURCH
Copyright © 1986 by Herald Press, Scottdale, Pa. 15683
  Published simultaneously in Canada by Herald Press,
  Kitchener, Ont. N2G 4M5. All rights reserved.
Library of Congress Catalog Card Number: 86-3133
International Standard Book Number: 0-8361-3403-6
Printed in the United States of America
Design by David Hiebert

91 90 89 88 87   9 8 7 6 5 4 3 2

To
brothers and sisters
seeking to communicate
the meaning of the atonement
across the many boundaries
which divide humanity

Contents

INTRODUCTION

PRINCIPAL BIBLICAL IMAGES

CONTEMPORARY IMPLICATIONS

Foreword

At the very center of the Christian faith is Jesus, a crucified Messiah. All the wisdom and the power of God have been revealed in him. Apart from such wisdom and power no genuine Christian experience is possible.

Unfortunately, Western Christianity has been so conditioned by Constantinian presuppositions that it has failed to take into account the centrality of the crucified Messiah. It has been far more preoccupied with worldly wisdom and worldly power than with faithfulness to the gospel of the kingdom. It has concentrated on the salvation of the individual soul but has frequently disregarded God's purpose to create a new humanity marked by sacrificial love and justice for the poor.

Without the crucified Messiah at the center, Christianity becomes triumphalistic. It shuns suffering. It therefore avoids confrontation with the wise and the powerful of this world. As Dietrich Bonhoeffer saw it, this type of Christianity is based on cheap grace—grace without the cross, grace without discipleship, grace without Jesus Christ.

Nothing more radical could ever be suggested to people who have adjusted themselves to Constantinian Christianity than that which is proposed in this book: to reconsider the meaning of the cross. A serious illness requires a strong medicine!

For many years the author has lived in Latin America and Spain, where evangelical Christians, even in modern days, have sealed their witness to Jesus Christ with their own death. Could it be that in order to understand the meaning of the cross (and the meaning of the gospel) one needs to become personally acquainted with the suffering of the weak?

Those of us in Latin America cannot cease to be surprised at the many changes that have taken place here in the past few years within Constantinian Christianity. Of all the changes, however, the most amazing is undoubtedly one closely linked with the rediscovery of suffering as the badge of true discipleship. One cannot but hope and pray that the same kind of rediscovery may be made by Christians everywhere, especially in countries where the Constantinian accommodation has proliferated.

To this end, this new book by John Driver should be a great help. I do not know any other book on the atonement that does so well in showing the intimate relationship between the suffering of the crucified Messiah and the suffering of those who bear his name, between the saving work of Christ and his power to transform every aspect of life, between a theological understanding of the cross and an epistemology of obedience.

In the classical theories on the atonement, the work of Christ was unrelated to God's intention to create a new humanity. Driver here demonstrates that the covenanted community of God's people is the essential context for understanding the atonement. The reconciling work of Christ creates a reconciling community where all the barriers that divide humankind break down.

Driver's book is an invitation to look at the cross, not merely as the source of individual salvation, but as the place wherein begins the renewal of the creation—the new heavens and the new earth that God has promised and that the messianic community anticipates. May many readers heed its message!

—C. René Padilla
Buenos Aires

Author's Preface

As radical evangelicals, we all owe a considerable debt to evangelical scholars such as Leon L. Morris (*The Apostolic Preaching of the Cross*, 1955; et al.) and others who nearly a generation ago contributed substantially to a return from the vagaries of liberal Protestantism to a more biblical understanding of the meaning of the work of Christ. In this they have rendered a real service to the Christian church as a whole. However, the terms of this discussion were not conducive to a really radical return to a full-orbed biblical perspective. The focus of the conversations was largely limited to linguistic and doctrinal questions with which the doctrine of the atonement has traditionally been defined, such as the concepts of propitiation and expiation, the wrath of God, sacrifice, satisfaction, and others.

As a consequence of this somewhat limited definition of the problem, the Constantinian presuppositions of the principal theories of the atonement were left largely unquestioned. The essentially missionary context of the New Testament was not allowed to play a prominent role in understanding how the apostolic community used the wide variety of images to communicate the meaning of the work of Christ.

The continuing demise of historic Christendom and the increased urgency to find ways of communicating the meaning of the work of Christ in non-Constantinian situations, coupled with a fresh vision of the gospel being caught in radical evangelical movements of renewal, has furnished the occasion to move beyond the positions clarified by L. L. Morris and others to the articulation of a more full-orbed vision of the saving work of Christ. This vision seeks to be more fully freed from the presuppositions of Constantinian Christendom which have so often influenced the doctrinal understandings of the atonement and more fully in accord with the biblical missionary context. It is a vision which seeks to reflect more faithfully the pluralism of the New Testament.

11

INTRODUCTION

1

A Radical Evangelical
Approach to the Doctrine
of the Atonement

Since the time of their earliest confessions Christians have declared that "Christ died for our sins in accordance with the scriptures" (1 Cor. 15:3). Variations of this theme also appear in a number of the earliest Christian hymns recorded in the New Testament (Eph. 1:7; Phil. 2:7-8; Col. 1:20; 1 Pet. 2:21). But these statements, found in both confessions and hymns, are testimonies to the reality of the death and resurrection of Christ and to its saving efficacy in the life of the Christian community rather than rational definitions of the meaning of the death of Christ.

Judging from the writings of the New Testament, Jesus' followers experienced his life, death, and resurrection as the source of at-one-ment before they understood it. They saw and experienced this reality personally in Jesus' ministry to Judaism's outcasts, in the community-creating experience of Pentecost, and in the missionary ingathering of Gentiles in Palestine, Samaria, Syria, and finally in Asia Minor and Greece. From the earliest days of the primitive community in Jerusalem, the apostles began to find and use images to communicate and to explain the reality which they had experienced. They drew these images from the Old Testament, and just as Jesus had done, they also adapted the Old Testament and its images to the realities of their message. In this context a number of motifs appeared to aid new disciples in understanding the meaning of Jesus' messianic work, specifically his suffering and death.

Images of the Atonement

Rather than defining the church by means of dogmatic statements, the New Testament describes the church through the use of a series of complementary images which, taken together, reflect with remarkable detail the nature and mission of the church (cf. Minear, 1960:11-27).

The New Testament describes the atoning work of Christ in a similar way. Rather than simply offering formal dogmatic assertions, the New Testament writers employed a series of images (pictures) to depict the saving work of Christ and to interpret its meaning. While modern Western readers tend to favor literal definitions and cogent theories in order to clarify their understanding, this is not the biblical approach.

The mode of thought which characterizes the New Testament is dominated by recourse to pictures, analogies, and images, rather than employing merely prosaic language. Furthermore, New Testament use of imagery is solidly rooted in the story of the believing community. New Testament writers consistently reach back into the Old Testament for images to communicate their understanding of the work of Christ in the ongoing salvation history of God's people.

The terms *image* and *metaphor* are not used here as an alternative to the literal or real meanings of the work of Christ. The terms certainly do not refer to mere figments of the imagination in the minds of believers. By image we refer to terms or concepts whose meanings are not exhausted by the strictly literal sense of the term. New Testament descriptions of the work of Christ in terms of vicarious suffering, sacrifice, conflict and victory, ransom and redemption or liberation, reconciliation, or justification may be seen as pictures which point to, illuminate, and communicate a reality which is bigger than the terms themselves. No single term (or combination of terms, for that matter) is capable of wholly containing the meaning of the atoning work of Christ.

Some ambiguity will remain in our definition of image. When we ask for an absolutely clear definition of the concept, we assume that the New Testament is interested in distinguishing with clarity between imaginal and non-imaginal use of terms. However, this modern concern to separate sharply figurative and non-figurative expressions is foreign to the New Testament. The use of images such as dispersion, circumcision, and temple for the church illustrates this point. These basic images of the church are also non-figurative geographic, medical, and architectural references. The same is true of a term such as *redemption* which can refer to the historical reality of liberation from Egyptian slavery or to the concrete manumission of a slave, as well as all that God has done in Christ to free people from oppression by the powers of evil.

In the New Testament we note a certain priority assigned to the use of imaginal concepts. Words with decidedly factual connotations were filled with figurative meaning to the point of almost displacing the non-figurative usage. Images such as adoption and sonship illustrate this tendency. This, of course, is in contrast to the marked bias of nineteenth-century rationalism and Protestant orthodoxy, for example, in favor of concrete terms whose meanings could be more easily defined rationally.

The task of distinguishing clearly between figurative and non-figurative usage of language is difficult. The term *temple* illustrates this point. The word may refer to a particular building at a specific time in a certain place, but at the same time it can refer to the divine-human relationships which characterize the people of God. The concrete and the figurative meanings are interdependent and contribute to one another. Therefore, to insist on separating the figurative from the literal components appears useless. Furthermore, we may expect that vital images will carry more factual freight than first imagined, and that terms which appear to be primarily literal may also bear imaginistic meaning. It is therefore possible to affirm the rich variety of meaning which all of the metaphors applied to the death of Christ and its benefits communicate without undervaluing the literal connotations of those images.

The tendency to insist that terms be either metaphorical or ontological introduces a polemic into our understanding of the New Testament confessions of the meaning of the death and resurrection of Christ which is more akin to modern philosophical presuppositions than to biblical modes of expression.

Redemption, for example, refers to a concrete, observable, historical event in the life of God's people. Redemption is also clearly an image in that it refers to a restored relationship with God which is not equally visible in the same historical sense. When the New Testament writers applied this concept to the meaning of the death of Christ, they brought the imaginal power of this figure to the forefront. The redemption metaphor includes both literal and imaginal aspects of the saving work of Christ.

Likewise, reconciliation is a concrete reality in which relationships are restored among human groups alienated from one another. To reconcile means literally to bring people into council again, and this calls for restoring broken social relationships. But reconciliation is also an image in that its meaning surpasses the realm of observable concrete reality. It refers also to a restored relationship with God which may not be equally visible on a strictly historical plane. As a saving work of "God in Christ," the reconciliation image surpasses the boundaries which separate the purely metaphorical from the exclusively prosaic, embracing both in the process of understanding the work of Christ.

What special functions do images perform in the communication of the meaning of the death and resurrection of Christ?

First, metaphorical language generally carries the ability to communicate more powerfully (and more imaginatively) than purely prosaic language. This is certainly no less true of the images with which the apostolic writers understood and communicated the meaning of the saving work of Christ.

Second, images are also useful in understanding a reality which is not particularly amenable to purely objective observation or evaluation. Realities which rise out of the operation of divine forces of necessity require imaginal language to communicate that which is inherently mystery. The people of God have used images to understand and communicate the salvific activity of God.

Third, images also contribute powerfully to the self-understanding of God's people. The images used in the New Testament to understand and communicate the saving work of Christ are potent forces in the creation of the church's sense of identity. To know ourselves to be liberated, forgiven, redeemed, reconciled, justified, and adopted into the family of God is an essential foundation for adequately perceiving and soundly basing our identity. These images are rooted in the experience of salvation history. When authentic experience fades, the images tend to lose their meaning. On the other hand, they furnish a forceful means of recalling God's people to their roots in the life, death, and resurrection of God's Son.

Images undoubtedly fulfill these functions more effectively than do merely formal dogmatic assertions. The plurality of images used to understand the work of Christ is essential. The apostolic community allowed all to stand in a complementary relationship rather than attempting to reduce them to a single theory or a dogmatic statement. The value of any one of these images depends on allowing it to remain in relationship to all of the rest. Insofar as they have been held together, they have communicated powerfully the the meaning of the death and resurrection of Christ.

Where these images have become separated from an authentic experience of the saving work of Christ, their function has tended to become a mirror for self-contemplation or a yardstick to measure orthodoxy. This kind of separation robs the images of their power. But when properly connected, they enable us to perceive the mystery of the meaning of the life, death, and resurrection of Christ and to relate that perception to our own "missionary" lives. These images can thus speak powerfully to the church, recalling it to paths of faithfulness.

Conflict-Victory-Liberation Motif

A primary metaphor the early church used to explain the work of Christ was the conflict-victory-liberation motif. This image, as we observe from the Gospels, is rooted in the earliest experiences of the apostles with Jesus. We must recognize that this is a real conflict and victory, and by speaking of it as image or metaphor we do not detract from its reality but seek to enhance its meaning by including dimensions which are not readily apparent. Jesus himself understood his messianic mission in terms of conflict. His ministry began with temptation, conflict with the enemy. This theme is continued in a prominent way throughout the Gospels.

This image also has roots in the Old Testament. The theme of colossal conflict between God—on behalf of his people—and enslaving evil powers can be traced from the experience of liberation from Egypt all the way through the post-exilic prophets. Christ's victory over the powers is at the heart of one of the earliest of the Christian confessions (Phil. 2:9-11). This is the tradition which Paul developed into a major metaphor for understanding the work of Christ. This was an image which probably spoke to Christians of Gentile origin as well as to those of Jewish background, a factor which undoubtedly accounts for its continuing popularity in the post-apostolic period of the church's history.

Vicarious Suffering

The suffering-servant figure from the prophet Isaiah was probably the earliest image used by the apostolic witnesses (Daly, 1978:56-57). This was only natural, since they recalled that Jesus himself had understood his messianic mission and suffering in these terms. This metaphor predominates in the earliest of the Christian hymns (Phil. 2:7; 1 Pet. 2:21-25) and is the dominant Christological motif in the earliest apostolic preaching (Acts 3:13,26; 4:27,30). It also provides the theological content as well as wording for the institution of the Lord's Supper.

The fact that most of the uses of this image to describe the life and death of Jesus are contained in the Gospels seems to indicate two things. First, this was the primary way in which Jesus himself understood his messianic mission. Second, this image was considered essential in the apostolic church well into the second generation of the movement. This observation assumes the thesis that the Gospels reflect faithfully the content of apostolic preaching and were written to be read among converts of the Gentile mission during the period embraced by the fifth, sixth, and seventh decades of the first century.

In the Gospels Jesus' messianic mission is introduced and identified by use of references to the Servant Songs of Isaiah. These include his commissioning through baptism (Matt. 3:17), his announcement of the messianic program (Luke 4:18-22), his ministry of healings and exorcisms (Matt. 8:16-17), and his allusions to his approaching suffering and death (Mark 10:45; 14:24). The Lamb of God motif, so important in the Johannine writings, most certainly finds its primary basis in the servant poem of Isaiah 53.

Archetypal Images

Several archetypal images in the New Testament are applied to Jesus. These include representative man, pioneer, forerunner, and firstborn. Although in terms of frequency of use these Christological titles are relatively minor, they are closely associated in their contexts with references to the death of Christ and contribute substantially to our understanding of the work of Christ.

Jesus is referred to as "the one man" or "the last Adam" in Romans 5:12-21 and 1 Corinthians 15:20-22,45-49. Behind this vision of Christ as representative man stands the Hebrew concept of corporate personality. In this perspective Christ is viewed as the bearer of the destiny of humanity. Christ's representative role as the new Adam includes his vicarious death in absolute obedience to the will of the Father, a death in which we too participate. He is also representative in his resurrection. Redeemed humanity will eventually be conformed to his image. Christ, the representative man, creates a new humanity through his death and resurrection which constitutes a new social reality, a reconciled and reconciling community (Eph. 2:11-22). Jesus' death is a representative death. This image is especially useful for understanding the sense in which Christ's death is "for us." In this sense the suffering and death of Christ are not instead of ours, but rather they are viewed as representative and as a pattern to which we must be conformed. Thus Jesus' death calls for our death, the death of the old humanity, and his resurrection is the beginning of a new humanity.

Archegos, variously translated as author, leader, and pioneer, appears four times in the New Testament; in every case it refers to Jesus Christ and his saving work (Acts 3:15; 5:30-31; Heb. 2:9-10; 12:2). As *archegos* Jesus was recognized as the founding leader of the kingdom in which the primitive community held its citizenship. Through his obedience "unto death for everyone" Jesus became the originator of a new family of brothers and sisters (Heb. 2:9-11). Jesus is the founder of this community of faith by virtue of his role as pioneer of faithfulness. By his faith-obedience to God, even unto death, Christ perfected faith in God's unconditional love which alone is able to overcome the barrier of human sin. As perfector of our faith, Jesus is both the once-for-all actualization of God's love in salvation history and the source of his community's faithful obedience to the point of suffering (Heb. 12:2-4).

Another Christological title, *prodromos*, which occurs only once in the New Testament (Heb. 6:20), refers to Jesus as the "forerunner on our behalf." Since the phrase translated "on our behalf" *(huper hemon)* appears to be practically a technical term in the New Testament for understanding the meaning of the death of Jesus, forerunner is an image which contributes to our understanding of the meaning of the work of Christ. In this context, Jesus, who "learned obedience through what he suffered" and "became the source of eternal salvation to all who obey him," is seen as the forerunner in his suffering unto death: the prototype of the believers' obedient running.

The term translated "firstborn" *(prototokos)* appears five times in the New Testament and in three of these occurrences is an explicit reference to the saving death of Christ (Rom. 8:29; Col. 1:15,18; Heb. 1:6; Rev. 1:5). This particular Christological title points to the supremacy and uniqueness of Christ and his saving work as well as to his relationship to the "many brethren" in the new family of God which comes into existence through his work. The essential element in Christ's supremacy is his obedience unto death. This is the supremacy of Christ which the church joyfully confesses, since he is the one "who loves us and has freed us from our sins by his blood" (Rev. 1:5).

Martyr Motif

Another important New Testament image for understanding the meaning of the life and death of Jesus is the martyr motif. Although this motif has been assigned relatively little importance in the history of the church (with the exception of the earliest centuries), there are reasons to believe that it was an important image for the New Testament community. The gospel message of God's saving intention for humankind is called "the testimony *(marturian)* of Jesus Christ." This phrase is a striking feature of the book of Revelation where it appears seven times. It is probably best understood as referring not so much to a witness *to* Jesus, but rather as Jesus' testimony or witness. In line with this, Jesus Christ is called "the faithful witness *(martus)* . . . who loves us and has freed us from our sins by his blood" (Rev. 1:5-6). Jesus is the one who has preeminently shown himself to be utterly faithful in fulfilling his mission: to reveal God's character and saving intention as these are seen and experienced in his kingdom. Jesus was obedient in his mission even to the point of risking death.

When we recall that in the New Testament the same term covers both witness and martyr, we are provided with another of the early church's keys for understanding the meaning of both the life and death of Jesus. The New Testament depicts Jesus as witnessing faithfully to the coming of the kingdom of God even to the point of his death on the cross, to the point of becoming a curse according to the contemporary Jewish perspective. Jesus is the authentic witness-martyr in both of the principal senses of the term.

But the descriptive phrase "the faithful witness" is not limited to Jesus in the New Testament. In Revelation 2:13 the term is applied to the Christian, Antipas. The witness unto death of Jesus is the revelator's clue to understanding martyrologically the witness of Jesus' servants. Satan is overcome "by the blood of the Lamb [through the witness unto death of Jesus] and by the word of their [Jesus' servants] testimony, for they loved not their lives even unto death" (Rev. 12:11).

While the martyr motif is set forth explicitly in Revelation, it is implied in the Gospels and the Epistles where the witness of Christians is described in terms of participation in Messiah's suffering.

The *martus* family of terms in Revelation sheds light on both the biblical understanding of the meaning of Jesus' death as well as its view of the mission of his people. The revelatory-saving mission of Messiah required faithfulness to the Father, whose mission it was, even to the point of suffering and death at the hands of God's enemies. For the people of Messiah, faithfulness to their Lord in his mission in a world which has fallen under the dominion of Satan calls for a witness sealed by suffering and even death.

Sacrifice Motif

Ritual motifs of sacrifice were also used in the early church to understand the meaning of Christ's death. Although this motif may not have enjoyed the early popularity of the servant and conflict-victory images in the primitive community, it was also an early and important way of interpreting the work of Christ. It surely finds basis in Jesus' own understanding of his messianic mission and death.

The Old Testament sacrificial rituals of the burnt offering, the Day of Atonement ritual with its sin offering, the Passover sacrifice, the sacrifices with which the covenant was inaugurated at Sinai, and even the offering of Isaac, all contribute to the rather complex sacrificial motif with which the New Testament writers described the death of Jesus. This image is particularly prominent in Paul's writings, but it is also found in the synoptic Gospels (especially in the institution of the Lord's Supper), Peter's letters, the Johannine writings, and Hebrews.

Paul understood Jesus' death largely in terms of Passover and sin offering imagery, the two rites which the Jews of the New Testament period associated most closely with redemption and forgiveness. The phrase generally translated "for us" *(huper hemon)*, which is a technical phrase when associated with sacrifice, is common in Pauline writings.

A good example of Paul's application of the sacrificial motif to Jesus' death is 2 Corinthians 5:21: "For our sake *(huper hemon)* he [God] made him [Christ] to be sin [i.e., a sin offering] who knew no sin, so that in him we might become the righteousness of God." Romans 8:3 surely carries the same meaning, and in Romans 3:25 expiation can also be understood as means of expiation or sin offering.

Hebrews, more than any other New Testament book uses the sacrificial image to understand the work of Christ (Heb. 8:1-10:18). Christ is compared to both the high priest and the bloody sacrifice by which the sins of the people were expiated. But Hebrews makes it clear that the work of Christ is much more than an upgrading of the Old Testament sacrificial system. It is an image to help understand the ministry of God's Messiah who, in contrast with all who went before, achieved eternal redemption.

While Jesus did not pass judgment on the Old Testament forms of sacrifice explicitly, and a few texts even seem to presuppose that they will be continued (Matt. 5:23f.), his sayings concerning the transient nature of the temple imply that sacrifice is secondary and is destined to be transcended. In the New Testament, the Christian community, the locus of both divine and human reconciliation into fellowship, becomes the temple.

In reality, in the New Testament both temple and sacrifice are spiritualized and applied to the life of the new people of God. In the writings of both Paul and Peter, as well as Hebrews, sacrifice becomes a motif for understanding the nature of life in the Christian community—praising God, doing good to others, and living in communion with others, which includes the dimension of economic sharing (Rom. 12:1-2; 1 Pet. 2:4-10; Heb. 13:15-16).

So according to the New Testament, sacrificial motifs are important for understanding and illuminating the meaning of the work of Christ, but just as in the case of other individual images, they are incapable of exhausting or defining that reality. In fact, they spill over into descriptions of life in the body of Christ.

Expiation Motif and the Wrath of God

In ancient Israel's worship, there was one place above all others where God's presence was made manifest among people: the space above the cover of the ark of the covenant. Here at the mercy seat (*hilasterion*) the presence of Yahweh with Israel was actualized. Here Yahweh met the representative of his people during the ritual of the Day of Atonement. God had made sufficient provision for his people so that their sins and ritual impurities might be forgiven or expiated (*hilaskomai*), thus neutralizing the effects of the evil in their midst.

Joining the images of mercy seat and expiation in this way seems contradictory to modern readers. Mercy seat conveys the image of a throne from which the merciful God grants mercy or forgiveness. On the other hand, expiation is generally understood as a performance by the guilty person, or some kind of suffering inflicted on the guilty person, or some sort of payment in order to make restitution for the evil which has been caused. Therefore mercy seat and expiation are anything but synonymous in their commonly understood metaphoric senses. In the biblical use of the terms, however, we discover that the term for mercy seat is also translated expiation in the New Testament (Rom. 3:25), indicating a basic common meaning which totally escapes the modern Western reader.

For Christians of Jewish origin, mercy seat or expiation became a metaphor to elucidate the meaning of Christ's life, death, and resurrection on their behalf. Judging from the limited use of this image in the New Testament, it probably did not become as popular as other metaphors used to describe the work of Christ. Paul used this metaphor along with others to explain the meaning of the death of Christ (Rom. 3:25), and John twice used this metaphor to explain the work of Christ who had lived, died, and risen from the dead in order that forgiveness of sins and love for one another might characterize his community (1 John 1:7—2:2; 4:10-11).

Redemption-Purchase Motif

The redemption of Israel from Egyptian bondage was the point at which God's saving grace was most sharply focused in the Old

Testament. This redeeming act of God was to become a paradigm for God's saving action in favor of his people throughout their history.

So redemption was not originally a mere image or metaphor. It was a term used to describe a historical reality in the life of God's people as well as to refer to the manumission of slaves. This reality is what gives the image its metaphorical strength when it is applied to freedom from sin. The relationship between reality and metaphor is much stronger in the case of redemption than it is in some of the other images.

Therefore New Testament writers quite naturally would have picked up this image in order to describe the saving work of Jesus Christ. The experience of the early church was that Jesus Christ had indeed freed the new people of God from slavery to sin, to Satan, and to the evil powers. Therefore the metaphor of ransom, redemption, or purchase was especially appropriate. It was an image which could be applied personally in a meaningful way, as well as be used in its primary corporate sense as referring to the redemption of God's people. For Christians of Greco-Roman background the image was also meaningful since the manumission of slaves was carried out among them through the payment of a ransom, a purchase price. Here, too, the image was that of purchase out of slavery to become servants (slaves) of God.

Reconciliation

The reconciliation motif differs from other New Testament motifs for understanding the work of Christ in that reconciliation is not an image like the others. To "re-concile" means literally to bring people together into council again. This calls for restoring relationships. Reconciliation can be distinguished from other images in that this motif is not really an image. It is, rather, a real description of restored relationship which happens between people. It is figurative as an image of restored relationship with God only in the sense that the reality of God as a person is conceived of metaphorically; therefore alienation from God and restoration to relationship with God are realities described by metaphorical terms. But that two persons are reconciled is not an image; it is a reality. Reconciliation is a functional description of restoration to "council" relationships.

It is therefore perfectly understandable that the reconciliation motif would become especially appropriate to describe the meaning of the work of Christ when, as a result of the mission to the Gentiles, the church became a body made up of many nations. As one might expect, all twelve of the New Testament references to this image are found in the Pauline Epistles. In four of the five passages where the reconciliation motif is used, Paul refers to the new creation or the new humanity in which both Jews and Gentiles are reconciled into one body through the work of Christ (Eph. 2:14-16; 2 Cor. 5:17; Col. 1:20; 3:10-11).

In addition to this application, reconciliation was also used to describe God's initiative taken through Jesus Christ in reconciling humankind unto himself (2 Cor. 5:18-20). So this motif, scarcely used in contemporary Greco-Roman or Jewish circles, became a fundamental concept to explain the meaning of Jesus' saving life, death, and resurrection. The striking thing about the use of this metaphor in the New Testament is that in every case God graciously takes the initiative and, overcoming people's hostility, reconciles them to himself. This stands in sharp contrast to all pagan religious practice where people seek to achieve reconciliation by appeasing the hostility of the gods.

Justification

Another image, also firmly based in the history of God's people under the old covenant, was used especially in Paul's epistles to explain the meaning of Christ's passion: justice or justification, righteousness or setting right, and/or making righteous. The essential character of biblical justice is quite clearly stated in Micah 6:1-8, just one representative passage from the Old Testament. It is the form which relationships should take within God's covenant community. The foundation of these relationships is found in God's saving action.

The only adequate response to God's saving initiative is to act in a way which reflects God's character, to obey God's law with covenant faithfulness. This, rather than Roman legal understanding, is the background against which Paul's use of this metaphor is to be understood. Jesus is the clearest revelation of God's righteousness (Rom. 1:16-17). Paul understood that through Jesus' covenant faithfulness unto death people are made righteous (Rom. 3:21-26). Jesus' death is the point at which the revelation of God's righteousness comes into clearest focus. The cross was the result of Jesus' reversal of human values and relationships in his kingdom proclamation and activity. So a direct relationship exists between the life of Jesus, described in the Gospels, and the justification which results from his death and resurrection.

Adoption-Family Image

Sonship, or adoption, was another metaphor with which the early church understood what God does for people's salvation through the work of Christ. In three of the five passages in which the term appears in the New Testament, adoption is linked to redemption (Rom. 8:23; Gal. 4:4-5; Eph. 1:5-7), and in one of these passages it is explicitly related to Christ's death (Eph. 1:5-7). In Galatians 4:4 adoption is a parallel to the word *redeem*. This seems to indicate clearly that adoption was considered to be an image to describe the atoning work of Christ. Through the work of Christ we are brought into God's family.

While the use of this particular image is limited to Paul's epistles, the family metaphor is one of the most important New Testament figures for describing the new people of God. Brothers and sisters are the most common designation for the people of God in the New Testament. This family image is based on the relationship of Yahweh to Israel in the Old Testament; later and more directly it is based on the relationship of Jesus to divinity (Son/Father). In two of the five adoption passages the term *Abba* appears, underscoring the depth of intimate relationship with God which results from the work of Christ. Although this image has not generally been recognized as a metaphor for understanding the atoning work of Christ in the history of Christian thought, it apparently served this purpose well in the early church.

These appear to be the principal motifs which illuminated the primitive church's understanding of the meaning of the work of Christ—not of his death alone, although this is often the center of focus, but also of his life and resurrection. But we have good reason to think that *they were not looked upon as definitions which served to set limits to the meaning of Christ's atoning work*. In the New

Testament the reality of Christ's work in history and experience is primary. Subsequently, in the ongoing life of the church, metaphors which were drawn from the experience of God's people in the old covenant—or which were rooted in Jesus' own self-understanding as Messiah—were used to elucidate their understanding of Christ's work.

In the later history of the Christian church this process was reversed. Certain metaphors, as they were interpreted, were invested with dogmatic authority, becoming definitions of the meaning of Christ's atoning work. At times one particular image has become dominant and has been used almost exclusively to capture the meaning of Christ's death. At other times another metaphor has caught the imagination of its interpreters and gained ascendency.

Problems in the Church's Understanding

Constantinianism

A fundamental shift within the Christian church became especially notable during the fourth and fifth centuries. This new situation came to be called Constantinianism for Constantine, the Roman emperor at the time when the Christian movement was granted official toleration. However, the process toward Constantinianism had begun before the time of Constantine and continued long after him.

Constantinianism reflects the change from a scarcely tolerated and often persecuted missionary minority movement into an established social institution with the power to determine (sometimes by persecution) life within its own ranks as well as in society. In the process of change the ethics and the doctrines of the church were gradually adjusted to adapt to the exigencies of the new situation. The emperor himself became a Christian and began to exert his power in behalf of the church; all society was christened.

This was a situation notably different from that which the New Testament envisioned (see Mark 10:42-45). The most noteworthy changes came in the social ethics of Christians. For example, during the century following Constantine the church moved from being a persecuted, barely tolerated movement to a persecuting majority. At the beginning of the fourth century Christians systematically opposed military violence. By the beginning of the fifth century those who participated in the Roman legions had to be Christians.

During this period the meaning of being a Christian was gradually changed. Rather than being essentially a movement of Christlike people, the Christian church was composed of all those who confessed the Apostles' Creed, who accepted the apostolic canon, and who obeyed the apostolic successor, the bishop of Rome.

A similar change occurred in the understanding of salvation and the saving work of Christ. The benefits of the saving work of Christ were objectified in the sacraments. Baptism and the breaking of the bread became the sacraments of Christian initiation and of the altar. The immediacy of the spiritual and moral experience of the saving work of Christ became dim as the benefits of the death and resurrection of Christ came to be applied sacramentally, logically removing it one step from actual personal experience. In relation to the atonement a process began which gradually led to explaining the meaning of the death of Christ in the thought categories of the sacrament of penance.

An anecdote from officially Christian Spain may help us to appreciate some of the effects of Constantinianism on the way in which the saving life, death, and resurrection of Jesus Christ are understood. The story comes from the period immediately following the death of Francisco Franco, the twentieth-century military dictator who ruled Spain with an iron hand for nearly forty years. He had been a faithful Roman Catholic Christian, of course, and during the course of his life and immediately prior to his death he availed himself of the saving benefits of the church.

Shortly after Franco's death this slogan appeared in large black letters on a wall in Gerona, a city in northeastern Spain: "God can't be trusted. Franco is in heaven." The words of this dissenter to both the regime and established church in Spain express in a startling way a concern which believers, who insist on taking seriously the New Testament vision of the work of Christ and the salvation it bestows, intuitively perceive. The full-orbed New Testament meaning of the saving death and resurrection of Christ, and their consequences for the salvation of God's people and the restoration of creation, have come to be perceived as an abstract "saving" transaction which allows sinful and violent people and fallen structures to remain substantially unchanged. If this is what the saving life, death, and resurrection of Christ means, the logical conclusion is that the utterly faithful God of the Bible is no longer trustworthy.

This event happened in Spain with its Roman Catholic version of established Christianity. But the situation which has prevailed in Protestant lands of Constantinian orientation is not really different in substance. Here, too, the work of Christ has been interpreted as an abstract "saving" transaction which allows sinful and violent people (especially the powerful) and corrupted structures to remain substantially unchanged. The literal ethical components of Christ's saving work have gradually atrophied, and the transcendent aspects, especially of sacrifice and expiation which lent themselves more easily to sacramental expression, became almost exclusively the lens through which the saving work of Christ was viewed. The practical results of this Constantinian shift in the way of perceiving the atoning work of Christ soon appeared. Admittedly un-Christlike people could be assured of the benefits of the saving death of Christ, bereft of its power to transform.

Demand for Rationality

The theological orientation of individuals or groups often seems to determine their preference for the metaphor or metaphors with which they illuminate their doctrine of the atonement. This temptation to choose from among the metaphors, in the interests of clarity or rationality, has served to impoverish the church's understanding of the atonement. What to logical modern Western minds may appear to be a defect in the New Testament is, in fact, a strength. The images which appear in the New Testament were most certainly used because they were needed to elucidate the work of Christ in some particular place and in some special situation. No image by itself is capable of carrying all of the meaning of the reality of Christ's saving work.

We will therefore do well to allow all of the images to stand in juxtaposition with one another, each making its particular contributions to our understanding, rather than to try to force all (or at least as many as we can make fit) into a rational theory of the atonement. While the interest in logic has certainly characterized the history of Christian thought in the West, this does not seem to have been a primary concern of either the Old or the New Testament.

However, simply to make use of all of the biblical metaphors is not sufficient. They should also be understood, insofar as this is possible, in their biblical sense. This fundamental rule covers all literary interpretation. The following example related to our study will serve to illustrate the importance of this hermeneutical principle.

The Misconception of Law

The juridical motif of justification is an important image in the biblical understanding of the atonement. However, in the history of the Western church this key image has generally been interpreted from the perspective of a Roman concept of law, coupled with the typical Western preoccupation with the problem of guilt. In the Bible, law was understood as covenant law, the expression of God's intention for relationships within his redeemed community. Law in ancient Israel did not require a static or meticulous perfection, but it supposed a covenant relationship in which were provisions for forgiveness and repentance and where God was gracious. In Judaism we observe a deformation of covenant law in the direction of legalism. This deformation of law was what both Jesus and Paul denounced so forcefully.

A similar misunderstanding of law occurred in the Christian church from around the third century onward. Instead of holding to the concept of biblical covenant law, the paradigm for understanding juridical metaphors became the Roman concept of law which was not only distributive but predominantly retributive. Law, rather than primarily reflecting God's intention for right relationships within the community of grace, became a system of just reward and equivalent retribution. Therefore transgression of the law required just punishment rather than the kind of forgiveness and repentance which had characterized covenant law at its best. This makes a place for the sense of guilt which from Augustine onward has become so prominent in Western Christianity. This problem of guilt became the central focus in the juridical image for understanding the atonement. Luther's well-known struggle with his sense of guilt in his desperate search for a gracious God was a part of this Augustinian legacy. Paul's juridical images were read from the perspective of the struggles of conscience we find in men such as Augustine and Luther (Stendahl, 1976:78-96).

Preoccupation with Guilt

However, when one approaches the biblical text without this Western legal bias, one finds that Paul had a remarkably robust conscience (Phil. 3:6). Paul's Damascus-road encounter was a messianic conversion in which he realized that Jesus was Messiah, not a conversion in the sense of restoration from the effects of a plagued conscience. When Paul talked about forgetting what was behind him (Phil. 3:13), he meant not his shortcomings in his attempt to obey the law, but his achievements as a righteous Jew. A faithful response to the utterly faithful Messiah characterized Paul's life from that point onward. Rather than merely being concerned about the question of juridical guilt, Paul was profoundly committed to establishing obedience in God's community (Rom. 8:4; Eph. 2:10; Gal. 1:4; Titus 2:11-14; Phil. 2:12-15). This concern accounts for the extensive "ethical" sections generally found in Paul's epistles. Rather than being viewed as practical and secondary applications of Paul's doctrine of justification, these passages would be better understood as concrete descriptions of the way in which the righteousness of God is realized among people.

To understand law as basically a system of just retribution and sin as primarily guilt which deserves punishment is to read the New Testament from the post-biblical perspective of Roman law and a Western sense of guilt.

This concept of law is an understandable consequence of the Constantinian vision of church and society. With the christening of the entire society, law was dislodged from the context of grace which had always characterized biblical covenant law. Therefore it became relatively natural to transfer the legal concepts of punishment and guilt from secular society to the church's self-understanding.

In the biblical perspective of God's gracious covenant which provided the context of his saving relationship with his people, God's wrath was in reality his response to covenant violation in the interests of protecting this merciful and loving relationship. However, with the fading of the biblical vision of covenant, God increasingly came to be viewed in terms of the ancient Greek and Roman deities whose wrath called for appeasement and whose anger must be placated by religious means.

The Constantinian situation also made it necessary to place salvation within the reach of all of society, more or less as it was, since by political and ecclesiastical definition it was Christian. Therefore the means of salvation came to be basically sacramental. In Roman Catholicism the process was understood as *ex opere operato,* achieved in the operation of the sacrament itself. The sacraments, in and of themselves, were viewed as vehicles of God's saving grace. In Constantinian Protestantism salvation came to be understood in sola-fideistic terms; justification by "faith alone" came to mean "being declared righteous even though one is not." (The term *solafideism* here is understood to refer to a practically unilateral emphasis on the fact of "salvation by faith alone" to the point of neglecting the biblical meanings and consequences of a living faith and the wholeness of salvation.) In both cases, the means of grace were more easily placed within the reach of all, for all practical purposes. In Catholicism guilt was understood as indebtedness and dealt with by means of the penitential process of attrition, confession, satisfaction, and absolution. In Protestantism the guilt was removed through forensic justification—a legal declaration of righteousness, as if one were already righteous, even though it was not yet the case. In reality, it was a legal fiction.

The absence of a covenanted community of God's people as the essential context for understanding the atoning work of Christ became the occasion for reinterpretation of biblical images and categories in terms of the practices and thought patterns of Western Christendom. Old Testament sacrifice was understood as a means to placate the anger of God; this function was transferred to Jesus as lamb of God. This explains the disproportionate emphasis on the sacrament of the Lord's body in Catholicism as well as long-standing belief in Protestantism that "the only thing really essential to our salvation is the death of Christ, as an innocent victim."

It was not only necessary that sin be expiated. The righteous anger of God must also be propitiated. In light of this need, the biblical image of redemption, or of being ransomed, from slavery to sin was transferred into being freed from indebtedness to God.

The most logical and rationally appealing theory of the atonement, as well as the most widely influential in Western Christianity, was conceived and has been perpetuated in this Constantinian matrix. In this new social situation more than 1,000 years removed from the New Testament, St. Anselm elaborated this theory in the High Middle Ages in an attempt to articulate an explanation of the death of Christ which was compatible with the sacramental practice of medieval Catholicism. And, as we have noted, this theory, with some adaptations, has also proved to be useful within established Protestantism.

A Radical Evangelical Understanding of the Atonement

The thesis of this study is that a radical evangelical approach to understanding the atonement will make a real difference in the way the church sees its mission. In a freely committed covenant community, the category of law can once again be restored to the function it was intended to fulfill in ancient Israel and in the New Testament community.

In the perspective of the new people of God, the entire mission of Messiah becomes of fundamental importance. The salvation of God's community depends on the life, death, and resurrection of Christ in their entirety.

We must distinguish clearly between the kinds of images for understanding the saving work of Christ which appear in the New Testament and theories of the atonement which have developed in Christian history. Images are pictures of a reality which is bigger than themselves. Therefore images stand in complementary relationship to one another. On the other hand, a theory is based on a systematic analysis, elucidation, or definition of a concept and is a conception or series of propositions formed by speculation, deduction, or abstraction and generalization from the facts as these have been observed. The urge to formulate theories is understandable, but the church runs the risk of deforming or partializing the reality which it seeks to understand more clearly.

All of these images employed by the writers of the New Testament are essential to our understanding of the atonement. They all carry the authority of apostolic witness; all have proved their usefulness in the life of the church; all are necessary for a full-orbed biblical understanding of the meaning of Christ's life, death, and resurrection on our behalf. But these images must be understood in the specific biblical context of their symbolic meaning. This calls for radical interpretation which goes beyond the relatively recent theories and interpretations of the atonement all the way back to the biblical roots themselves.

According to the New Testament, knowledge grows out of obedience, rather than leading to obedience, as Western people have generally imagined. Therefore this calls for an epistemology of obedience. God's original intention for humankind was the creation of communion. Every strand of New Testament literature makes it clear that God's purpose with humanity is still to establish obedience in his communion. Only in the context of this faithful community is the true meaning of the saving work of Christ experienced and understood and integrated into its ongoing life and mission.

2

Review and Critique
of Principal Theories
of the Atonement

The first chapter contained a brief résumé of the principal images which the New Testament writers employed in order to describe the saving work of Christ. Before reflecting on these images in more detail, we will now review and critique several of the principal theories of the atonement which have been developed in the course of Christian history.

An image is a picture or a figure which is used to convey the meaning of a reality which may be bigger than the image itself. It seeks to understand and communicate the reality without attempting to gather all aspects into a rational or systematic whole. The New Testament allows a number of images to stand in complementary relationship to one another in order to depict the meaning of the work of Christ.

On the other hand, the theories of the atonement with which we will be dealing are human post-biblical constructions which try to explain in rationally satisfactory ways things which are not explained in a fully logical way in the biblical material itself. A theory includes an intentional concern for consistency and logic with a view to being able to protect itself from other less adequate formulations. While the urge to formulate satisfactory theories is understandable and in many instances may prove useful, inherent limitations must be recognized. While a theory may attempt to take into account all the biblical material included in the images, it goes beyond them in proposing answers to questions about system, verifiability, coherence, and consistency.

Classical Western Christianity has produced three major theories of the atonement. The first to arise was the so-called dramatic theory which sought to understand the saving work of Christ in terms of the cosmic drama of conflict and victory. This theory flourished especially during the early period of Christian history, between the second and the sixth centuries, but it has also received renewed attention in the twentieth century, thanks to the work of theologians such as Gustaf Aulén.

The two remaining theories were not systematically articulated until the end of the eleventh century and the beginning of the twelfth century. Anselm of Canterbury (1033-1109) developed what has been called the satisfaction theory. It is also known as an objective view, since it concentrates on what the saving work of Christ accomplishes outside of one—the removal of a concrete barrier "out there," so that *God becomes the object* of reconciliation and Jesus Christ, on behalf of humans, is the subject.

Peter Abelard (1079-1142) articulated the view which has come to be called the moral-influence theory. It is also known as a subjective view since it concentrates on what the saving work of Christ accomplishes inside of one—changing the person from hatred and rebellion to love and obedience, so that *God is seen as the subject* of reconciliation and people are the objects.

While Abelard's theory seems to have enjoyed considerable popularity during the Middle Ages, Anselm's view has gradually become the predominant view in Western Christianity. So, although Anselm precedes Abelard by thirty or forty years chronologically, we will consider Abelard's subjective theory before dealing with Anselm's objective view. Since Anselm's satisfaction theory has proved to be much more adequate and influential in the subsequent history of the church than Abelard's has been, we will need to treat Anselm's theory in considerably more depth. For this reason we will review Anselm's theory last and will treat it much more fully than the other principal theories.

In the descriptions of the three principal theories of the atonement which follow, we will not attempt to reinterpret these representative positions. We simply seek to summarize the commonly held understandings of these theories in order to set the stage for suggesting a fresh look at our understanding of the work of Christ from a decidedly different perspective.

In the pages which follow, the three theories will often be compared with each other, not for the purpose of making value judgments as to their relative usefulness as theories of the atonement, but in order to clarify the variety of concepts and perspectives which they have contributed to the attempt to understand the meaning of the saving work of Christ.

The descriptions and comparisons of these three representative theories will also serve to highlight their strengths and weaknesses, the truths as well as the partial truths which they contain, and their relative adequacy or inadequacy for understanding biblically the meaning of the work of Christ. This kind of historical review is necessary in order to set the stage for a radical evangelical approach to the question. It seeks to be radical in the sense of being intentionally concerned to discover the roots of the meaning of the work of Christ as they are found in the New Testament witness and evangelical in the sense of seeking to be faithful to God's ultimate Evangel, Jesus Christ.

I. Classic Dramatic View (Conflict-Victory)

The oldest theory of the atonement which developed in the Christian church has been called the classic or dramatic view. The Swedish theologian Gustaf Aulén has set forth the principal features of this theory under the dramatic term, *Christus Victor* (Christ is Victor), in a book first published in 1931. The central theme of this view is the idea of the work of Christ as a scene in the divine cosmic drama of conflict and victory.

This conflict-victory motif seems to have predominated among Western church leaders from the second to the sixth centuries as an image for understanding the incarnation and especially the death and resurrection of Christ. Christ the Victor fights against and triumphs over the evil powers of the world, the tyrants under which humankind is in bondage and suffering, and in him God reconciles the world to himself (Aulén, 1969:4). The cross is seen as the struggle between Jesus and his enemies—or between God, in the person of Jesus, and his enemies. Behind the Romans and the Jews were spiritual powers, principalities, powers, rulers of this present age. This view draws, of course, upon the Pauline references to the cosmic struggle against the powers, the flesh, the law, and the rulers of darkness.

While objective theories of the atonement tend to emphasize almost exclusively Christ's death and subjective theories underscore the importance of Christ's life, the dramatic view sees Christ's saving work as a continuous divine operation. In addition to the death of Christ, this view stresses the incarnation as a whole. Jesus' resurrection is viewed as "the manifestation of the decisive victory over the powers of evil, which was won on the cross; it is also the starting point for . . . the gift of the Spirit, for the continuation of the work of God in the souls of men" (Aulén, 1969:32). So Christ's life, death, and resurrection are all understood as critical aspects of the ongoing divine struggle with the evil powers which enslave people.

The classic view sees sin primarily as submission to evil powers and the resulting enslavement at their hands. This is in contrast to objective views in which sin is understood basically as transgression of divine law and to subjective views in which the focus is more on spiritual and moral immaturity. Sin, in the classic view, is corporate as well as personal. Here the tendencies toward individualistic understandings of sin and salvation are less apparent than in either the objective or the subjective theories.

In the classic theory God is clearly viewed as the author of the saving work of Christ. In some subjective views, such as those of theological rationalism, God tends to become a benign partner whose atoning and forgiving work "is made dependent upon the ethical effects in human lives" (Aulén, 1969:139). For objective views, such as Anselm's, God appears primarily as an offended plaintiff or judge since the emphasis falls on people's guilt and the subsequent penalty. Therefore Christ, as God-man, offers satisfaction to God on behalf of humanity. But according to the classic theory, God, through Christ, is clearly the Reconciler. Although the full humanity of Jesus is never in doubt in the classic view, Christ's suffering and death are not ascribed to him "as human," but rather "as God" since his work consists in the conquest of all powers who are in opposition to God. Aulén cites Luther as saying, "This is not the work of any created being, but of almighty God" (Aulén, 1969:106).

In this connection we should also note that Roman Catholic, Reformed, and Lutheran confessions have all repudiated the ancient

Patripassian heresy which assumed that the divine nature itself suffered. In line with this the "Form of Concord" quotes Luther as saying "that our Saviour to suffer must become man" (Hodge, 1898:483).

Other elements included in this classic understanding of the saving work of Christ are the ideas of ransom and the "deception of the Devil" (Aulén, 1969:47). The ways in which the early church leaders developed these images vary, but the general understanding runs as follows: All humanity has fallen under the power of the devil who is able to afflict and to put to death. He could not be expected to give them up unless he received a ransom in return. Jesus Christ came to offer himself as that ransom for the lives of all who have been taken captive by the devil. Satan, supposing that he could extend his power by killing the Son of God, took Christ in exchange for the lives of humanity and killed him instead. According to most versions of the theory, Satan had rights over enslaved humanity and could justly demand a ransom. But Satan, deceived by Christ's humility, grabbed the opportunity and put him to death. However, Christ could not be held (cf. Acts 2:24), and the drama reaches its climax in his resurrection in which he wrenches himself free from Satan's grasp. The deceiver at last has been deceived.

Eventually this understanding of the work of Christ began to fall into disrepute. For one thing, it granted certain rights to the devil, assuming that he has certain things coming and that even God must respect these claims. Another objectionable element in this image has been its dependence on the use of fraud. God deceived Satan who thought he was getting something in return for giving up his claim on humanity. This idea of the deception of the devil occurs frequently in both the Eastern and Western churches. Augustine used the simile of the mousetrap. Mice are enticed into the trap by the bait; in this case Christ is the bait by which the devil is caught. In other cases Jesus was perceived as the baited hook snapped up by the devil. Therefore, although this was the first image to be developed with a certain amount of logical clarity in the second century, it did not come to enjoy universal long-range support.

In spite of disagreement over the least acceptable aspects of this image, it does have some positive features. In broad outline it does describe the awful nature of the conflict between God and the powers. It communicates something of the seriousness and the depth of human sin in its corporate as well as its personal dimensions. And it points to the tremendous cost of the struggle which God undertook for humanity's salvation. In contrast to Anselm's theory, which is abstract and highly rational in its approach, the classic view depends much more on descriptive images such as the ransom figure within the general *Christus Victor* motif which, in a sense, is also itself an image. The classic view is basically dramatic in the way it portrays the saving work of Christ.

In spite of the objections which the ransom-deception images provoke, the metaphor has some basic meanings. First, the picture does serve to deny that God proceeds by brute force to accomplish purposes by compulsion. Furthermore, God does not stand outside the drama, but is rather its chief actor who overcomes evil, not by almighty fiat, but by giving of his own Son in divine self-oblation, by the method of self-offering (Aulén, 1969:53-54).

Second, the image also asserts the fundamental responsibility of humanity for its sin. Slavery to sin and the devil is not blamed on the devil. Humanity's enslaved state is the consequence of its own sin, and being under the wrath of God is another way to describe this condition. To describe the devil as an enemy, beguiler, and usurper, and also as possessing certain rights over humanity is to assert simultaneously that the devil is God's enemy and that he is also the executant of God's judgment (Aulén, 1969:54-55).

Indeed, one of the strengths of the classical view is the idea that the devil has, in a certain sense, some rights over humans. God has given to the devil these rights by granting to humans the kind of freedom in which they are capable of selling themselves to the devil. And when one sells oneself to the devil, one really belongs to him. The reality of human bondage to a power that won't let one go unless some new and stronger force is brought to bear is portrayed well in the Bible by the concept of a personal devil.

Third, when those of earlier generations referred to the deception of the devil in their image, it was not necessary to find in God the source of this deception. This is an image, and it does not lend itself to the literal interpretation of all of its details. Behind these seemingly fantastic speculations lies the thought that the power of evil ultimately overreaches itself when it comes into conflict with the power of God (Aulén, 1969:55). Evil loses the battle precisely at the point of its pretended victories. While this was probably not in the minds of the church leaders who expressed the view, it speaks indirectly to the question of the real nature of power and authority, a question with which both Jesus and Paul dealt in a decisive manner.

As we have seen, Anselm's theory is objective inasmuch as it presupposes an objective barrier between God and humanity which must be removed by a satisfaction offered from humankind's side. In other words, God needs to be reconciled to the world. The classic view sees God as reconciling us by struggling against the powers. But the classic view also speaks of God as being reconciled to the world as well as reconciling the world. In this sense the classic theory is also objective.

However, this barrier is not abstract, as in Anslem's view. It is rather the real barrier which takes the form of the power of these fallen structures to execute God's judgment. God's wrath is expressed in the oppression of humankind at the hands of evil powers in all of the various forms in which they present themselves. Although they rule by God's permission, they are bitterly opposed to him. Therefore these evil powers constitute a barrier between humanity and God. Christ's struggle was not merely against personal temptation in order to qualify as a blameless sacrifice for sin or to be able to serve as a perfect moral example. Jesus did combat personal temptation successfully, but he did it in the larger context of his struggle with these powers. In his victory Christ has broken the dominion of these powers. The barrier of their domination has been abolished, although their existence continues provisionally until the parousia. Inasmuch as God's wrath is expressed through the instrumentality of the powers of evil, it is possible to say that in this conflict against the powers, "God is at once the Reconciler and the Reconciled. His enmity is taken away in the very act in which He reconciles the world unto Himself" (Aulén, 1969:35).

The nature of a theory of the atonement is to attempt to systematize and understand in a logically satisfying way the reasons for and the meaning of the saving work of Christ. Needless to say, the conflict-victory motif has not really satisfied this demand for a rational construction in which the rich variety of biblical material can be systematically accounted for. In reality the classic dramatic theory was built almost exclusively around the biblical conflict-victory image. Herein lies its strength as a motif for understanding biblically the meaning of the work of Christ and its weakness as a theory which attempts to bring together all the strands of biblical material into a logical system of thought. Insofar as it has claimed to be a theory for understanding the saving work of Christ, the dramatic view has failed to convince.

II. Abelard's Subjective View (Moral Influence)

Peter Abelard (1079-1142) enunciated another way of under-standing the meaning of the work of Christ less than a generation after Anselm had described it as an objective satisfaction offered to God in humans' behalf. As we have pointed out in the preface to this section, although Anselm precedes Abelard chronologically, we will consider Abelard's subjective view before dealing with Anselm's theory. Since the satisfaction theory has proved to be much more adequate and influential in the subsequent history of the church than Abelard's view has been, it will be necessary to treat Anselm's theory in considerably more depth.

For Abelard the primary significance of the cross was not the re-moval of an objective barrier between God and humans, thereby rec-onciling God, but rather a demonstration to humanity of God's matchless love. In Jesus' self-sacrificing death, humanity is touched by the limitless depths of God's love. This subjective effect on us is the key to Abelard's understanding of the work of Christ.

Abelard rejected the traditional view that Christ had come to pay a debt to the devil as well as Anselm's theory that Christ had come to offer a satisfaction to God. Abelard also held a different view of sin. For him the essence of sin is more in people's evil intentions than in their actions. It consists in agreeing to the evil inclination of the mind. Abelard saw the work of Christ as providing both an example of, as well as an occasion for, teaching about the love of God. Through the power of Jesus' example, people are moved to love God, whose forgiveness is based on limitless love and is given in response to the intercession of the risen Christ.

While Anselm developed the idea of the reconciliation of God in the death of Christ with the use of legal categories, Abelard thought of a reconciliation of humanity with God expressed in terms of the moral disposition of the two parties toward each other. So the ethical dimensions of Christ's life and death receive more emphasis. Instead of the honor of God and the conservation of God's legal rights in relation to humankind, essential elements in Anselm's theory, Abelard underscored the love and ethical righteousness of God. While Anselm elaborated his theory with the whole human race in mind, Abelard described the work of Christ on behalf of the elect who will sooner or later believe in the saving work of Christ. This difference in basic presupposition helps explain at least some of the differences between Anselm and Abelard (Ritschl, 1872:35).

Abelard's paraphrase of Romans 3:22-26 reflects his thought.

> Inasmuch as no one can be justified before God by fulfillment of the ceremonial law, God has accordingly by His alliance with human nature in Christ, and by the surrender of Him to suffering and death, given proof of the highest love towards us, and awakens in those who by faith discern, or have in former times waited for this deed of reconciliation, such a degree of love to God and their fellowmen as forms an indissoluble bond of union with God, and constitutes the ground of forgiveness of sins formerly committed (Ritschl, 1872:36).

Abelard never got around to saying why the incarnation and death of Christ were necessary for our reconciliation, although he did refute the classic idea of redemption out of the power of the devil by the death of Christ on two grounds. First, Satan never acquired any rights over humankind which had to be provided for by an equivalent ransom. Second, since redemption by Christ is valid only for the elect, they really could not have been in the power of the devil (Ritschl, 1872:36).

Abelard's understanding that reconciliation takes place in people's free response to the revelation of God's love in the life and death of Christ does not mean that it is the result of human effort. Although their decision to love God is free, it is because from the beginning they have been the objects of the divine decree of election to salvation. Insofar as humans are reconciled by means of their free personal appropriation of Christ's reconciling act, it is subjective. Insofar as this free response is made because people are objects of the divine decree of election, atonement is objective (Ritschl, 1872:37).

The love of God which awakens a response of love in humans is the ground of their justification. Abelard viewed God's justice more in ethical terms than in legal ones, so justice does not stand in opposition to God's grace. In his incarnation and death Christ has been the representative of the love of God toward us. But this is not all. In his intercession the risen Christ is our representative before God. Therefore Christ is viewed as the mediator of reconciliation.

Abelard was the principal medieval exponent of this theory which has come to be called the moral-influence view. During the Middle Ages Abelard's theory was preferred over Anselm's satisfaction theory, thanks to the influence of Peter Lombard (Ritschl, 1872:24). In the modern period, especially since the rise of theological liberalism in the nineteenth century, the subjective view has enjoyed rather widespread popularity. This is seen in the thought of such exponents as the nineteenth-century German theologian Friedrich Schleiermacher and the twentieth-century American "social gospel" theologian Walter Rauschenbusch. Differences such as the concept of election, for example, exist between the thought of Abelard and the vision of modern exponents of the theory, but the principal characteristics of the view remain intact.

God is—and has always been—a loving and forgiving God. Therefore there is no need to propitiate God or to appease his anger or to offer him some satisfaction. The problem is in humans. They are self-centered, rebellious, turned in upon themselves, and closed to God. The death of Christ is the example or dramatization that brings home to us God's love for humanity. The power of example in Christ's cross makes us willing to accept the forgiveness which God has always wanted to give us.

As we have already observed in relation to the classic view, the subjective view also contains strengths and weaknesses. A tendency of Abelard and later liberal theologians is to focus on the life of Jesus as well as on his death. Although some liberals apparently stressed the importance of Jesus' life to the point of underrating the importance of his death, Schleiermacher, for example, insists on the principle that Jesus' life is a unity with his death. Jesus' perfect obedience in death is viewed as "the crown of his active obedience" in his life (Schleiermacher, 1928:453).

Anselm and orthodox theologians who follow him have seen Jesus' suffering as a satisfaction for human sin. They see Jesus in his death bearing the weight of divine wrath as a penalty decreed by God. But for Schleiermacher the penalty of sin or the "justice of God" is found in the evils of human society. A race which has turned away from God experiences all sorts of suffering due to poverty, war, famine, and crime. In the experience of these evils humanity feels God's wrath (Schleiermacher, 1928:315-24).

Walter Rauschenbusch further developed the implications of this view of divine wrath for our understanding of the death of Christ. Jesus did not bear our sins in accordance with some abstract legal formula. Rather, Jesus bore them by direct experience when he was persecuted and killed by the forces of religious bigotry, political power, injustice, and violence. Due to the corporate nature of sin and the solidarity of evil and guilt, all people everywhere are equally guilty and in need of forgiveness. But Jesus' death was not merely a passive submission to the powers. In his life and death of absolute opposition to them Christ became the highest revelation of God's love and exposed the power of sin in all its ugliness (Rauschenbusch, 1917:259, 267-68). On the other hand, in his conflict with the worst manifestations of the power of evil, Jesus responded with absolutely self-denying love. So the cross is also the highest revelation of divine love.

Liberal theologians find dynamic, organic, relational language more useful to describe the meaning of Jesus' life and death than the legal categories of the orthodox satisfaction view. Whereas for the Anselmian view, as we shall see more fully, Christ's righteousness is legally declared to belong to us even though we do not actually become righteous, for the moral-influence theory redemption is seen as the actual increase of God-consciousness. Through the presence of the life of Christ in us the impulse to fulfill God's will is active in us. Living fellowship with Christ makes a real moral difference. Only in this sense do the exponents of the moral-influence theory talk about the "imputation of Christ's righteousness" (Schleiermacher, 1928:254-55; cf. Ritschl, 1966:547).

A notable difference between the Anselmian and Abelardian theories relates, of course, to their views of human sin. According to the moral-influence theory, sin tends to be a relative lack of God-consciousness. Rather than conceiving of sin as transgressing God's honor and thereby creating a humanly insurmountable barrier between God and humanity, it appears to be simply a question of relative distance between what God wants us to be and what we are. In contrast, the Anselmian vision makes a sharp distinction between God's will and humans' disobedience and undersores more sharply the need for God's initiative in humans' salvation.

The Abelardian/liberal emphasis on the subjective effect of Christ's death upon us stands out in sharp contrast to the objective character of Anselm's view—that the prime effect of Christ's death is upon God. Considerable New Testament support exists for this aspect of the subjective view. "God shows his love for us in that while we were yet sinners Christ died for us" (Rom. 5:8). In Romans 8:32-39 Paul speaks of God "who did not spare his own Son but gave him up for us all." He goes on to illustrate the concrete way in which this demonstration of love subjectively empowers God's people to face all sorts of adversity. In fact John writes that we really never knew what love was until we beheld it in the life and death of Christ (1 John 3:16). And in the following verse John makes explicit reference to the "moral influence" of Christ's death on our actions. Even in 1 John 4:10, where we have one of the two New Testament occurrences of the term *hilasmos*, variously translated as "propitiation" or "expiation," the death of Christ is not interpreted in terms of the objective satisfaction theory in which its effect on God is underscored but in terms of the subjective effects in which the concrete moral action of God's people is modified through the power of God's love manifested in the death of his Son.

While the subjective theory does call attention to the reality of the effect of Christ's death upon us, it does not tell us why the death of Jesus was necessary in order to reveal the love of God. Was there no other way to show this love? Logically, one could argue that if Jesus' death was not functional, it was not really necessary. The subjective view, in its strictest logic, does not really quite answer the question of why Jesus had to die. It does, however, call attention to the fact that Christ's death does offer a dramatic and powerful example of God's love, and it does in fact exercise a moral influence which has proven to be extraordinarily efficacious.

But neither Abelard, with his emphasis upon the moral influence of Christ's saving work upon the elect, nor the later theologically liberal emphasis on reconciliation as free personal appropriation of Christ's reconciling act really come to grips with the biblical view of the enslaving power of evil and the bondage to sin which requires redemption.

Furthermore, both Abelard's theory and modern liberal views tend to play into the hand of modern individualism. (Anselm is not exempt from this charge either.) Neither the cosmic and spiritual nor the corporate and systemic dimensions of evil are dealt with adequately in the moral-influence theories of the atonement.

Perhaps the most telling criticism of Abelard's moral-influence theory is that its application was to individuals within Christendom where one's salvation was one matter (basically sacramental) and the moral influence of Christ's supreme example of love for a person was another (following Christ). This theory does not really relate the work of Christ to the creation of the community of the new covenant and the concrete shape of that community's discipleship. It does not do justice to the biblical vision of God's covenant love and righteousness which redeem and create a covenant people who reflect God's character.

Newer liberal versions of the moral-influence theory are guilty of the same inadequacy. Individuals respond to God's love in neo-Christendom settings or in a vague universalism of the parenthood of God and the familyhood of humanity. The moral-influence theory leaves the work of Christ unrelated to God's community-creating intention which is so prominent in both old and new covenants. As we shall see later, Anselm's view suffers from the same deficiency.

So while the Abelardian view must surely be commmended for its attempt to bring in the ethical and moral concerns, these are not integrally related to the creation of the new messianic community. The correction which this theory calls for is not to play down its moral concerns but to make the ethical and moral aspects even more foundational along biblical lines. The nature and the concrete shape of the discipleship of the Christian community needs to grow directly out of the concrete nature of the saving work of Christ—as it does in the New Testament. The reconciling act of Christ literally creates a reconciled and reconciling community (Eph. 2).

III. Anselm's Objective View (Satisfaction)

The classical statement of the satisfaction theory of the atonement goes back to the medieval theologian Anselm of Canterbury (1033-1109), who gave expression to it in his book *Cur Deus Homo?* Although in its classic formulation this theory appeared more than 1,000 years after the emergence of the Christian church and it does not reflect the manner in which the work of Christ was understood in the writings of early church leaders, and in spite of certain inadequacies which appear when it is subjected to scrutiny from a broader biblical-theological perspective, it has become the most influential view for understanding the atonement among Western theologians. Anselm's line of argument has been central in Orthodox Protestantism and is reflected in the writings of Martin Luther, John Calvin, and Charles Hodge, to mention only a few. From these sources it has established itself as basic to the doctrinal understandings of conservative Protestantism and modern evangelicalism.

Protestantism has not only tended to reaffirm the satisfaction view but has made it more dominant and more nearly a test of faith than had been the case in the Middle Ages. This has been true for both established and free church Protestants, for Lutherans, Calvinists, and Arminians alike. The Thirty-nine Articles of Anglicanism, for example, contain one of the most forthright statements of the Anselmian penal satisfaction theory: "Christ . . . was crucified, dead, and buried to reconcile his Father to us, and to be a sacrifice, not only for original guilt, but also for the actual sins of men" (Art. II). "The offering of Christ once made is that perfect redemption, propitiation, and satisfaction for all the sins of the whole world, both original and actual, and there is none other satisfaction for sin, but that alone" (Art. XXXI) (Schaff, 1877:486-516). The subjective view has gained popularity principally within the past one hundred years in circles within this broader climate where theological liberalism has been dominant, but in recent decades its importance has declined.

Anselm's view is generally described by the technical terms "objective" and "satisfactionist." It is called objective because the primary reason for the death of Christ was to remove the barrier between humanity and God which had been created by sin. Its objectivity lies in the fact that this barrier is not viewed as being in humans. Rather, this barrier is conceived of as being either in God or in the moral order of things between God and humanity. The barrier is clearly located outside the sinner. Christ's work is seen as directed primarily toward this barrier which is an objective reality quite independent of our subjective feelings about it.

This view is called satisfactionist because Christ's death is understood as satisfaction rendered to God. The term comes from the Latin, meaning "to do enough" or "to do what needs to be done." Christ's death allows God to forgive people's sin within the scope of justice and regularity which the moral structure of the universe requires (Anselm I, 12).[1] Thus satisfaction is the prime category for understanding the work of Christ.

The logic of Anselm's theory can be briefly set forth as follows: The sin of humanity consists in "not rendering to God what is His due," that is, subjection to God's will. In other words, sin is the transgression of God's law. This is seen as a debt which both people and angels owe to God. "Therefore everyone who sins ought to render back to God the honor he has taken away, and this is the satisfaction which every sinner ought to make to God" (I, 11). "Right order" does not permit God mercifully to "remit sins without payment for the honor which has been taken from Him." To remit sin unpunished is not befitting of God, so "it is not within the scope of His liberty, or kindness, or will, to let go unpunished the sinner who does not repay to God what he has taken away" (I,12). By his nature God must preserve "the honor of his own dignity" (I, 13). God's honor is sacred, in Anselm's view. One is impressed by the fact that in this view God is the captive of his own honor. God's liberty, kindness, and will, for example, are all subordinated to the importance assigned to his honor. "Either the sinner pays of his own accord, or God takes it from him against his will" (I,14). Without satisfaction the sinner cannot be restored (I,19).

Furthermore, in the interests of justice, satisfaction must be at least equal to the sin committed against God (I,23). In fact the only satisfaction which is adequate is death because that is the nature of guilt. This was the understanding from the beginning: "The soul that sins, that man shall die." So the only satisfaction possible to humanity is the punishment of death. Since humankind obviously cannot make satisfaction and God cannot simply remit what humans cannot pay ("It is impossible for Him to be merciful in this way," since they would be denying the justice of God's nature [I,25]), there must be "a complete satisfaction for sin, which no sinner can make" (II,4).

This penalty can be paid by another person. But obviously no one with a debt can pay another's debt. But if there were a sinless person who would not have to die for his or her own sin, then if that person died, the merit of that person's death could be applied to the guilt of someone else. If, in addition to being innocent, that person were more than human, then his or her death might apply to all people. In reality Anselm set out to explain the incarnation rather than to develop a theory of the atonement. Why did God become human? The answer is so that this kind of saving work could be done. By being a human, God could die the kind of death humans die. By being innocent, that person could apply his death to the account of others. By being divine, his merit is sufficient for all humanity.

The whole universe is of insufficient value to pay the penalty for violating God's honor. The only solution, then, is that the price to be paid to God for the sin of humankind be something greater than all the universe besides God. Therefore none but God can make this satisfaction (II,6).

A satisfaction is required "which no one can make except God, and no one ought to make except men. It is necessary that one who is God-man should make it" (II,6). In Christ's death this satisfaction is made, so now God can, with justice, forgive sinners their whole debt (II,20). God became a blameless man who could thereby die willingly and credit his death to all those who become eligible for that credit. The theory is articulated largely in forensic (courtroom terms) and commercial categories. In Anselm's time those who benefited from this transaction were those who received the sacraments. In Protestant orthodoxy they became those who believe, those who are saved by faith alone.

In addition to being a satisfaction, Christ's death is also, in a sense, an example—although this is really not essential to Anselm's logic. By enduring "with uncomplaining patience injuries, and insults, and the death of the cross with robbers, brought on Him on account of the righteousness which he kept with perfect obedience, he gave men an example that on account of no trials which they can experience should they turn away from the righteousness which they owe to God" (II,18).

Variations on Anselm's theory

In the course of the church's history, several variations have appeared which logically fall within the scope of the Anselmian satisfaction theory. The following appear to be the principal variants.[2]

The first understands satisfaction in the narrow sense in which God is seen as the plaintiff. In forensic terms, humans are guilty and God is the offended party. God requires satisfaction, not in the sense of fitting punishment but rather in terms of commensurate reparation. In this case the compensation is death due to the nature of the offense. So the cross of Christ takes the place of the life that God was demanding as compensation for the offense.

This is the variant which Charles Hodge seems to call "pecuniary satisfaction." However, he held that "the satisfaction of Christ was not pecuniary, but penal or forensic; a satisfaction for sinners, and not for those who owed a certain amount of money" (1898:471). Hodge did, however, grant that an analogy exists between "pecuniary satisfaction" and "juridical or legal satisfaction." It consists of (1) the effect produced which is the certain deliverance of those for whom satisfaction is made, (2) the fact that a real equivalent is paid, and (3) the guilty party is freed through the making of this satisfaction. Therefore Hodge states "that by analogy it is right to say that Christ assumed and paid our debts" (1898:487).

Another variant within the satisfaction family is called the penal view. Here punishment is understood in the narrow sense. God is seen as both judge and prosecutor in a criminal proceeding rather than as plaintiff in a damage suit. Since humans have broken God's law, they must be punished. They are found guilty in this legal sense, and Christ is made to suffer the penalty. "He made him to be sin who knew no sin" (2 Cor. 5:21) is interpreted as Christ being made to be the one who carries actual guilt and punishment for guilt. God as prosecutor or judge is satisfied when the punishment has been discharged. In line with this view, Protestant confessions of faith assert that the death of Christ reconciled God to us. God as prosecutor or judge is satisfied by the penalty borne by Christ on behalf of sinners, and his righteous anger is mollified, his attitude is changed, and his concern for justice is met. For Charles Hodge, Christ's satisfaction was fundamentally penal or forensic (1898:471). "The essence of the penalty of the divine law is the manifestation of God's displeasure, the withdrawal of the divine favour. This Christ suffered in our stead. He bore the wrath of God" (Hodge, 1898:473).

A third variant within the satisfaction group is called governmental. Here God is viewed as ruler or legislator rather than plaintiff or judge. Why does the ruler or legislator say that there must be compensation or punishment? It is not because he is offended (as the plaintiff) nor because he has righteous anger (as judge or prosecutor). On the contrary, he is concerned for the welfare of his citizens. He makes laws requiring punishment because the maintenance of the public order demands it. The common welfare requires rules which must be obeyed. Disobedience cannot be passed over lightly. The seriousness of sin must be demonstrated. To demonstrate the seriousness of sin a penalty must be attached to infractions. In this case satisfaction is necessary to assure the ongoing seriousness of the moral order of the realm in which God is ruler and legislator. So God can't simply forgive and forget.

Judging from the emphasis that the governmental variant of the satisfaction theory receives in the work of Charles Hodge, it must be of central importance. "By the satisfaction of Christ is meant all He has done to satisfy the demands of the law and justice of God, in the place and in behalf of sinners" (Hodge, 1898:470). Christ's sufferings are called punishment because they are for "the satisfaction of justice" (Hodge, 1898:474). "When, therefore, it is said that the sufferings of Christ were vicarious, the meaning is that He suffered in the place of sinners. He was their substitute. He assumed their obligation to satisfy justice" (Hodge, 1898:475).

Evaluation of Anselm's Theory

As we have seen, Protestantism has tended to reaffirm the Anselmian satisfaction theory in its main thrust. Conservative Protestantism has granted it a dominant place in orthodox doctrine and has even tended to make it a test of faith. It is therefore crucial to evaluate in depth the strengths and weaknesses of this theory.

At first sight a number of considerations appear to favor this view. First, it appears to answer the questions, Why was the death of Jesus absolutely necessary? Why could nothing else save us? With the logic inherent in the judicial image, it demonstrates that the blameless death of Christ was an absolute necessity. In this way God's holiness and love could be reconciled. Second, it certainly appears to take sin more seriously than the subjective theories of the atonement. Third, at first sight, it appears to be somewhat parallel to other images such as sacrifice and the shedding of blood and to redemption as the payment of a price for liberation. It attempts to integrate these metaphors into its vision of the work of Christ.

However, under more serious scrutiny not all of these apparent strengths stand up to the test of faithfulness to the biblical vision as well as might be desired. Furthermore, on the negative side are a number of damaging criticisms to which the satisfaction theory is vulnerable. In the interest of clarity these criticisms may be grouped as exegetical, theological, historical, and practical.

Exegetical

By defining lostness as offending God's honor or holiness and the death of Christ as the satisfaction for God's offended honor, this view abandons the New Testament affirmation that God is the agent, not the object, of reconciliation (cf. 2 Cor. 5:18-20). In fact precisely at this point the Christian gospel is different from all other approaches to God. Other religions see God as angry and needing to be appeased. The gospel reveals God taking the initiative for our salvation. Humanity, not God, needs to be reconciled.

The Anselmian view that Christ's death is a substitute for our death is not reflected in the New Testament with absolute clarity. The concept of substitution must be deduced from the biblical language and metaphors which are employed. Christ certainly died for us, in our behalf; in this sense he died as our representative, or substitute.

Substitution, as it has traditionally been employed in this context, does not give sufficient emphasis to what is of primary significance in the work of Christ—that God was the subject. Substitution, in Anselm's theory, is too one-sided. It sees Christ only as humanity's substitute. This is surely true. But by itself it conjures up pagan visions of Jesus standing in humanity's place and pleading with an angry God. Jesus, in his death, represented not only humanity to God but also God to humanity. In this sense "representative" is most surely a better term than "substitution," as it has come to be understood in the Anselmian view.

Substitution in this view is also too narrow a concept. It is too individualistic to represent adequately Paul's thought. While it is true that Christ "gave himself for me" (Gal. 2:20), it is more faithful to Pauline theology to say that Jesus represents humanity so that his death is our death. Christ died not so much instead of humankind but as a human and for humanity (cf. Dunn, 1974:139-41).

Proponents of this theory find in the biblical "for-us-ness" of Christ's death a concept compatible with the theory of satisfaction, but in so doing they tend to interpret biblical language in a way which makes it fit into a basically non-biblical metaphor.

According to the Anselmian view, the guilt of past sin makes the atonement necessary. Such an overriding preoccupation with guilt in the New Testament does not appear. This, as we have seen, seems to be a primary concern which colors Westerners' reading of the biblical texts. In the New Testament the lostness of humanity is defined around the foci of humanity's separation from God and their inability to do good. According to the satisfactionist vision, salvation is primarily remission of guilt and the cancellation of punishment. Our purpose is not to deny the presence of a concern for the remission of guilt in the Bible (2 Kings 24:1-4). However, in the New Testament perspective we find a primary emphasis on reconciliation, on the reestablishment of the communion and obedience which have been destroyed, and on discipleship.

In fact the Old Testament sacrificial system seems to show that God's purpose for humanity is reconciliation and obedience rather than merely the cancellation of guilt. When the imagery of sacrifice is applied to the task of understanding the work of Christ, we often forget that Old Testament sacrifice in general is not concerned exclusively with the problem of humanity's guilt. The central feature of the Old Testament concept of atonement can be described as a process whereby the creature-Creator relationship, which has been disturbed or violated by the creature, is restored by the Creator to its proper harmony. Furthermore, it seems clear that this atoning process came to be particularly associated with the blood rite of the sin offering. This was God's gracious provision for restoring relationships broken by unwitting sins and averting danger to the welfare of the entire community (Lev. 4:3,13,27). As for the guilt-offering, it was not so much a vehicle for the rehabilitation of the guilty as it was a provision for making reparations. Forgiveness in the Old Testament, as well as in the New, is a gift of God's grace. It is not something to be earned through sacrifice.

The church has usually assumed that the biblical language and symbolism of sacrifice are especially compatible with the Anselmian theory of the atonement. The satisfaction theory calls for a death, and the sacrificial system requires the death of animals. However, to approach the meaning of Old Testament sacrifice from the perspective of satisfaction is to run the risk of misunderstanding it.

Only in the case of the scapegoat was sin specifically placed on the animal, and in this case it was not sacrificed but chased into the wilderness as bearer of Israel's sin. On the other hand, when a man brought a flawless lamb to the temple and laid his hands upon it, he was not placing his guilt on the sheep and then having it sacrificed in his stead. Rather, he was identifying with the purity of his gift and offering himself to God (Lev. 4:32-35). In this case the primary concept would be that of representation or identification, rather than simply substitution as the Anselmian view has generally understood it. Leviticus 17:11 seems to show that the real center of Old Testament sacrifice was not substitutionary death but the offering of life, of which the blood is the bearer (cf. Heb. 9:22). The sacrificial system of the ancient Hebrews is complex and has given rise to more than one theory for understanding its rich variety of meanings. However, the easy juxtaposition of satisfaction through juridical punishment with the meaning of the sacrificial rites of the Old Testament which makes the Anselmian theory so appealing is not really supported by the biblical sources.

To place the expiation of juridical guilt at the center of God's saving purpose, which is the effect of the Anselmian satisfaction theory, does a grave injustice to the biblical evidence. Removal of guilt is an important biblical concern, but it does not seem to be the center of focus. All strands of the New Testament message make clear God's purpose for humanity to establish obedience in his communion. The prophetic vision of messianic hope gave obedience precedence (Jer. 31). The synoptic Gospels' description of the kingdom offers the same view (Matt. 5-7; 19; Luke 14). Peter (1 Pet. 2:2-4), Paul (Rom. 8:4; Gal. 1:4; Eph. 2:10; Titus 2:11-14; Philem. 1:12-15), John (John 15:9-10, 16-17; 1 John 3:5-10; Rev. 19:8), and Hebrews (9:13-14) all concur in this vision. Forgiveness in the sense of removal of impediments to communion with God is certainly a part of God's purpose, but we do not find a dominant preoccupation with guilt and satisfaction. The central concern of the Anselmian theory for guilt and its removal would appear to find inspiration more in Western concepts of justice and punishment than it does in the Bible and its world of thought.

Another example of the way in which the Anselmian vision does violence to the biblical perspective is the way in which the biblical concept of redemption is treated. People have generally thought that the idea of redemption fits particularly well into the Anselmian view. Redemption here is freeing from indebtedness or confinement, to use the commercial and forensic images. However, in the New Testament redemption is to free from slavery, including slavery to sin. Freed from the servitude of sin, we become the servants of God. So biblical redemption is really a change of masters (cf. Ex. 3:12), and when the New Testament uses this metaphor, it is one of the strongest expressions of the truth that the concern of God in the atonement is our obedience rather than simply our guilt (1 Cor. 6:20; 7:23; Rom. 6:17-22).

Theological

These exegetical criticisms of the Anselmian view are simply underscored when we approach it from a more systematic theological perspective. When it is viewed from the perspective of the kind of consensus which arises out of bringing together the strands of biblical thought into a meaningful whole, the inadequacy of the satisfaction theory is again apparent.

Anselm's satisfaction theory moves us in the direction of a tritheistic doctrine of God. The idea that God is a Trinity composed of three personalities who are able to carry out transactions among themselves is certainly not biblical, nor is it congenial with the best of Christian tradition. The Nicene Creed points toward the oneness of the Godhead (the deity of Christ and the Spirit), not in the direction of threeness. So the idea of the Father and Son as having separate wills and identities to the point of being able to hold transactions with each other has no grounds in the New Testament nor in the best of the church's doctrinal heritage.

If the principal question were, as Anselm stated it, how to have a valid death, then when the requirements are met through the innocence of the victim, the problem is essentially solved. But this way of posing the problem is in danger of assuming an *opus operatum* (i.e., that the benefit is automatically bestowed by virtue of the work already done) view of Christ's death and · also tends toward universalism (i.e., it is a universally valid death whether people want it or not). The Anselmic view can logically lead to universalism. This logical tendency toward universalism which grows out of understanding the work of Christ primarily in terms of a valid legal transaction on behalf of humanity is counteracted in Calvinistic circles by a doctrine of election which restricts the effects of the saving work of Christ to the elect.

Historical

The exegetical and theological criticisms of the Anselmic view are further underscored when we see that a number of the underlying presuppositions of the Anselmic theory really find their rootage in the Constantinian Christendom of the period rather than in the world and thought of the New Testament.

Penance. Anselm's satisfaction theory seems to have grown out of the penitential practice of the medieval church. Concepts such as punishment, merit, redemption, and satisfaction are taken from the realm of individual applicability and then used to describe the saving action of the God-man in covering the sin of all humankind. Anselm uses the language and the concepts of the medieval sacrament of penance to understand the atonement. The work of Christ is seen as becoming a vicarious oblation of utter obedience which takes the place of humanity's disobedience, thus satisfying the honor of God's justice.

Penance is a human work which seeks to earn good standing with God, and Anselm begins his logical construction by asking, "What human work can have saving merit?" The answer he gives is "only the work of God incarnate." But in Anselm's construction Christ's death remains a human initiative directed Godward. This, of course, is the reverse of the biblical view.

Grace. Anselm's view of the atonement also presupposes a medieval understanding of sacramental grace. His formulation of objective cosmic-historic atonement presupposes the medieval subjective, experiential, sacramental means of appropriating the effects of that act. This kind of grace is imparted in the context of Christendom where people are viewed as individual sinners. There is no vision of a redeemed disciple community such as the one reflected in the New Testament and the best of the evangelical tradition. The Anselmian vision of the atonement was easily adapted to classical Protestantism, which simply perpetuated the presuppositions and realities of Christendom.

People were perceived as individuals within Christendom. Whereas individuals in medieval Catholicism sought to appropriate the benefits of the saving work of Christ through the sacraments, in the Protestant tradition these benefits were bestowed by faith alone, which ideally meant a gracious saving relationship of trust and obedience. However, given the Constantinian character of classic Protestantism, all too often it meant solafideism, in which faith tended to be perceived as a purely spiritualized confidence which sought to appropriate the benefits of Christ's saving work as a legal transaction which lay entirely outside the experience of the believers, or, somewhat later, as intellectual assent to right doctrine.

Anselm's objective satisfaction theory proved to be equally acceptable to both medieval Catholicism and traditional Protestantism because of their common Christendom character. In a situation in which everyone in society needs to be considered Christian, an objective, easily applied theory for understanding the work of Christ has been found to be equally attractive. The saving benefit of the work of Christ was applied sacramentally in Catholicism and by means of the sacraments and solafideism in the case of classic Protestantism.

Roman juridical system. Anselm's theory is developed with the presuppositions and categories of the Roman juridical system in the context of a Christendom where these were applied in both secular and religious life. Anselm thinks like a Roman lawyer who, as the theologian that he is, succeeds in working pardon into a legal system of just punishments and rewards. The triumph of this theory of the atonement in terms of satisfaction lies in its compatibility with Western legal structures which formed the underpinning of medieval Christendom and orthodox mainstream Protestantism.

One example of this basic compatibility between Western juridical structures and the Anselmian view can be found in the church's traditional approach to the exercise of discipline. While the New Testament clearly points in the direction of the restoring function of discipline (Matt. 18:15-20), in the church's tradition discipline has generally been perceived as just retribution, pedagogy, and defense of the church's honor. In fact, Roman law provided the conceptual categories for the church's sacrament of penance. Terms such as punishment, merit, satisfaction, and absolution which have characterized Roman Catholicism's penitential system have come directly from Roman legal theory and practice.

While Protestants have rejected the penitential system as such, they have accepted Anselm's application of its conceptual basis to their understanding of the saving work of Christ. In the practice of church discipline, Protestantism has often proceeded more in the spirit of Western law than in the gracious spirit of biblical covenant, which is revealed most fully in the saving work of Christ.

The widespread Christian defense of the practice of capital punishment offers another example of recourse to secular Western legal concepts for our way of understanding how God deals with sin and the appropriate way for the state to deal with crime. The biblical data pertinent to this issue are hotly debated among Christians. However, the fact that most Western Christians have traditionally assumed the position which is most compatible with Western legal theory and practice seems to lend credibility to the view that Christendom has indeed depended strongly on secular juridical categories for its understandings of the work of Christ and matters of ecclesiastical and civil discipline.

On the other hand, the New Testament shows remarkably little concern for the legal systems of the time and the need to keep them intact. Jesus chose the publicans and others outside the pale of the socioreligious structures rather than the scribes and Pharisees. The apostolic writings continue to show that the novelty of Jesus' gospel is his attitude which breaks through the bounds of established justice. In fact, God's grace flexes and supersedes the rigidities of legal systems. By taking the categories of Roman civil law rather than the biblical vision of covenant law as his model for understanding God's dealings with humankind, Anselm arrives at conclusions which run counter to the gospel.

Sin. What we have said about Anselm's appropriation of presuppositions and categories from the Roman legal system is applicable to other borrowings. His understanding of the nature and the enormity of sin against God is portrayed by concepts drawn from the Germanic feudal ideas of personal honor. As we have already noted in our brief review of Anselm's *Cur Deus Homo?* God himself is the captive of his own honor. Even God's kindness and liberty are subject to divine honor. This is a medieval Germanic idea about God in which it is not God's grace or mercy or saving or liberating intent but God's pride which is the foremost attribute of divinity.

Germanic legal concepts are also present in Anselm's conviction that the enormity of sin depends on the relative worth or position of the offended party. His understanding of redemption was probably determined more by contemporary Irish and Germanic legal concepts than by the biblical view (Williams, 1957:246).

It certainly is understandable that Anselm would want to articulate the meaning of the work of Christ in the categories of his time. However, the intrusion of all of these extra-biblical ideas from the arena of contemporary medieval social, legal, and religious practices has served to vitiate fatally Anselm's satisfaction theory. As we have seen, Anselm's theory has exercised a vast influence on the church since the Middle Ages, and in somewhat modified forms, it continues to be influential in conservative Protestantism.

Practical

A fourth set of objections to Anselm's theory comes from the practical area of the Christian vocation to discipleship and mission.

Ethics. As we have already pointed out, the Anselmian view was formulated in the church-state context of medieval Christendom where sacraments meant more than ethics for salvation. The Protestant version of the satisfaction theory was adapted in a similar church-state context of established Protestantism where a quite one-sided emphasis on justification by faith alone tended to sideline concerns for moral seriousness. These traditions have always had difficulty in relating sanctification to justification, since their definition of the meaning of the work of Christ has meant that they are conceived of as two different realities. For some traditions sanctification is strictly a second Christian experience after justification. For others it is logically simultaneous but practically subsequent and not really indispensable. Others include a subsequent sanctification by means of a new legalism. As long as justification and sanctification are both logically and practically separated from one another, justification will continue to be exclusively applied to the sinner rather than to the saint. This separation is not unrelated to certain emphases which deny any real difference between sinner and saint. So there is the doctrinal possibility of being justified without being righteous and of being saved without being sanctified, positions which are unacceptable from the perspective of the New Testament.

Discipleship. A series of New Testament texts speak of the Christian's sufferings or cross as being in some sense parallel to Christ's (Matt. 10:38; Mark 8:34f.; 10:38f.; Luke 14:27; John 15:20; 2 Cor. 1:5; 4:10; Phil. 1:29; 2:5-8; 3:10; Col. 1:24f.; Heb. 12:1-4; 1 Pet. 2:21f.; Rev. 12:11). From the perspective of a strictly satisfactionist view of the work of Christ, these texts make no sense at all.

On the other hand, these texts are sometimes misconstrued by the liberal tradition in Protestantism along the lines developed in that classic of American liberalism first published in 1896 by Charles M. Sheldon, *In His Steps*. This book rather simplistically attempts to translate discipleship into the relatively easygoing terms of the American way of life. It sees "what might be in the world when once the new discipleship had made its way into the conscience and conscientiousness of Christendom" and envisions individual disciples as ennobling the nation's patriotism (1937:239).

Yet the concept of discipleship is most clearly brought out in those passages which refer to Jesus' sacrifice. The Christian's cross certainly does not placate the offended holiness of God, nor is the Christian's suffering a kind of transaction with God. The traditional solution to this apparent dilemma has been to interpret the cross of the Christian pastorally as some form of personal suffering which Christians have in common with all humanity—recurring headaches, grouchy neighbors—but which, in the case of the Christian, fulfills a pedagogical function. Another way out of this hermeneutical dilemma is to interpret the work of Christ in other than satisfaction concepts and to recognize the ethical dimensions in the saving work of Christ, pertinent for both the life and the mission of God's people in the world.

The existence of this dilemma explains why many proponents of the Anselmic theory sidestep the issues which rise out of the relationship between radical discipleship and the work of Christ. Teaching about discipleship falls into the category of Christian living and is treated as useful but not indispensable. Preaching about the work of Christ alone is seen as the essential gospel and is indispensable for salvation as it is understood in satisfactionist terms. In the perspective of the New Testament, as radical evangelicals see it, the work of Christ is clearly understood to affect discipleship in the context of the community of the new covenant.

Universalism. Another practical shortcoming is the potential for universalism, inherent in Anselm's satisfaction theory, which can undercut the seriousness of Christian mission and pastoral care. This does not need to happen, nor does it always happen, but logically the satisfaction theory is vulnerable to this danger. What has been done has been done for all, for the whole universe. The death of Christ is a divine-human death which is all that is needed for everybody. If someone does not receive it, the problem lies elsewhere. It is not because the work of Christ is not universally adequate. This implicit universalism does not, in fact, always cut the nerve of mission or pastoral care any more than Calvin's predestinarianism cuts the nerve of moral commitment. But it somehow takes off the pressure.

In fact this can be observed in Christendom situations, be they Roman Catholic or Protestant. The benefits of the work of Christ can quite easily be made to satisfy the needs of the entire population either through sacramental ritual or by solafideistic appropriation of the fully adequate once-for-all death of Christ.

IV. Other Approaches

We have reviewed the three principal ways in which Christians have attempted to understand the saving work of Christ. The first comes from the early centuries of Christian history. The other two were articulated by medieval Catholic theologians at the beginning of the twelfth century. Most other views have been anticipated by or included in the three theories which we have reviewed. Two possible exceptions to this are the incarnational and the dynamistic views, reviewed here in broad outline.

Incarnational

The incarnational view is rooted in the thought of the early church leaders and is found in the Eastern Orthodox Church and in some Anglican circles. According to this view humanity is saved not by the death of Christ, as such, but by Christ's incarnation. God has come into humanity and shared the lot of humankind even to the point of death. Through Christ's sharing of our mortal life, humanity receives immortality. Athanasius expressed it this way: "The Word became man in order that we might be made divine."

In this view Jesus died because all people die. We were really saved at Bethlehem. In fact, a more thoroughgoing statement would be to locate the point of human salvation at the annunciation, at the time of conception. The High Orthodox churches actually do celebrate the feast of the incarnation on March 25. This view does not really explain why the death of Christ was necessary for our salvation. It does not do justice to the New Testament witness of the fact that something is unique and special about the death of Christ.

Dynamistic

Another approach to understanding the atonement might be called the dynamistic view. While it cannot be identified with the thought of any one exponent, it has been present in one form or another in a wide variety of contexts and streams of thought. It sees evil as a power which is able to reproduce itself with a certain amount of autonomy. It is not identified closely with persons or structures, as in other theories. It is much more than mere guilt. It is an evil force which, let loose in the world, keeps multiplying and bearing its evil fruit. The only way to neutralize this evil force is to let it spend itself against some barrier or be absorbed by some buffer or be deprived of the medium in which it grows.

Some scholars feel that this view underlies the ancient conception of sacrifice. Evil deeds or words unleash a chain of destructiveness in the world. Blood sacrifice is conceived of as a barrier which breaks or neutralizes the evil force and averts further havoc. Old Testament interpreters differ as to whether this kind of dynamic view was held by the ancient Hebrews. Be this as it may, the concepts and practices of the Hebrews were certainly shaped by their experience of Yahweh and his saving actions on their behalf.

Another context in which this view appears is the thought of Friedrich Schleiermacher (1928) and of Douglas Clyde MacIntosh (1927). Evil has the power to reproduce itself, and this happens until its impact is absorbed or counteracted, thus interrupting the causal chain. This happens when someone is ready to absorb evil rather than passing it on. Evil is deprived of the reaction of hate which it needs as a medium in which to grow. This is what Christ did supremely. This is also what Christians are called to do, enabled by the power of Christ. So the supremacy of the sacrifice of Christ is not that it is of an altogether different nature than the cross of the Christian, but it is prior to it in point of time and is its source of empowerment and motivation.

In modern times the dynamistic view has commended itself to some Christians who work in the area of psychotherapy or psychodynamics, especially by those who seek to relate theology to psychotherapy or counseling to theology. These, too, use terms such as power or force to refer to evil and good in human and divine-human relationships. In this vein some speak about the deep psychological dimensions of the work of Christ.

The dynamistic view shares some points of similarity with the classical motif of conflict and victory. However, here the powers are allowed to spend themselves against the victim, rather than being broken by the superior power of Christ as Lord. In common with the satisfaction view, the power of sin is objective in that it is not limited to the individual personalities of its instruments. But the dynamistic view describes this objective power in cosmic images rather than forensic ones.

In favor of this view is the fact that it affirms the meaningfulness of our suffering as a part of the same combat of Christ against the powers. Biblical expressions which see Christ "made sin for us"—as a victim of wrath—also fit this theory. Current ways of thinking about nonviolent social action as "breaking the vicious spiral of violence" fit this image, as do modern psychiatric views where the therapist absorbs the hostility of another, thus facilitating healing.

The difficulties which this view faces in seeking to explain the work of Christ include its limited capacity to describe the power of sin as a force which can be neutralized or buffered. The image is not able to express adequately the personal and sociopolitical dimensions of the death of Christ. The idea of a simple cause-and-effect chain of consequences which propagates evil and can be checked or reversed by another cause has obvious limitations as an image for understanding the work of Christ. Nevertheless, fruitful insights can be gotten from this view which is both ancient and relatively modern. While it is not able to explain the atonement by itself, it does offer some apparently valid clues to interpreting the work of Christ.

V. Plurality of Images a Strength

Objective views of atonement stress that God, as Ruler of the cosmos, must punish sin and reward goodness. The cross of Christ is understood in legal terms as vicarious satisfaction for sin. Subjective views stress the love of God toward humanity. The supreme expression of this love is the life and death of Christ. He is the source of new and powerful moral and spiritual vitality. The classical view finds the key to understanding the work of Christ in a cosmic conflict between God and the forces of evil. Christ's death and resurrection are understood as the victorious struggle against the evil powers.

These three apparently incompatible approaches to the work of Christ are actually complementary. The questions they pose are all important: whether and how God is loving and just, whether and how the way God has loved us in Christ determines the way his people express love, whether and how God combats evil and brings about deliverance.

The urge to define with precision the meaning of the saving work of Christ has resulted in views incapable of expressing the rich variety of meaning found in the New Testament. The plurality of images for understanding the work of Christ in the New Testament should be recognized for the strength that it is.

PRINCIPAL BIBLICAL IMAGES FOR UNDERSTANDING THE ATONEMENT

3

Conflict-Victory-Liberation Motif

A primary way by which the New Testament describes the work of Christ might be called the conflict-triumph motif.[1] Salvation occurs when God pours out righteousness—his own life-giving power—in such a way that both God's people and all creation are delivered from the forces of evil and established in God's kingdom. In a number of New Testament passages the work of Christ is specifically described in terms of victory over evil powers (Gal. 4:3-9; Eph. 1:19-22; 2:14-16; 3:7-13; 6:12; Phil. 2:9-11; Col. 1:13-14; 2:8-15; 1 Pet. 3:18-22).

While these powers may be a difficult reality for modern people to grasp, they were taken seriously in the New Testament era when they were understood as invisible, spiritual forces which enslave and oppress people in a bondage from which they are unable to break free themselves. These forces were understood to lie behind many of the religious, social, and political institutions. In fact, the earliest confession of faith—Jesus is Lord—was also a denial of the loyalty claims of all other powers.

The synoptic Gospels describe Jesus' messianic mission in terms of conflict with another power. This is a key theme in Jesus' ministry. The temptation narratives in each of the Gospels set the stage in which Jesus' mission, conflict with the devil or tempter, is carried out (Matt. 4:1-2; Mark 1:12-13; Luke 4:1-2). Prominent among Jesus' messianic activities were the healings and exorcisms which were seen as aspects of this conflict. Casting out demons by the power of God's Spirit was a sure sign that God's kingdom had come into their midst (Matt. 12:28). Metaphors of conflict describe Jesus' mission (Matt. 12:29). Jesus warned of another kingdom, another way, another master, who vied for humankind's loyalty. "You cannot serve God and mammon" (Matt. 6:24). Freedom from bondage to these powers was essential to the coming of the kingdom.

One of the hallmarks of the Gospel narratives is the repeated report of Jesus casting out evil spirits or demons (Mark 1:26; et al.).[2] While these demons were regarded primarily as individual beings in Judaism, Jesus seems to have changed these contemporary ideas, stressing their solidarity with Satan. Satan is pictured as an enemy with power (Luke 10:19) who rules over a kingdom (Luke 11:18) whose soldiers are demons (Mark 5:9). Rather than viewing evil in terms of fortuitous and isolated individual manifestations, Jesus saw it as a unity whose source is "the enemy" (Mark 10:19) who disrupts creation and holds humankind in his grip.

Jesus enters this world, enslaved by Satan, with authority (Mark 1:27) and does battle with the evil one. Jesus' exorcisms are depicted in the Gospel of Mark as battles (Mark 1:23-28). The parable of the duel with the "strong man" points in the same direction (Mark 3:27; Luke 11:21). Someone has suggested that Isaiah 53:12b where a variant translation could read, "He shall have the strong men as spoil," may well be the background for this parable of Jesus (Jeremias, 1971:94). In Luke 13:16 Jesus describes a healing as a loosening of the bonds of Satan's victim.

These victories of Jesus over the powers of evil mark the dawning of a new era of salvation and anticipate Satan's destruction (Mark 1:24). "But if it is by the finger of God [The parallel passage in Matt. 12:28 reads "Spirit of God."] that I cast out demons, then the kingdom of God has come upon you" (Luke 11:20). The healings and exorcisms of Jesus contribute in an anticipatory way to Satan's destruction.

To proclaim the kingdom is to be given authority over the powers of evil (Mark 3:14f.). In fact this is a characteristic of Jesus' commission to his disciples (Mark 6:7; Matt. 10:7f.; Luke 10:19f.). At the conclusion of the disciples' mission, in which demons were subject to them in Jesus' name, Jesus saw "Satan cast from heaven" (Luke 10:18). The apostolic proclamation of the kingdom is seen as the beginning of Satan's annihilation.

In the ministry of Jesus and his disciples evil spirits are rendered powerless. Satan is being destroyed (Luke 10:18). Paradise, in which "nothing shall hurt you," is opening up (Luke 10:19), and the names of the redeemed are in the book of life (Luke 10:20). Already in the present time the new age is dawning and Satan is being vanquished. Although he still exercises power, it has been decisively broken.

In Acts these demonic powers in conflict with God's Messiah are identified as people and human institutions set against God (Acts 4:24-28). The notable way in which the primitive community recalled the words of Gamaliel, "You might even be found opposing God" (Acts 5:39), express with a fine sense of irony the conflict of Messiah and his community with the powers. Peter reflects the understanding of the apostolic community: "God anointed Jesus of Nazareth with the Holy Spirit and with power; . . . he went about healing all who were oppressed by the devil, for God was with him" (Acts 10:38).

Old Testament Origins of Conflict Image

The New Testament image which views the work of Christ in terms of conflict, victory, and liberation is solidly based in the Old Testament vision of God's saving activity. The theme of colossal conflict between God—on behalf of his people—and the enslaving evil powers can be seen in its sharpest Old Testament focus in the experience of liberation from Egyptian bondage as reported in the book of Exodus.

The biblical story reports Israel's liberation from Egypt as a confrontation between Yahweh, the God of Israel, and Pharaoh and the gods of the Egyptians. "And you shall say to Pharaoh, 'Thus says the Lord, Israel is my first-born son, and *I* say to you, "Let *my* son go that he may serve *me*"; if *you* refuse to let him go, behold, *I* will slay *your* first-born son' " (Ex. 4:22-23, emphasis mine). The real conflict is between Pharaoh and the God of Israel who had sent Moses. More than Israel's freedom is at stake. It is a question of who controls history—Yahweh, Lord of his enslaved people, or Pharaoh, the incarnation of the sun god and master of Egypt.

This struggle theme between God and Pharaoh is repeated over and over in the story. It is set forth in Moses' charge, "The Lord, the God of the Hebrews, sent me to you saying, 'Let *my* people go, that they may serve *me* in the wilderness; and behold *you* have not obeyed' " (Ex. 7:16, emphasis mine). In the narrative which follows, this theme is reiterated constantly. "Let *my* people go, that they may

serve *me*.... Behold, I will plague all *your* country with frogs"
(8:1d-2). "Let *my* people go, that they may serve *me*.... Behold, I
will send swarms of flies on *you* and *your* servants and *your* people,
and into *your* houses" (8:20d-21, emphasis mine). This contrast is explicitly continued in the verses which follow (9:13-15; 10:3-4).

The climax of this confrontation between the God of Israel and
the powers which ruled Egypt is found in the events of Passover. For
that reason the salvation of God's people in the exodus is commemorated in the "sacrifice of the Lord's passover" (Ex. 12:27).
That Isaiah picks up the theme of the lamb again in a new conflict-
victory situation on the occasion of the return of God's people from
Babylonian exile is certainly no mere coincidence (Isa. 53:7). Following the prophetic vision, the messianic community came to recognize the value of this image to describe God's new saving and liberating work on their behalf in the person of Jesus, the "lamb of God,
who takes away the sin of the world" (John 1:29).

The chief significance of the work of Christ was that he won the
decisive battle, the turning point in God's struggle with the forces of
opposition. This struggle was waged throughout the Old Testament.
It continued in the early church and is still being waged in our time.
It is the war of the lamb against all the principalities and powers of
Satan's kingdom.

The origin of the biblical view of evil forces called principalities,
powers, or rulers of this world need not be posited in the supposed
ignorance and superstition of a culturally immature and naive
people. Nor is it the result of uncritical borrowing from pagan
sources. Although the terminology is not identical, the same concept
is found in the Old Testament. Evil in the Old Testament was
regarded neither as an illusion nor as the absence of good. It was far
too powerful and real. However, these powers are ultimately judged
by God (Pss. 89:6-7; 82). The term "Lord of hosts" may be a
reference to God's superiority over subordinate powers. Israel's worship of foreign gods should not be construed merely as a religious sin
in the narrow modern sense of the term. It was a matter of adopting
the ways and values represented by these gods which amounted to a
denial of God's covenant righteousness in social relationships (Judg.
10:6). Punishment for this unfaithfulness consisted of allowing Israel
to be oppressed by the forces they were worshiping (10:7-9).

Disobedience to Yahweh never resulted in Israel's becoming free to determine their own way. They always became subservient to other values and powers, enslaved to other gods. Israel was saved by turning back in repentance to Yahweh, who delivered the nation from the dominion of these powers. While these powers exercised some positive functions in the maintenance of social order in the life of the nations, and they may have been used by God to discipline and punish people when they did evil, they exceeded their functions and drew to themselves the loyalty and obedience which belong to Yahweh alone.

New Testament Understandings of Conflict

New Testament references to Satan, demons, principalities, and powers are more frequent than they are in the Old Testament. Their reality is assumed, so one has to search for specific indications of their character and operation. They exist as power capable of personal activity. They are, by their nature, deceptive. The devil is the "father of lies" (John 8:44) who blinds the minds of unbelievers (2 Cor. 4:4), who disguises himself as an "angel of light," and "his servants also disguise themselves as servants of righteousness" (2 Cor. 11:14-15). A number of New Testament passages affirm the fact that the powers are religious forces. They are called "elemental spirits" or "basic principles" (stoicheia) which are in reality enslaving (Gal. 4:3,9). These elements are presented as Jewish religious customs (Col. 2:8, 16, 23). This does not mean that everything the powers represent is intrinsically opposed to God. But insofar as they call for ultimate allegiance, these institutions and customs call God's people away from him.

Furthermore, as in the Old Testament, powers in the New Testament are political. Jesus was confronted by the one who holds the "kingdoms of this world" (Luke 4:5-6), the one called the "prince of this world" (John 12:31). According to Paul, the rulers of this passing age are doomed to destruction in the end (1 Cor. 2:6-8; 15:24-25). The people of God are struggling against "the world rulers of this present darkness" (Eph. 6:12). Meanwhile, Jesus is Lord, exalted "far above all rule and authority and power and dominion" (Eph. 1:21; cf. 1 Pet. 3:22).

The contradictions of life in a fallen world are evident in the functioning of these powers. As structures of created existence they are needed to provide the personal support and social cohesion necessary to ongoing human life on this planet. But these structures created for human well-being (Col. 1:15) have usurped the role of master and have enslaved those whom they should be serving. The New Testament seems to be more interested in returning the powers to their proper roles under the lordship of Christ (1 Cor. 15:24-25; Phil. 2:10; cf. Rev. 21:24-26) than their annihilation, as such. However, their ultimate instrument of threat and control, death, shall be stripped from them (1 Cor. 15:26).

Understanding Sin

In the Gospels sin appears in the form of demonic and human forces which opposed Jesus and his kingdom. Paul also speaks of sin as an enslaving, deceiving, and humanly irresistible force which leads to death. Therefore any understanding of sin which concentrates merely on the individual level is not broad enough, and any concept of Christ's atoning work which concentrates on individual salvation alone is not deep enough to do justice to the biblical vision of both realities.

Paul repeatedly regarded sin as a force, a power locked in a struggle of transcendent dimensions. It is a struggle of life and death. God's righteousness and Spirit are ultimately bound up with life (Rom. 5:17-18,21; 6:4,13,22-23; 8;2,6,10). Sin is inseparably connected with death, its certain consequence (Rom. 5:12; 6:21,23; 7:5,11; cf. 1 Cor. 15:56; Eph. 2:1). Paul spoke of sin and death as "reigning and having dominion" (Rom. 5:14-17,21; 6:12,14). These terms, reign *(basileueto)* and dominion *(kurieusei)*, are parallels of "kingdom and lord." The choice between sin and righteousness is the choice between two kingdoms and two lordships.

Sin enslaves us (Rom. 6:6,16,20), and we can obey sin instead of Christ (Rom. 6:16-17). Sin deceives and kills (Rom. 7:11) and makes war and takes captives (Rom. 7:23). Sin is a deadly power which only the "Spirit of life in Christ Jesus" is able to overcome (Rom. 8:2). Paul speaks of dying to sin (Rom. 7:4,6) and of participating in the righteousness and resurrection life of Christ (Rom. 5:10; 6:14; 8:10), referring to what the synoptic Gospels call repentance from sin—a decisive change of lordship over all aspects of our lives.

Traditional Catholicism has seen sin as essentially turning away from the eternal God to temporal goods. Sin has also been viewed as the absence of the good rather than an active evil force. Therefore sin is defined negatively, so that its results are primarily immorality and disharmony.

The Reformers placed more emphasis on sin as active unfaithfulness and disobedience against God. Therefore sin and salvation have to do essentially with decision for or against God, not merely with choices for or against personal or social values. In this the Reformers were surely moving in the right direction. However, they were not sufficiently critical of sin's corporate character. The problems of individual sinners were taken seriously, but sinful structures, institutions, movements, and ideologies were not equally challenged.

Protestant orthodoxy has regarded sin as "transgression of the law," so both sin and atonement are viewed from the perspective of legal categories. Broken commandments are the consequences and evidence of sin. But while legal categories can describe certain aspects of sin, they are not capable of grasping its essence.

To view sin as merely the sum of the disobedience of sinners and the work of Christ as merely reconciling to God individuals alienated by their sin does not take seriously the biblical view of sin. On the other hand, simply to understand sin in terms of impersonal structures and Christ's work as the unmasking and defeating of these powers in their various institutionalized forms fails to recognize the personal dimensions of the problem. The conflict between God and sin in the Bible is not merely a battle between a personal power and an impersonal force of evil. We are tempted to try to explain evil in purely impersonal terms. But the biblical struggle is a titanic confrontation of wills. Only the energizing power of the Spirit of God operative in our wills can free us from the deadly domination of the powers.

The Power of Law

Law can and does become for fallen humanity an enslaving and deceiving power.[3] Paul includes law among the powers from which Christ came to free us. Being "under the law" is parallel to being "slaves to the elemental spirits" (Gal. 3:23, 25; 4:3). Christ's redemption is for "those who were under the law" (Gal. 4:4) as well as those who "were in bondage to beings that by nature are no gods" or "elemental spirits" (Gal. 4:8-9). Being freed from the law and being freed from the powers are comparable experiences (Col. 2:14-23).

Paul writes that Christ "has broken down the dividing wall of hostility" between Jews and Gentiles "by abolishing in his flesh the law of commandments and ordinances, that he might create in himself one new man in place of the two, so making peace (Eph. 2:14-15). The Jewish law, as well as pagan religious observances, was capable of regulating one's life and determining values and ultimate loyalties. Paul proclaims that just as Christ's death dethroned pagan religion, it also dethroned the law as the supreme way to God. This does not mean that biblical law is intrinsically evil. As a description of God's righteousness intended for the life of his people, the "law is holy, just and good" (Rom. 7:12). As a principle of self-justification it becomes one of the most dangerous of the powers which war against God's people. As the structure which legitimates oppressive self-centered values of fallen humanity, it becomes the vehicle of sin leading to slavery and destruction.

Christ's Victory Ushers in New Life

Christ's exaltation over the principalities and powers is at the heart of the earliest Christian confessions (Phil. 2:9-11). People in the world of the first century understood that their destinies were largely controlled by supernatural beings, many of them malevolent. The news that Christ's cross had "disarmed the principalities and powers" (Col. 2:15), that his resurrection had placed him "far above all rule and authority and power and dominion" (Eph. 1:21; cf. 2:1-2, 3:10; 6:12), that "neither death, nor life, nor angels, nor principalities . . . nor powers . . . will be able to separate us from the love of God in Christ Jesus our Lord" (Rom. 8:38-39) was good news. This deliverance from the powers was not peripheral to the gospel. The work of Christ meant freedom from these oppressive powers (Gal. 4:3-9; 5:1).

While these powers were most certainly thought of as personal entities, they were also much more than that. Since the religious, social, and political spheres of ancient life were all intimately interrelated, these beings were the controlling forces behind the values, ideologies, and social and political structures which held societies together. In modern times we might call them the state, politics, class, social struggle, nationalism, public opinion, accepted morality, ideas of decency, democracy, human traditions, or fixed social codes.

Judging from the biblical testimony, God's wrath seems to be executed primarily through the malevolent control which the principalities and powers exert over our lives. Our sins take forms which are both personal and social. Each of us has turned away from God, and we find ourselves under the domination of the powers. God's wrath is also manifested in forms which are both personal and social. These include such things as drug abuse, alcoholism, sexual immorality, hunger, poverty, and warfare. These come upon us because we go along with the social, economic, and ideological forces characterized by selfishness, injustice, and greed. Searching for ways to escape or gratify our existence, we fall victim to the powers from which we hoped to gain our well-being.

Jesus came proclaiming God's kingdom: a reign of justice, peace, and love which, by its nature, was in sharp conflict with life under the powers. In fact, because of this conflict Jesus was crucified. If we view them from this perspective, we see a continuity between Jesus' life and death. They are both phases of the same struggle which God has waged against his enemies throughout biblical history.

The death of Christ reveals the true nature of the powers. As Acts 4:25-28 and Luke 24:40 remind us, these were the state and the established religious institutions. Inasmuch as they order social and economic life and provide some degree of peace and stability, governments portray themselves as benefactors of the people (Luke 22:25). However, in reality they all perpetuate injustices and inequalities to some extent and are built upon the illegitimate exercise of power which forcibly subjugates at least some. But Jesus contrasted the way of the kingdom of God with that of governments (Matt. 20:20-28 and parallels). By both teaching and example he exposed the malefactor image of political power.

The religious powers of Jesus' day were personalized in Ananias, Caiaphas, the Sanhedrin, and many lesser scribes, Pharisees, and Sadducees. Like all religious powers, they sought to bring the comfort and blessing of God to the people. Religious institutions tend to perceive of themselves as true servants and representatives of God. However, the veiled self-interest and thirst for power of the religious practitioners are manifested for what they really are by the presence of God's Servant who with authority (Matt. 7:29) revealed God's will in contrast to the religionists of the establishment. The reaction of both state and religious institutions was the cross. So in Christ's death the true nature of the powers is most clearly revealed.

A traditional interpretation of 1 Corinthians 2:6-8 has held that Christ wished to deceive his enemies as to his true nature through his incarnation. As an early church father put it, "Christ concealed himself under the veil of our nature, in order that, as happens with greedy fishes, together with the bait of the flesh, the hook of the Godhead might also be swallowed" (cited in Aulén, 1969:52). This view obviously contradicts our understanding of the nature of God and his dealings with humanity. The powers were deceived, not because God acted inconsistently with his nature, but because of the falsehood of their own assumptions about the nature of God's love and the character of authority.

Jesus as Messiah refused to exercise violent regal power, but as servant was characterized by self-giving sacrificial love. He exposed and criticized the ways of the powerful as being contrary to God's way for his people. Their reaction indicates that the powers did not understand Jesus' way. They saw him as a threat to them and their structures, so they tried to destroy him. The disguise of Jesus was not his human nature, but the revelation that God's way is the servant way, something that the powers (with their presuppositons about the exercise of authority and the maintenance of social order) did not grasp. The violence of their reaction unmasked them.

Judged from the perspective of human values, the cross was anything but a victory. But in keeping with the vision of Jesus, the early church saw in the cross the climax of the battle which God has waged throughout the centuries (Col. 2:14-15).

Christ's victory over the powers is fully appreciated in the New Testament from the perspective of the resurrection. An early Christian confession speaks of Jesus as being "vindicated in the Spirit" (1 Tim. 3:16). This is far more than a mere judicial verdict. In the reality of the resurrection God has the last word; the defeat of the powers is made real and passes into the experience of the people of

God (Rom. 1:4; 8:11; Phil. 2:9-11; 1 Pet. 3:18). The victorious resurrection of Jesus was a judgment on God's enemies, a revelation of God's power and the establishing of his kingdom.

Jesus' messianic way has been vindicated (Acts 2:24). This is the message which led to repentance and forgiveness of sins (Acts 2:37-38; 5:31). In other words, judgment, understood as God's great reversal announced by Jesus, has already taken place for people. This is also true of the powers. Jesus "disarmed the principalities and powers and made a public example of them, triumphing over them" (Col. 2:15). His lordship over them is recognized (Phil. 2:9-11). God's power was manifested "in Christ when he raised him from the dead and made him sit at his right hand in the heavenly places, far above all rule and authority and power and dominion, and above every name that is named, not only in this age, but also in that which is to come; and he has put all things under his feet" (Eph. 1:19-22). God's people are participants in this victory (Eph. 2:6-7). The resurrection of Christ makes clear the meaning of what happened on the cross. In Christ God has challenged the powers and has shown himself to be stronger than they.

Participation in Christ's death and resurrection does not merely result in forgiveness and a clean slate before the Judge. It is inseparable from living and walking in Christ's resurrection power (Rom. 6:4; cf. 6:5-23; Gal. 2:20; 6:15). So when Paul writes of Jesus being "raised for our justification" (Rom. 4:25), it is not merely a reference to a clean judicial slate, but to the real possibility of both being set in right relationship and being made righteous. In Jesus' resurrection the righteousness of God is revealed as that power which establishes and sustains the life of the kingdom among God's people. This is the basis for the various expressions of *koinonia* as a prime characteristic of God's people—in the Jerusalem community (Acts 2:43-47; 4:32-37) and in the Gentile world (Gal. 3:28). The Spirit of the resurrection of Jesus is the one who continues to energize all of the community's ongoing fellowship, worship, and witness.

From the fourth century onward, after the church found itself allied with secular power, the military metaphors which form a part of the larger biblical conflict-victory motif could be applied literally to the warfare of Christians. However, during the pre-Constantinian period these military metaphors were images which permitted the messianic community to understand the reality of its warfare in terms of its participation in the "war on the Lamb" (Rev. 17:14). In their participation in this conflict the people of God are limited to the instruments which Jesus employed in his victory over the enemy. Throughout Christian history generally only those parts of the church which were freed from the alliance with worldly power have been able really to understand the conflict-victory image in its radical New Testament sense.

The conflict-victory motif portrays the work of Christ as the climax of God's conflict with all of the powers of evil which seek to undermine his original intention, already manifest in creation, of communion with his creatures in the context of human community. The victory takes the form of liberation from all forms of enslaving relationships, be they personal or institutional. This victory means the re-creation of new possibilities for communion with God and with others—the new community in which animosities are overcome and in which the life of the kingdom of God has already begun to become a new possibility.

Healing in Christ: Victory and Wholeness

The attitudes toward sickness and healing which predominated in the ancient world are admittedly complex. Illness seems to have been understood in earliest times as the attack of an invisible spiritual assailant. Among the Egyptians, and later among the Greeks, the art of healing was put on a more rational basis. But the ancient Greeks also had gods of healing, and the goal of their activity was the reestablishment of human happiness, rationally understood. But in general, ancient ideas of healing fluctuated among superstition, religion, and science with the boundaries between them remaining somewhat fluid (Oepke, 1965:195-99).

In ancient Israel Yahweh was seen as Healer in both a literal and a figurative sense. Yahweh commissioned priests (Lev. 13:49ff.; 14:2ff.) and prophets alike (2 Kings 5; Is. 38:21.) to serve as his agents. In the context of God's gracious covenant, however, prayer was seen as the chief means of healing. The Psalms abound with examples of complaint, petition for healing, and thanksgiving that God has heard (Pss. 6; 16:10; 30:2f.; 32:3f.; 38; 41:3-4; 51:7f.; 103:3ff.; 107:17ff.; 147:3).

In light of the global view of persons held among the ancient Hebrews, it is easy to understand how terms for healing came to be used in both literal and figurative senses. Indispensable to healing is the forgiveness of sins—dependent, of course, on repentance and conversion. Therefore healing and remission of sins are closely linked (Isa. 6:10; Pss. 6:2; 30:2; 41:4). In a context in which well-being consists of fellowship in the covenant community of Yahweh, restoration to wholeness carries spiritual, physical, social, and personal dimensions. The climax of this Old Testament view of the God who heals through the instrumentality of his anointed agents (Zech. 11:6; Jer. 6:14) is reached in the Servant Songs of Isaiah (53:4-5; 61:1). Here the vicarious suffering of the servant of Yahweh, which is seen as an expiation for the sins of many, is also described as the source of healing.

This is the motif which the New Testament picks up in order to interpret the messianic mission of Jesus (Matt. 8:17). According to Matthew's version of Isaiah 53:4, "He took our infirmities and bore our diseases."[4] As God's Messiah who brings in the age of salvation, Jesus' activity is prominently described as healing. Hardly any other image describes the work of Christ which is so strongly impressed in the early Christian tradition as that of healer. All of the Gospels describe Jesus' healing activity. His healings and exorcisms are sure signs that the messianic age is dawning and that Jesus is Messiah (Luke 7:21ff. and parallels).

It is possible to recognize a kind of "framework of oriental symbolism as a reference to the time of salvation" (Oepke, 1965:204) in the New Testament's emphasis on the physical healings which Jesus effected, yet it is difficult to see how such a thoroughgoing spiritualization of the healing of the sick is any more acceptable than a similar spiritualization of salvation from sin. In the stories of healing by Jesus which appear in the synoptic Gospels, the terms generally translated "to save" (sozo and diasozo) occur eighteen times to describe how the sick are healed and the demon-possessed are liberated (Foerster, 1971:990).

Although this usage of the terms seems strange to modern readers, it apparently related well to the intentions of the Evangelists. To be made whole in the community of Messiah was, in effect, to be saved. Jesus' words to the woman with the hemorrhage are especially instructive: "Daughter, your faith has made you well (lit., "has saved you," *sozo*); go in peace and be healed *(hugies)* of your disease" (Mark 5:34). This usage of the terms is all the more striking when we note that Jesus spoke practically the same words to the prostitute in Luke 7:48,50: "Your sins are forgiven . . . your faith has saved *(sozo)* you; go in peace." To be made whole by Jesus was much more than a mere matter of correcting a physical defect. It was a question of new relationship in the community of the Messiah who heals and saves. In the messianic community we find wholeness which is physical as well as moral and spiritual.

Jesus' miracles of healing are presented in the Gospels as signs rather than spectacles. They are powerful signs that the age of salvation, anticipated by the prophets, is beginning to be fulfilled (Matt. 11:5; Isa. 35:5f.; 61:1). According to the Gospels, Jesus' endowment with "the power of the Spirit" enabled him to perform exorcisms and healings (Luke 4:14, 36-41). Furthermore, these works of liberation and healing are interpreted in the context of the biblical vision of cosmic conflict against the powers of evil (Matt. 12:28; Luke 11:20; see Grundmann, 1964:301). The healings and exorcisms performed by Jesus are themselves partial victories of God's reign, and every partial victory is a foretaste and guarantee of the final victory still to come. Jesus is the pioneer who perfects fallen creation by means of a new creation (Oepke, 1965:213). Healings are so much a part of the messianic activity that they are regularly listed along with preaching the gospel (Matt. 4:23; 9:35). Apparently no sickness or weakness lies beyond the power of Jesus.[5]

In the Gospel narratives the process of healing itself is never the most important element. It is rather the fact that this is a manifestation of the power of Jesus which makes plain the inbreaking of God's kingdom into a suffering world—in the person and activity of Jesus, God's kingdom is coming. The real miracle lies beyond the one which is immediately evident in the healing. In fact the New Testament exercises a remarkable degree of sobriety in reporting the details of Jesus' works of healing. The center of focus is rather the victory in the conflict with forces which struggle for mastery over the cosmos (Beyer, 1965:131).

Jesus' healings are best understood from this perspective of cosmic conflict. In this context, then, the disciples are commanded to heal and to cast out demons (Matt. 10:8; Luke 10:9); they are given power over evil spirits (Matt. 10:1; Mark 3:15; Luke 9:1). In Jesus' name, therefore, the apostles continue this healing activity as a part of the ongoing battle with the powers of evil following the ascension and Pentecost.

The fact that Jesus commissioned his disciples with power to heal need not be understood primarily in terms of special endowment with extraordinary powers, but rather as an expression of Jesus' intention that they be effective witnesses of the imminent kingdom of God in both word and deed. In the power of the eschatological Spirit the apostolic community continues the conflict against the powers of evil; this includes the struggle against physical illness as well as other manifestations of human fallenness (Acts 3:1ff.; 5:14-16; 8:7; 9:32ff.; 14:7ff.; 28:8ff.). This gift of healing is an operation of the exalted Christ who is active in their midst through his Spirit (Acts 3:16; 9:34; Rom. 15:18ff.).

Jesus recognized a certain connection between sickness and sin (Mark 2:5 and parallels; John 5:14). But he broke with the rigid dogma of his time which saw illness as a direct retribution for sin. Therefore Jesus set illness in a different perspective (John 9:3f.; 11:4; cf. Luke 13:1ff.). People who suffer illness and calamity in a world in which evil powers exercise their influence dare not be charged arbitrarily with culpability. A simple relationship of cause and effect cannot be established in all cases with certainty. However, illness is clearly an evil which contradicts God's intention for creation. It is undoubtedly a part of the "groaning of travail" of "the whole creation" to which Paul refers (Rom. 8:22).

Through the work of Christ we are freed from bondage to sin. However, the full enjoyment of this freedom will finally be ours only in the *parousia*. The power of evil which manifests itself in all sorts of human illness and suffering has also been broken by the work of Christ. But similarly, the full realization of this victory awaits the manifestation of the Son of Man in the last day. Meanwhile, in this hope we are being saved and healed as we await with steadfast assurance our final redemption. In this situation the Spirit sustains us even in our weakness *(asthenia)* (Rom. 8:18-26).

The New Testament applies the motifs of vicarious suffering (Isa. 53) and conflict-victory in a holistic way to its understanding of the work of Christ. The work of Christ effected the physical healing of the sick as well as the moral and spiritual wholeness of the sinful. While the church has never forgotten that healing in its deepest sense includes forgiveness of sins, a notable tendency in the church has been to assign a figurative or spiritual sense to healing when it is associated to the work of Christ.

However, when the church takes with New Testament seriousness the motifs of vicarious suffering and conflict-victory as images for understanding the work of Christ, then all of the forms of wholeness—physical as well as spiritual, social, and personal—will be greeted with joy as signs which anticipate the full realization of God's reign. Since the new creation and the new humanity are expressions of a new reality which is already present in our midst, then we may expect concrete signs among us which anticipate the future. In this sense, therefore, we confess with thanksgiving that wholeness is the work of Christ, potentially and in reality.

4

Vicarious Suffering

As one reads the description and interpretations of the life and death of Jesus in the New Testament, the close relationship which these bear to the Servant Songs of Isaiah becomes apparent. These passages become keys for understanding the meaning of Christ's life and death for Jesus himself as well as for the early church. The Servant Songs are found in Isaiah 42:1-4 (5-9); 49:1-6; 50:4-9 (10-11); and 52:13—53:12. Isaiah 61:1-2 is sometimes considered a fifth Servant Song. The relationship between this passage and the other songs is evident (cf. Is. 42:1; 42:7; 50:10-11). Both Jesus and the apostles used the images in these passages to interpret the meaning of Christ's messianic mission.

The Servant of Yahweh

The identity of this servant of Yahweh has been the object of much discussion. Some indications are that the reference is to Israel as God's people or perhaps to a remnant of the people (Isa. 49:3; cf. 41:8; 44:1-2; 45:4; 48:20). However, the notably personal characteristics assigned to the servant seem to point to some historic person among the prophets, past or present. Some have speculated that the reference is to the prophet himself, with the fourth poem being written after his death. Be this as it may, he must have been a person of some public relevance.

By the beginning of the Christian era some Jews quite possibly interpreted the songs messianically (Stuhlmueller, 1968:378; cf. Hengel, 1981:59). However, the suffering described in the fourth song was seen as falling on Israel (and in part upon the Gentiles). The Dead Sea Scrolls seldom, if ever, make use of these songs, and the Targums tended to turn the suffering one into an enemy of God. Vicarious expiatory suffering[1] was evidently not an integral part of official Judaism's messianic doctrine. The combining of the suffering-servant motif with the messianic concept of the Son of Man seems to have been Jesus' unique contribution (Stuhlmueller, 1968:378). And this, for our purposes, is of fundamental importance.

The New Testament from the beginning describes and interprets Jesus' saving mission in terms of the suffering-servant motif. Each of the Gospels begins on this note. The synoptic Gospels describe Jesus' messianic commission in terms of Isaiah 42:1 (Mark 1:11; Matt. 3:17; Luke 3:22). John associates Jesus with the lamb of the fourth Servant Song (Isa. 53:7).[2] (In Aramaic the same term, *talya* carries the meaning of "lamb" and "servant." John the Baptist may have intentionally used this term which carried the two meanings, but the Evangelist, writing in Greek, had to choose one of the terms for his Gospel. As a messianic title, Lamb is found only in the Gospel of John and Revelation.)

In the key passage which Luke uses as an introductory summary of the contents of his Gospel (4:18-30), Jesus identifies his mission in terms of the fifth Servant Song (Isa. 61:1-2; cf. 42:2; 58:6). In Matthew 8:16-17 Jesus' healing ministry is interpreted according to the servant vision (Is. 53:4). This is not a mere case of proof-texting. According to the biblical perspective a connection exists between the alleviation of physical evils and the expiation of sin. The same servant bore our diseases and "bore the sin of many" (Isa. 53:12). The low-key servanthood nature of Jesus' ministry is interpreted in terms of Isaiah 42:1-4 (Matt. 12:16-21), and the response to Jesus' public ministry is summed up with texts drawn from Isaiah 53:1 and 6:9-10 (John 12:37-43).

In Luke 22:37 Jesus himself interprets his impending passion with a specific reference to Isaiah 53:10. Unmistakable echos from the Servant Songs are present also in Jesus' allusions to his suffering and death (Mark 8:31; 9:12b,31; 10:33f.,45; 14:21). The "many" of Mark 10:45 ("to give his life as a ransom for many") is strongly reminiscent of the fourfold "many" in Isaiah 52:14-15; 53:11-12. The early church certainly understood Jesus' messianic ministry in terms of the servant motif (Luke 24:26f.; Acts 8:32,35), and primitive apostolic preaching refers specifically to Jesus as servant (Acts 3:13,26; 4:27,30). The servant motif characterized primitive hymns and confessions of faith. We find many examples in the writings of both Paul and Peter (Phil. 2:7; 1 Pet. 2:21-25; 1 Cor. 15:3-4).

While Paul with some frequency adapted the servant image to himself (Acts 13:47; Gal. 1:15; Rom. 15:21), he also applied it to the death of Jesus. "Who was put to death for our trespasses" (Rom. 4:25) appears to be a free quotation from the Septuagint version of Isaiah 53:12, and the phrase "for us" in the Lord's Supper formula in 1 Corinthians 11:23-25 is most certainly an adaptation of the "for us" and "many" motif which is so prominent in Isaiah 52-53. As we have already noticed, references to Jesus as "lamb of God" and as "a lamb ... slain" are most certainly inspired by the image in Isaiah 53 (John 1:29,36; Acts 8:32; 1 Pet. 1:19; Rev. 5:6; 13:8; 14:5). Even in Hebrews 9:28 we find an allusion to Isaiah 53:12.

So a servant soteriology appears to be a fundamental characteristic of the earliest Christian reflection on the meaning of the life, death, and resurrection of Christ. It seems equally clear that this current of interpretation finds its source in Jesus himself.[3]

The Servant Vision of the Servant Songs

Traditionally, the two aspects of the servant vision which have illuminated our understanding of the work of Christ are the vicarious nature of the servant's death (Isa. 53:12; Mark 10:45; Eph. 2:13) and the servant's mediatorial role in establishing the new covenant (Isa. 42:6-8; 1 Cor. 11:25). However, another probably more fundamental way in which the Servant Songs illumine the New Testament understanding of Jesus' messianic role is the reality of God's kingly rule and the method of its establishment. Therefore, we will review the thrust of the Servant Songs to see what further light they throw on our understanding of the work of Christ.[4]

Isaiah 42:1-4. The servant is Yahweh's chosen one, endowed with the Spirit and commissioned to carry out God's saving intention: "Bring forth justice to the nations" (1). The methods employed by the servant in the fulfillment of this mission are quiet, unobtrusive, nonviolent, and persistent (2-3). In spite of the apparent ineffectiveness of this strategy and reason for discouragement and seeming failure, the fidelity of God's servant shall not waver until the righteousness of God's covenant intention is established throughout the earth (4).

Isaiah 49:1-7. Yahweh's servant has been called from birth and destined for a mission. Here the servant is Israel, in whom God will be glorified (3). In spite of the apparent fruitlessness of any efforts, God will vindicate the servant's labor eventually. The servant will not only "restore the preserved of Israel," but will be "a light to the nations, that [God's] salvation may reach to the end of the earth" (6). God's "Holy One," the servant so "deeply despised, abhorred by the nations" (7), will finally become the object of praise and obeisance of the world's rulers.

Isaiah 50:4-9. The servant is an obedient disciple of the Lord God (4-5a). In fact, this obedience involves suffering violence and ignominy; but even in the face of suffering, the servant does not draw back, confident that in the midst of conflict God will finally vindicate (8-9).

Isaiah 52:13—53:12. The poem is divided into three parts. Yahweh speaks at the beginning (52:13-15) and end (53:11-12), and the middle "we" section is spoken by either Israel or the nations (53:1-10). The song begins with Yahweh's announcement of the exaltation of the servant (52:13). But this exaltation follows an utterly astonishing humiliation. For the nations and their kings it is an unheard of, unimaginable reversal of things which they will eventually come to see and understand (52:15).

The appearance of the servant, like that of a desert scrub bush, is unattractive (53:2). The servant suffered unimaginably at the hands of humans to the point that it was supposed that it was a result of divine displeasure (53:4b). But they come to see that the servant's suffering was vicarious and restoring. He has become their sin-bearer (53:6).[5] In the innocent suffering inflicted upon him he remained nonviolent. By oppressive and unjust means his life was taken. He was wrongly judged to be an evildoer. Yet, somehow the saving intention of God lies behind the innocent and vicarious suffering of the servant. "He makes himself an offering for sin" (53:10).[6] This suffering is vindicated in the emergence of God's people. Yahweh declares that the servant's suffering is redemptive, and participation in the community of the righteous one means to share the righteousness which characterizes both God and God's people (53:11). Finally, Yahweh declares that the servant's way of innocent, vicarious suffering has become the way of true power and conquest (53:12). The servant is Lord!

Isaiah 61:1-2. The servant of the Lord is the herald and agent of God's kingly rule in which relationships are ordered according to God's covenant intention expressed in Sinai and underscored in the sabbatical and Jubilee provisions, or "the year of the Lord's favor" (2). It is a rule characterized by righteousness and the glory of God (3).

As we have already indicated, the contribution of the Servant Songs to our understanding of the work of Christ has been largely limited to seeing his death as a vicarious expiation for sin. But a more careful reading which sets aside for the moment the presuppositions of later theories of the atonement gives us a basis for a fuller vision of the work of Christ. The servant way is inherent in God's kingly rule among humankind.

The important themes of the Servant Songs can be summarized as follows. (1) The servant of Yahweh was God's agent to the nations (Isa. 42:1,4,6; 49:1,6; 52:15). (2) The task to which the servant was commissioned was to bring Yahweh's justice—or salvation (49:6)— to the nations (42:1,3,4,6; 53:11). (3) The servant was anointed with the Spirit of Yahweh (42:1; 61:1) in order to effect his ministry nonviolently by means of Yahweh's word (42:2-3; 49:2; 50:4-5; 61:1-2). (4) The servant faced growing opposition, persecution, and death which he accepted patiently in the pursuit of his task (42:4; 49:4; 50:6-9; 52:14—53:12). (5) The servant achieved his purpose of bringing justice to the nations only by Yahweh's intervention in reversing the judgment of the nations and elevating him to a place of rule (49:4; 52:13-15; 53:11-12). (6) Kings and nations confessed their rebellion and acknowledged that the suffering of the servant was on their behalf, that "with his stripes they are healed" (53:1-10).

One cannot help noticing the difference between the servant in these passages and another agent anointed by God, Cyrus (Isa. 45:1). He exercises power by means of the traditional instruments of coercion available to the rulers of this world. Cyrus is called a shepherd, and he even fulfilled God's purpose in the restoration of Jerusalem (44:28). However, God's justice is established through the servant. The servant, rather than Cyrus, is elevated to be Yahweh's ruler. Yahweh's intention in the elevation of a servant to kingship is that the nations acknowledge a new kind of political leadership and authority based on a new kind of power, the power of servanthood. The prophet-servant equipped with Yahweh's word and committed to vicarious and innocent suffering, rather than King Cyrus, is elevated as Yahweh's ruler.

The function of the servant is emphatically set forth in the first Servant Song: "He will bring forth justice to the nations" (42:1); "he will faithfully bring forth justice" (42:3); "he will not fail . . . till he has established justice in the earth" (42:4); "I have called you in righteousness . . . I have given you . . . a light to the nations" (42:6). A paraphrase of this passage assigns the same function to Yahweh (51:4-5). So we may understand justice *(mishpat)* here as the politics of God: the way in which relationships are ordered in God's kingdom. The kingly characteristics of the servant are so directly contrary to the reign of a ruler such as Cyrus that there is little wonder that the servant meets with opposition, persecution, and death. The same is true of Jesus in his historic encounter with the powers in Jerusalem (cf. Acts 4:25-32).

The climax of the Servant Songs in Isaiah 52:13—53:12 is the elevation of the servant to kingly rule (53:12). God's servant is made king in a reversal of values which is humanly astonishing. This is the main point of the passage. Expiation and vicarious innocent suffering of the servant should be interpreted within this context. Hope for the nations, whose politics of violence and power is a turning of "every one to his own way" (53:6), lies in the servant who suffers to reverse the meaning and practice of the exercise of power and thus to bring God's justice or salvation. This means, among other things, that peace, justice, and salvation, the concrete shape of the kingdom to which the messianic mission points, are all tied integrally to the atoning work of Jesus. They are not peripheral concerns essentially unrelated to his saving work.

Variations of the Servant Vision

Jesus' redefinition of the meaning of authority and service is given in all of the Gospels (Matt. 20:24-28; Mark 10:41-45; Luke 22:24-27; cf. John 13:13-15). It is found in the same context in which he describes his mission "to give his life as a ransom for many" (Mark 10:45). This theme is underscored in the fourth Servant Song where the term *many* appears five times (Isa. 52:14-15; 53:11,12a,12c). The convergence of these themes in Mark 10:45 appears to confirm the idea that Jesus took both his understanding of authority and the concept of giving "his life as a ransom for many" from the Servant Songs.

An Old Testament parallel to the Servant Songs is sometimes found in the life and suffering of Jeremiah. "I was a like a gentle lamb led to the slaughter" (Jer. 11:19) is Jeremiah's evaluation of his situation in the midst of violent and murderous enemies. But a stronger parallel is found in Zechariah 9:9-10, which seems to reflect the same servanthood vision of kingship as the Servant Songs. While the Revised Standard Version does not indicate it, the terms *righteous one* (translated "triumphant") and *afflicted* (translated "humble") may well be direct allusions to Isaiah 53:7,11.

In later Jewish thought the idea of the propitiatory value of the sufferings of the righteous appears. But this has nothing in common with the servant vision of Isaiah. Here we have the thought of a God whose wrath is appeased by suffering. In 2 Maccabees 7:37f. the youngest of the martyr brothers offers his body and life for the laws of the fathers, praying that God will soon show propitiousness to the nation, "in order that in me and in my brothers the wrath of the Almighty, justly poured out upon our race may be appeased." In 4 Maccabees 6:27-29 Eleazar prays that his blood may be a sacrifice for the purification of the people: "Make my blood a purification for them and take my life as a ransom [*antipsuchon*] for their life." In 4 Maccabees 17:21-22 the martyrs in their sufferings "became, as it were, a ransom for our nation's sins, and through the blood of these righteous ones and their propitiating death, the divine Providence preserved Israel which before was evil entreated."

The difference between this propitiatory and substitutionary view of suffering on behalf of the nation, held by the Maccabees, and the vision of vicarious expiatory suffering outlined in the Servant Songs of Isaiah is obvious.

According to the Maccabean view, the death of these freedom fighters who were committed to the just cause of freeing their people was both vicarious and propitiatory. The wrath of God upon Israel was experienced concretely in their being handed over to the tyranny and exploitation of foreign domination. In this situation the appeasement of God's wrath meant freedom from the yoke of the heathen and the establishment of home rule, which in this case meant the imposition of the Hasmonean dynasty. In any event, it meant the reestablishment of rule by coercive power rather than the creation of a new alternative, such as that envisioned in the Servant Songs and espoused by Jesus.

Constantinian Christendom has by and large perpetuated this Maccabean vision. The Western church has generally passed over the image of vicarious expiatory suffering reflected in the Servant Songs and espoused by Jesus as a prime category with which to understand the work of Christ because it does not really fit into the Constantinian vision in which power is at the disposal of the church. For this reason the Maccabean view has been so congenial. Western Christianity has generally not really grasped the integral relationship between the vicarious expiatory suffering of the Messiah and the creation of a concrete new reality in which the rule of God takes a radically new social shape, in which lordship is servanthood.

The Maccabean vision can take a Constantinian form just as naturally as it fits in a revolutionary situation, since both focus on "appeasing the wrath of God" in unjust situations, but neither has the radical disposition to submit to the new social alternative of the suffering servant.

Traditional Western Christianity has been characterized by an overriding concern for understanding the work of Christ in terms of appeasing the wrath of God. But the creation of a new messianic community characterized, vertically, by unconditional dependence on the absolutely faithful covenant God who saves and provides for people and, horizontally, by uncoerced social relationships of agape love has been left largely to radical reform movements.[7]

This view of servanthood, the true path to God's justice and salvation in which God's people are restored to wholeness, inspired Jesus' messianic mission. The work of Christ reveals supremely the reality of God's rule among humankind established through the power of suffering servanthood.

The Lamb of God

Two terms are used in the New Testament to refer to Christ as Lamb. *Amnos* occurs four times in the New Testament (John 1:29,36; Acts 8:32; 1 Pet. 1:19). The term is always applied to Jesus who is compared with a lamb as one who suffers and dies innocently and representatively. *Arnion* is used 28 times in Revelation as a description of the exalted Christ. The designation of Messiah as a lamb does not appear in later Judaism, so we need not look to contemporary Judaism as the source of use of the term in the primitive Christian community. But where does the source of this unlikely messianic designation lie?

Lamb as Servant

First, Jesus himself, as well as the primitive community from the earliest period, saw in Messiah the servant of the Lord of Isaiah 53. Frequent references in the Gospels to the Servant Songs relate to Jesus' messianic activity. The early Palestinian church surely understood Jesus' messianic mission in terms of the servant image. In Isaiah 53:7 the servant who suffers patiently is compared to a lamb. This comparison is expressly related to Jesus in the primitive gospel proclamation of Philip (Acts 8:32). So Isaiah 53:7 may well be the origin of the earliest description of Jesus as a Lamb.

Second, the image of the lamb plays an especially prominent role in Johannine literature. In the Fourth Gospel Jesus was crucified at the moment when the Passover lambs were slaughtered in the temple (John 19:14). John 19:36 seems to be a direct allusion to the stipulation regarding the Passover lamb, "You shall not break a bone of it" (Ex. 12:46; Num. 9:12). Paul had earlier used the same figure to bolster the plea for the exercise of evangelical discipline in the Corinthian congregation. So it appears certain that the Christological image of the Paschal lamb was already well established (1 Cor. 5:7). The two lines of influence (the lamb of Isaiah 53 and the Passover lamb of Exodus 12) probably interacted in establishing the lamb as a metaphor for understanding the life and death of Jesus.

However, we have reason to think that the first of these two sources was primary. Jeremias has suggested that the Greek term translated "lamb of God" reflects an earlier Aramaic term, *talya* which carried a twofold meaning: (1) lamb and (2) servant or boy (Jeremias, 1964:338). So the original reference would have been to Jesus as servant of Yahweh. The double meaning of the term would explain the adoption or even the origin of the designation of Jesus as Lamb. This would happen only in bilingual or Greek-speaking areas, and interestingly enough, lamb, as a messianic title, is applied to Jesus only in the Fourth Gospel (two times) and Revelation (28 times). The use of the term in Acts 8:32 and 1 Peter simply compare Jesus to a lamb rather than using the term as a messianic title.

We can probably best understand John 1:29,36 in light of Isaiah 53:6,7,12.[8] In effect, John the Baptist was calling Jesus the servant of the Lord "who takes away the sin of the world." This is a remarkable reference to Isaiah 53:12 where the vicarious suffering of the servant of Yahweh is described. The Isaianic origin of the description of Jesus as Lamb is further substantiated by the synoptic parallel where Jesus' messianic mission is introduced by a reference to the Servant Song in Isaiah 42:1 (Matt. 3:17; Mark 1:11; Luke 3:22). So in light of its Old Testament roots, John 1:29 refers to the representative bearing of sin (cf. Isa. 53:12 [LXX]; 53:4,6,11), to vicarious expiatory suffering in behalf of many (cf. Mark 10:45).

Lamb as Sin-Bearer

Bearing "the sin of many" (Isa. 53:12) in vicarious suffering becomes for John taking away "the sin of the world" in the expiatory efficacy of Jesus' death (John 1:29). When the primitive community describes Jesus as lamb, it refers to the patience of his suffering (Acts 8:32), his sinlessness (1 Pet. 1:19), and the efficacy of his sacrificial death (John 1:29,36; 1 Pet. 1:19). Jesus was representatively obedient unto death, and by his vicarious death he cancelled the effects of sin for all humanity. Therefore Jesus' dying means the dawn of the time of messianic salvation (1 Pet. 1:20). As the blood of the Paschal lambs once played a part in the redemption from Egypt, so also Jesus accomplished redemption from the bondage of sin (1 Pet. 1:18). But the efficacy of Jesus' death is not limited to Israel, like that of the Paschal lamb, but it extends to the whole world, hopelessly fallen under the judgment of God (John 1:29).

We must remember that the lamb metaphor is descriptive rather than definitive in its application to Jesus. Furthermore, it is apparent that the servant image of Isaiah is primary in determining the meaning of the metaphor as applied to Jesus. This means that we should be careful not to give more emphasis to the Paschal lamb image than the New Testament does. In the final analysis, the person of Jesus rather than the metaphors themselves should define the substance of our understanding of his life and death.

Several additional observations can be made regarding the

Passover lamb as background for understanding the servant passages of Isaiah 42-53, as well as the work of Christ as lamb of God.

The liberation described in Exodus 12-15 was communal. The context for the celebration of the Passover was the "whole assembly of the congregation of Israel" in which the families participated (Ex. 12:6,3,4). The reality of this saving act of God was later to be commemorated by the people of God as a part of their ongoing experience of God's salvation (Ex. 12:14). But this commemoration was not merely ritual. In fact, the return from exile in Babylonia was seen as a new exodus (Isa. 42:9; 43:16-21; 51:9-11).

In the New Testament Christ's Passion is described literally as an exodus (Luke 9:31), and the life of the messianic community was understood in terms of exodus liberation (1 Cor. 10:1-4; Heb. 3:6-19). This understanding was so common that Paul could make a passing reference to "Christ, our Paschal lamb" without needing to explain it and without the risk of being misunderstood (1 Cor. 5:7).

In the Servant Songs of Isaiah the context of the ministry of the servant is a people among whom God's righteous rule is realized. Likewise, the context in which the Passover lamb was sacrificed was communal. It expedited the liberation of God's people from the bondage of Egypt. For the New Testament community this meant that the saving work of the Lamb of God results in the creation of a new people whose life is characterized by the righteousness which corresponds to God's kingdom.

Just as in the case of the suffering-servant image, Constantinian Christendom has had great difficulty in incorporating this communal dimension of the New Testament understanding of the work of Christ as Lamb of God into its practice and theology. At best the work of the Lamb of God was applied to individuals within Christendom. Again, the radical renewal movements have recovered the universal and communal dimensions of the saving work of the "Lamb of God who takes away the sin of the world" (John 1:29). In the context of covenanted community this salvation is fully personal because it is found within the community of the Messiah (John 1:36-37).

The Paschal lamb ritual was not originally a sacrifice in the sense of being taken to the temple for offering. The lamb was slaughtered, and its blood was smeared on the doorposts for a protective effect. It was eaten by the people as a meal, not simply turned over to the priests. It was a ceremony with a cultic dimension but without an altar or a mercy seat, which were located in the tabernacle or temple. It was a sharing of the life of the lamb with the family in the Passover commemoration. It was not essentially a matter of slaying the lamb *instead of* the family, but for the family.

No evidence seems to exist in the biblical text for not extending this meaning from the Passover commemoration to the prophetic description of the lamb who is led to the slaughter in Isaiah 53. The Isaiah passage has no explicit references to the kinds of instructions for the slaughter of the lamb and its disposition on the altar or dividing it among the priests of the type which we find in the common sacrificial rituals of the Old Testament. Undoubtedly, it is best to see as background for the slaughter of the lamb in Isaiah 53 the Paschal lamb which is slaughtered to be consumed by the people.

In John 6:48-58 Jesus invites the people to eat his flesh and drink his blood, and in so doing he essentially refers to himself as the Paschal lamb. The question of whether their eating is real or symbolic need not occupy our attention at this point. Rather, we should ask ourselves if we are not faced here with good reason to see the self-offering of the lamb of Isaiah 53, and ultimately the Paschal lamb, rather than one of the other sacrificial rituals of the Old Testament as background for understanding the institution of the Lord's Supper.

"Eating my flesh" and "drinking my blood" in John 6 is parallel to "taking the cross and following me" in the synoptic Gospels in that it occurs at the same point in the Gospel narrative, i.e., the moment when, after the crowds come to Jesus in the wilderness, the people begin to turn away from following him because of the hard sayings they hear him speak (cf. Matt. 16; Mark 8; Luke 9).

The offering of the lamb is a Paschal sacrifice rather than a temple sacrifice. Rather than simply being viewed as an expiatory sacrifice, it is perceived as a communal meal. The reason for eating the communal meal is to be strengthened to follow him whose flesh and blood we consume, whose essence we take into ourselves, just as those who participated in the first Passover received strength to follow the Lord in the Exodus.

In the book of Revelation, Lamb appears 28 times as a title for

Christ. The fact that the Lamb is described as having been slain (5:6,9,12; 13:8) shows that we cannot distinguish between the Lamb of the book of Revelation and the New Testament view of Jesus as suffering servant or Paschal lamb. The key to the identification of this "Lamb which is slain" as "Lord of lords and King of kings" (17:14) and who is "worthy to receive power ... and might and honor and glory and blessing" (5:12) is found in Jesus' own redefinition of authority and power (Matt. 20:25-28; Mark 10:41-45; Luke 22:24-27; John 13:13-15). The Lamb is the one who did "ransom *(agorazo)* men for God by his blood" (Rev. 5:9), in whose blood the robes of the redeemed have been "washed ... and made ... white" (7:14), in whose blood the "brethren ... have conquered" (12:10-11).

The use of this metaphoric title, "Lamb of God," for Jesus seems to underscore the centrality of the servant image reflected in the prophetic vision of Isaiah and concretely defined in the life and death of Jesus. A secondary allusion is found in the Paschal lamb of the Exodus. The Old Testament sacrificial system, as such, does not seem to offer substantial additional help for understanding the lamb image in its application to Jesus.

5

Archetypal Images

ORIGINAL

Several archetypal images in the New Testament are applied to
Jesus. These include Representative Man, Pioneer, Forerunner, and
Firstborn.[1] While they have not generally been related to the atonement in recent theology, these messianic titles apparently did play a
substantial role in the early church's articulation of the meaning of
the saving work of Christ. This is particularly true of the Pauline use
of the Representative Man metaphor.

Furthermore, all these images significantly relate the work of
Christ to the new life in Christ which the apostolic community
experienced with such intensity. Their usage simply underscores the
biblical concern for understanding God's gracious saving initiatives,
including the work of Christ, in the context of the experience of salvation in God's community.

new life

of the experience

Representative Man   *Jesus = ? the one man — Adam = one man*

According to the Gospels, Son of man was the title with which
Jesus most often referred to himself.[2] Although this title appears
nowhere in Pauline writings, Paul does gather up its meaning in
another set of similar terms whose use in the New Testament is exclusively Pauline. In Romans 5:12-21 Jesus is called "the one to
come," "that one man," or "the one man" repeatedly in contrast to
Adam, who is simply called Adam or "one man." In 1 Corinthians
15:45-49 Christ is called "the last Adam," "the second Adam," and
"the man of heaven," in each case in contrast to Adam. Similar to
Jesus' reference to the Son of man (Mark 10:45), Paul relates "the
last Adam" motif with that of the suffering servant of Yahweh who
brings "righteousness of life" (Rom. 5:12-21; Phil. 2:6-11) (Jeremias,
1964:141-43).

101

Pauline

Behind the Pauline use of these terms lies the Hebrew concept of corporate personality. According to this view, the life of the people or their corporate personality was focused synthetically in the person who occupied a position of headship, leader, or king. This was an important concept in the self-understanding of the people of God. This concept corresponded somewhat with other peoples of the ancient Near East. However, while the kings of Egypt, Mesopotamia, and Canaan were viewed as incarnations of their gods, in Israel the function of the king was simply charismatic (McKenzie, 1968:748). But as the "anointed of Yahweh," the king became the bearer, in a representative way, of Israel's destiny (Jer. 30:18-22). Psalm 69:6-12 offers a notable glimpse of this representative or mediatorial function of kingship in Israel. Deuteronomy 17:14-20 lists among the chief characteristics of this representative person that he be one of God's own choosing and whose principal virtue is obedience to God's intention for his people.

The relationship in the New Testament between the vicarious suffering and utter obedience of God's Anointed (Messiah) and the way in which the kingship of Christ is exercised is certainly not coincidental (cf. Phil. 2:5-11). "The Lamb will conquer them, for he is Lord of lords and King of kings, and those with him are called and chosen and faithful" (Rev. 17:14). The one who conquers is "the Lamb . . . clad in a robe dipped with blood" by means of the sharp sword which issues from his mouth (Rev. 19:9, 13,15). He is "King of kings and Lord of lords" (19:16). As the Anointed of God, Jesus carries representatively the mission and destiny of God's people. The saving work of Christ is not unrelated to the life and mission of his people. He carries in his suffering and ultimate victory the suffering and victory of God's people.

Solidarity in Death and Life

In Paul's understanding of Christ as the last Adam we observe three distinguishable dimensions. (1) Christ's representative role as the new Adam includes his vicarious death in absolute obedience to the Father (Rom. 5:12-21), a death in which we too participate. (2) Jesus is viewed as the new Adam from the perspective of his resurrection (1 Cor. 15:20-22, 45-49). From this perspective he is seen as the life-giving spirit and as the image to which redeemed humanity will eventually be conformed. (3) In the prison epistles (Eph. 2:15; 4:13,22,24; Col. 3:9), we find the expressions "new man" and "mature [or perfect] manhood." Here appears to be an overlapping of images. Christ is viewed as the Representative Man in which the people of God find their fullness (Eph. 4:13). God's people are also viewed as a new humanity, a concrete new social and spiritual reality which is, in fact, a community of reconciliation (Eph. 2:11-22).[3]

Paul in Romans 5:12-21 presupposes the biblical vision of corporate personality, including a solidarity of relationship with Adam in his fallenness. ("Adam" means "man" or "humanity.") But there is also a new solidarity of grace whereby, in his saving work, Christ is viewed as Representative Head of a new humanity characterized by righteousness. In view of Jewish speculation about an Archetypal Man, or a Heavenly Man, Paul's use of Adam and Christ in a representative sense would most certainly have been meaningful to his first-century Jewish readers (Barrett, 1968:374).

All humanity shares in the solidarity of sin and its result, death. This is not only because we all participate representatively in Adam, but *also* due to the fact that we all have sinned, too (Rom. 5:12). Furthermore, human sin is more than mere transgression of God's law. It is more fundamentally that exaltation of self which constitutes an idolatrous rebellion against God (5:13a).

But there is also a solidarity in grace through "the One to come," "the one man, Christ Jesus" (Rom. 5:14-15). Just as sin and death became universally established in the representative rebellion of Adam, so also grace and the new possibility of "righteousness of life" are open to all through the obedience of the New Representative Man, "the one man, Jesus Christ" (5:16-19).

Paul understands the work of Christ the Representative Man as obedience to the Father unto the point of death. The death of Christ is viewed as an act of obedience on our behalf, a view which is akin to the suffering servant of Yahweh motif, so important for Jesus in his messianic self-understanding as well as for the earliest Palestinian community. Furthermore, this representative character of Christ's work tells us something about the nature of the vicariousness of his death. Jesus' death was not instead of ours in the sense that Christians are thereby exempt from death. As the new Adam, Jesus' death and resurrection were representative, anticipating the possibility of our dying and being raised with him (1 Thess. 4:14; 5:10; 2 Cor. 5:15; 4:10; Rom. 14:9).

Jesus is the Son of man with whom the last age, the age of the new creation, has dawned. Adam was representative of the fall, of the old creation in which sin and death are universally shared. However, in Christ is a new beginning. This New Man, instead of idolatrous self-seeking, subordinated himself in utter obedience to God, obedient even unto death. Therefore Christ is the Representative Man in whom "many will be made righteous" (Rom. 5:19).

Paul's image of Christ as Representative Man in 1 Corinthians 15:20-22,45-49 is focused on his resurrection through which he is bearer of the possibility of life for all. In contrast to the first Adam, Christ—the "last Adam," the "man of heaven"—is both "life-giving spirit" (15:45) and Representative Man; it is to his image that redeemed humanity is destined to become conformed (15:49). This transformation has already begun to take place because it "comes from the Lord who is the Spirit" (2 Cor. 3:18; 4:10-12).

"By a man" and "in Adam" all humanity has representatively departed from its vocation according to God's original intention, and death has become our destiny. But now "by a man" and "in Christ" is resurrection and life. Christ is viewed as the representative bearer of life in whom all who are in solidarity with him receive life. The image of the firstfruits carries this meaning. The firstfruits is the offering of the first installment of the crop which representatively foreshadows and pledges the ultimate offering of the whole harvest.[4]

Neither of the two men mentioned here was simply a private individual. Each was an Adam, a representative man. What each of them was, others in their train have become. By nature the first were essentially physical and earthly. But those who participate in the new age, just as the last Adam, are spiritual and heaven-oriented. Christ's resurrection to a spiritual body, which has happened already, is representative of ours which is thereby assured by his.

In contrast to the fact that the first Adam became a living soul, the Last Adam became a life-giving spirit (1 Cor. 15:45). For Paul the resurrection means the Spirit and power (Rom. 1:4). In biblical thought spirit is not merely life but life-giving power (cf. John 6:63). Paul's line of reasoning in 1 Corinthians 15:45-49 does not merely serve to show that two kinds of bodies exist, but also to set forth the work of Christ through which alone it is possible to partake of the life of the age to come.

Representation, or solidarity, is a key concept which thoroughly colors Paul's understanding of Christ and his saving work. The fact that Jesus lived and died in history is of vital significance for Paul. The exalted contemporary Christ is one and the same as the Jesus of history. *Who* Jesus was, as well as *what* he did, is important for Paul. And here Paul insists in several ways that Jesus was the Representative Man. "Jesus became one with man in order to put an end to sinful man, in order that a new man might come into being. He became what man is in order that by his death and resurrection man might become what he his" (Dunn, 1974:126).

When Paul speaks about Adam and Jesus Christ, he refers representatively to two humanities. Adam represents what humankind might have been and what we are now: humanity made for communion with God but who has become the slave of self. Jesus represents a new kind of humanity: humanity which not only dies but lives again. In Christ humanity not only becomes spiritually alive, but also looks to a future life of communion with God. But Jesus' representative role covers the present as well as the future of humanity. Jesus represents what we are now, and by his obedience he represents what we may become.

In Romans 8:3 Paul speaks of God "sending his own Son in the likeness of sinful flesh and for sin." This does not mean that Jesus became guilty of sin. For Paul, flesh, as such, is not evil. It is rather humanity in its fallenness, subject to temptation, human appetites and desires, and death (cf. Rom. 7:5,18,25). In taking the form of sinful flesh, Jesus became representative of fallen humanity; he identified himself with humanity in its fallenness (Dunn, 1974:127-28). In this representative capacity Jesus served God's purposes as a sin offering for our sins (Barrett, 1957:56).

The primitive hymn in Philippians 2:5-11 also refers to Christ Jesus assuming the "likeness of men" and "being found in human form."[5] Among other things, this hymn reminds us of the early church's conviction that Jesus came not merely as a man, as one man among many, but as Representative Man not only subject to death but also obedient to God even to the point of death on the cross.

The biblical vision of humankind set forth in Psalm 8:4-6 was widely used in the early church in its testimony to Jesus Christ and his saving work (1 Cor. 15:27; Eph. 1:22; Phil. 3:21; Heb. 2:6-9; 1 Pet. 3:22). The writer to the Hebrews states the conviction that Jesus was *The* Man who fulfilled the destiny God had originally intended for humanity. Humankind had been created "lower than the angels" but has not yet been crowned with glory and honor and granted lordship over all things. However, in contrast, Jesus had fulfilled humanity's destiny. He too "for a little while was made lower than the angels," but he has been crowned with glory and honor "because of the suffering of death" (Heb. 2:8-9).

Jesus' representative role also surely underlies 1 Corinthians 15:27. Paul sees the fulfillment of Psalm 8 in Jesus Christ, the Representative Man (Barrett, 1968:359). Jesus entered upon his role as New Man only after having lived and suffered as a human. Adam missed his destiny because of sin; therefore his destiny became death (1 Cor. 15:21-22). Jesus Christ, after having lived out the destiny of Adam (death), created a new destiny (resurrection) in his role as the last Adam. In both cases his role was that of Representative Man in whom humanity participates through his death and resurrection (Dunn, 1974:129).[6]

Probably one of the clearest Pauline expressions of his understanding of Jesus Christ and his saving work in terms of Representative Man is 2 Corinthians 5:14-15: "One has died for all; therefore all have died." To say that Christ is Representative Man is to say that what is true of him in particular is true of humanity in general. To say that Adam is representative man in his fallenness is to say that all humanity is fallen. Therefore, when Paul says that Christ died as Representative Man he means that all humankind dies. We may suppose that had there been some other way for fallen humanity to overcome its fallenness Christ would not have died. Christ would have shown humankind how to overcome the fallenness of sinful flesh. But Christ, the Representative Man, died in solidarity with fallen humanity. The answer to the fallenness of sinful flesh is its destruction to death. So when Paul says that Christ "died for *(huper)* all" (5:14), without doubt he sees him as Representative Man. Paul does not say that all did not need to die because one died in their place. Rather, on account of the death of Christ all humanity became potentially dead in the sense described in verse 15. He died for us

that we might die to ourselves and live for him (Barrett, 1973:168).

In Christ's death he is representative of fallen humanity. In his resurrection Christ is representative of the new humanity, those who "live no longer for themselves" in the self-centered orientation which characterizes the life of fallen humanity, which was precisely the sin of Adam, who instead of living for his Creator sought to control life by and for himself. Relationships in the new humanity of the new Adam who died and who was raised again for us are characterized by love of the kind with which Christ himself loved us (2 Cor. 5:14a).[7] The kind of change described in this passage cannot take place "apart from the realm of actual obedience and unselfish living" (Barrett, 1973:169). In his death Christ, as human, represents all humanity in its fallenness. In his resurrection, Jesus Christ, as last Adam, represents all those who experience the life-giving spirit (1 Cor. 15:45) and brings into existence the new creation (2 Cor. 5:17) (Dunn, 1974:131).

Representation: Key to Understanding Sacrifice

While sacrifices were undoubtedly meaningful to pious and penitent worshipers in Israel, scholars have found it to be nearly impossible to discover a clear rationale for understanding the meaning of sacrifice in ancient Israel. Not unlikely, one of the values of sacrifice was its usefulness in effecting atonement, even though exactly how this happened remained shrouded in mystery.

As for Paul's use of the sacrificial image for understanding the meaning of Christ's death, the biblical concept of representation may well be a key to unlock its meaning (Dunn, 1974:131-37). The laying on of hands of the offerer, so prominent in the instructions for offering bloody sacrifices (Lev. 4), as well as in other ritual acts (e.g., Num. 8:10; 27:18,23; Deut. 34:9), appears to have had as its principal rationale some sort of identification or representation. Therefore the sin offering was thought to represent the one who was offering it.

In Romans 8:3 and 2 Corinthians 5:21 Paul views Christ in his death as a sin offering.[8] These are passages, as noted above, where the representative nature of the work of Christ is especially prominent. The following translation of these texts will serve to make clear the parallelism which Paul apparently intended.

God . . . condemned *sin* in the flesh *[of Jesus]*
In order that the *just requirement of the law* might be fulfilled in *us*
  (Rom. 8:3, 4).

For our sake God made the *Sinless One* into *sin*
In order that we might become the *righteousness of God* (2 Cor. 5:21).

Apparently for Paul to say that Jesus died as a sacrifice for our sins is the same as saying that Jesus died as representative of fallen humanity. His death signified the end of fallen humanity. It was representatively the destruction of sinners with their sin. But only those who, like the offerer of old, identify themselves with the sacrifice can experience the other half of the parallelism—the new life with Christ beyond the death of sin, that is, the righteousness of God lived in the solidarity of the body of Christ.

Representative Man: More Than Substitution

In his death Jesus represented not only fallen humanity, although, as we have seen, this was a part of Paul's view. Christ also represented God to humankind. That "God was in Christ" is absolutely fundamental to Paul's understanding of the saving work of Christ. For this reason representation seems to be a better term to describe the meaning of the work of Christ than substitution. As the term has been used traditionally, substitution has tended to be too one-sided (i.e., Christ in his death is viewed only as the substitute for sinners), as well as too narrow (i.e., Christ died as *my* substitute).

As we have noted, Paul saw Christ's death as that of Representative Man for humanity. Paul's point is not that Christ died *instead of* others, but *as* a human (2 Cor. 5:14). Therefore fallen humanity does not escape death. Either we die our own death without identifying ourselves with Christ, or we identify with Christ and die in the death of our representative; that is, his death works out in our life. Only insofar as this happens, do we live (Rom. 7:24-25; 8:10-13,17; 2 Cor. 4:10-12; Phil. 3:10-11; Col. 1:24).

Paul's conviction that it is necessary for Christians to share in the sufferings of Christ—and that this participation in suffering can be a benefit to others—arises out of his understanding of the representative character of Christ's death. That Christ died does not only mean that all have died, but that they must continue to work out the meaning of dying with Christ. To accept Jesus as Messiah is to be willing to share his suffering. In this sense, at least, the sufferings of Christ are not a substitute for ours, but a pattern to which we must be conformed (Hooker, 1981:82).

Jesus' death was the death of the old humanity, and his resurrection is the beginning of a new humanity. Fallen humanity cannot escape death. The only way through death to the other side, to the life of the Spirit, is through participation in Christ's death. So Jesus died, not so much as a substitute in place of humans, but as Representative Man on behalf of humanity in order to take us along with him into the new life of the Spirit (Dunn, 1974:141).

Archegos (Pioneer)

The title *archegos* appears four times in the New Testament, and in every case it refers to Jesus Christ and his saving work. Peter charged the people of Israel of having "killed the Author of life, whom God raised from the dead" (Acts 3:15). The charge is repeated in Acts 5:30-31, this time leveled at the Sanhedrin: "The God of our fathers raised Jesus whom you killed by hanging on a tree. God exalted him at his right hand as Leader and Savior, to give repentance to Israel and forgivness of sins." We read in Hebrews 2:9-10 that Jesus suffered death "so that by the grace of God he might taste death for every one. For it was fitting that he . . . should make the pioneer of their salvation perfect through suffering." In Hebrews 12:2 Jesus is described as "the pioneer and perfecter of our faith who . . . endured the cross." How does this term contribute to our understanding of the meaning of Christ's saving work?

In ancient Greece the term was applied to the hero of a city, to one who had founded the city and given it his name or served as its guardian. Therefore, *archegos* also carried the sense of captain.

In the Septuagint *archegos* is usually applied to the political or military leader of the people. It sometimes carries the meaning of head of a clan or tribe. Occasionally it is used in a figurative sense and translated variously as "father," "elder," and "beginning." In Judaism the term is applied mainly to the patriarchs but also to Adam and Noah.

As we have noted, in the New Testament the term is applied exclusively to Jesus and always in a context which deals with his saving death and resurrection. In Acts 3:15 and 5:31 the resurrection is cited as evidence that the title *archegos* is an appropriate one. Jesus is thus recognized as the founder of a kingdom in which the primitive community held its citizenship. The community not only bears his name, but also looks to him as its guardian. Through his resurrection and exaltation (the thrust of the Hebrews 2:10 and 12:2 passages) the community is assured, by witness of the Holy Spirit, participation in the power and the glory of its Leader and Savior (Acts 5:32).

While the term *archegos* itself is not used in relation to 2 Corinthians 5:17 and Ephesians 2:15, Christ clearly fulfilled the function of hero and originator in establishing the new creation and the new humanity.

In Hebrews 2:10 Jesus is called the *archegos* who leads many to the glory of salvation through his suffering. In his obedience unto "death for everyone" Jesus becomes the originator of a family of brothers and sisters (2:9-11). What is implicit in Chapter 2 becomes explicit in Hebrews 12:2ff. Not only is Jesus perfected through suffering, but he also becomes the one who perfects his followers in their suffering. Jesus is pictured as the founder of the community of faith by virtue of his role as pioneer of faithfulness. By his faith-obedience to God unto death Christ fulfilled or perfected faith in God's unconditional love which alone is capable of overcoming the barrier of human sin. So as perfecter of our faith Jesus is the once-for-all actualization of God's love in salvation history and the source of his community's faithful obedience to the point of suffering (12:3-4).

According to these passages, the saving work of Christ can be understood in terms of his role as *archegos,* the founder and preserver of a faithful and obedient people, a community in which repentance leads to forgiveness of sins, a participation in his glory, and a share in his witness to God's holy love even to the point of suffering.

Prodromos (Forerunner)

The term *prodromos,* translated "forerunner," occurs only once in the New Testament, in a reference to Jesus who "has gone as a forerunner on our behalf" (Heb. 6:20). The fact that Jesus is a forerunner for us *(huper hemon)* is of particular importance since "for us" is almost a technical phrase for understanding the meaning of the death of Christ in the New Testament. The fact that *prodromos* appears only here in the New Testament is not necessarily an indication of its lack of importance. On the contrary, it suggests that the term must have been chosen with care.

The earlier use of *prodromos* in the ancient Near East does not offer any particular help in determining its meaning and importance in the Hebrews text. In ancient Greece the term means literally "running before." The reference is generally to those who hurry on with others following. In the Septuagint the term applies to early figs (Isa. 28:4) and to the first ripe grapes (Num. 13:20).

For understanding the sense of *prodromos* in Hebrews 6:20 an especially helpful exercise is to take note of the context in which it is set. The term is employed at the end of an extensive parenthetical admonition which extends from Hebrews 5:11 to 6:20. The statement that Jesus is "designated by God a high priest after the order of Melchizedek" (5:10) appears to be the occasion for the extended parenthetical commentary in 5:11—6:20. An obvious question to ask when one is trying to interpret the conclusion of a parenthetical section is, What was the point of departure which furnished the occasion for the parenthesis? Following this procedure we notice that 6:20b certainly corresponds directly to 5:10 and that most likely 6:20a should be understood as corresponding to 5:8-9. Therefore, seeing Jesus as "a forerunner on our behalf" (6:20a) is best understood in light of the fact that "although he was a Son, he learned obedience through what he suffered; and being made perfect he became the source of eternal salvation to all who obey him" (5:8-9).

Furthermore, the phrase "for us" *(huper hemon)* in 6:20a also points in the direction of understanding this verse as a reference to Christ's saving work. Jesus, then, is seen as a forerunner in that he learned obedience through what he suffered. Jesus is the prototype of the believers' obedient running. Jesus ran as his community now runs. He reached the goal of his obedient running, a goal which is also possible for those who obey him (Heb. 5:9). This helps us to understand why the terms translated "to run" *(dromos* and *trecho)* became such an important part of the vocabulary of Christian edification in the early church.

When used in a figurative sense, "to run" commonly carries the meaning of prompt obedience in the Old Testament as well as in the Dead Sea Scrolls (Ps. 119:32) (Bauernfeind, 1972:231). This idea, rather than the Hellenistic ideas of athletic achievement, is probably uppermost in the Pauline use of this figure (*dromos* in Acts 20:24; 2 Tim. 4:7; *trecho* in Rom. 9:16; 1 Cor. 9:24,26; Gal. 2:2; 5:7; Phil. 2:16; Heb. 12:1).

Running is an emphatic form of walking, a term which also carries moral and ethical content in its figurative uses in biblical literature. So the figure is used to denote the whole life and conduct of believers. That this image should be applied to the saving work of Christ in Hebrews 6:20 is noteworthy. This concept is apparently akin to that expressed in the Christological title, *archegos*. In fact the running of believers is directly linked to the "pioneer (*archegos*) and perfecter of our faith" in Hebrews 12:1-2.

Prototokos (Firstborn)

The term *prototokos*, translated "firstborn," occurs six times in the singular form in the New Testament. The title is always applied to Jesus. (The term also appears twice in the plural form—Heb. 11:28; 12:23.) Only in Luke 2:7 is the term used in its natural literal sense (Jesus is the firstborn of Mary). This leaves us with five occurrences of the term as a Christological title for Jesus, and three of these are found in contexts with explicit reference to the saving death of Christ.

In ancient Greece the term was used more in the general figurative sense than in its natural literal intent. Therefore it conveys more the idea of privilege than of order of birth.

In the Septuagint the term is used frequently in the direct literal sense. In the Old Testament great importance is attached to the firstborn. In ancient Israel the land belonged to Yahweh; therefore he had a claim on the firstfruits as well as the firstborn. In this sense the term is also applied figuratively to Israel in order to show God's claim upon his people (Ex. 4:22). The term also carries in the Old Testament the idea of God's special favor toward his people as well as his anointed one, the king or the Messiah (Ps. 89:27).

Paul writes in Romans 8:29 of being "predestined to be conformed to the image of his Son, in order that he might be the firstborn among many brethren." Some scholars claim that discipleship is not in view here and that it is a matter of fellowship which results from being made like him on the last day. First John 3:2 is cited in support of this interpretation (Michaelis, 1968:877). However, this view runs counter to a considerable number of texts which call on believers to imitate Jesus concretely in his faithful obedience which leads to suffering. While conformity to Christ's image will surely become a glorious reality in the day of eschatological fulfillment, the relationship between the firstborn and the brethren alluded to in this text is also already a reality in the age of the Spirit (Rom. 8:14). In light of the emphasis on this kind of concern in early Christian exhortation which we find in the New Testament (e.g., "putting on Christ," "walking in the Spirit," "being in Christ") we may be sure that Paul is concerned that these "many brethren" bear some semblance of relationship to the firstborn.

Prototokos appears twice in the hymnic passage in Colossians 1:15-20. In 1:15 the term surely points to Christ as mediator in creation and therefore uniquely supreme over all creatures, rather than simply assigning to him priority in time as preexistent Lord.

In Colossians 1:18 "the first-born from the dead" can, of course, be a reference to Jesus' resurrection as the anticipation and prelude to the resurrection of the last day. However, here again the priority in time is not the only important element. In line with the predominant biblical usage of this term (an expression of prominence and rank), it also underlines the supremacy of the risen Christ. This meaning is reinforced by the context where Christ is described as "head of the body, the church" and "the beginning" *(arche)*. According to this passage, this supremacy is exercised in "making peace by the blood of his cross" (1:20).

To judge from its context, the reference to the firstborn in Hebrews 1:6 is to the supremacy of Christ over all others. The Son (1:2) is the unique and supreme agent in God's saving activity.

In Revelation 1:5 the primary reference does not appear to be priority in time, but rather the supremacy of the risen Christ. However, this text makes more explicit what was implicit in other uses of firstborn to refer to the supremacy of Jesus Christ. Here it is linked to his death, as was the case with the Colossians 1:15-20 passage. Christ is the one "who loves us and has freed us from our sins by his blood" (Rev. 1:5). Christ's obedience unto death, which was vindicated by God in the resurrection, is the essential element in his supremacy which is reflected in the title "firstborn."

The fact that this image is employed by Paul (Rom. 8:29), is found in the primitive hymn (Col. 1:15-20), and is used by the writer of the epistle to the Hebrews (1:6), the writer of the Apocalypse (Rev. 1:5), and in two contexts in relation to the death of Jesus, points to the widespread conviction in the early church that "the Lamb who was slain is worthy."

6

Martyr Motif

In the introduction to his Apocalypse, John anchors his eschatological vision of God's saving intention for humanity in the "testimony of Jesus Christ" *(marturian Iesou Christou)* (Rev. 1:2). A few verses later the writer expands the reference in order to give a preview of what the Messiah's witness implies. He refers to "Jesus Christ the faithful witness [*ho martus ho pistos*], the first-born of the dead, and the ruler of the kings of the earth ... who loves us and has freed us from our sins by his blood" (1:5).

The martyr motif has often been associated with a theologically liberal view of the saving work of Christ. In this perspective the death of Jesus was open to interpretation as simply the death of a good man, a well-intentioned Jewish rabbi who, due to a series of unfortunate circumstances, met a martyr's fate. A satisfactory response to this inadequate liberal view does not lie in simply ignoring the presence of this witness-suffering motif in the New Testament but in taking note of the importance assigned to the martyr motif in the New Testament writings and in attempting to understand the meaning of the image in a radical New Testament perspective.

The martyr motif, as a way of understanding the meaning of Christ's messianic mission and death as well as explaining the suffering of the primitive Christian community, plays a dominant role in the New Testament. In line with this, William R. Farmer has proposed the thesis that a prime criterion for determining which of the primitive Christian writings were to be admitted to the New Testament canon was the presence of the witness-martyr theme (cf. Farmer, 1982). In this chapter we will seek to set forth in biblical perspective the way in which the martyr image illuminates our understanding of the work of Christ as well as the mission of the church.

The family of terms generally translated in the New Testament as "witness" or "testimony," together with the corresponding verbs, is used in the majority of its occurrences in the technical sense of witness to ascertainable facts. But in the New Testament there is a progression in the use of the terms from this common secular sense to mean witness to truths and reality experienced, then to confession, and finally to suffering and death as a result of witness to this reality. In fact, the meaning of the terms seems to move back and forth between the senses of witness and martyrdom, meanings which are really complementary rather than mutually exclusive.

The passage referred to above (Rev. 1:2,5,6) offers an especially clear example of the multiple meanings of the terms. John sees his mission as "bearing witness [*martureo*] to the word of God and to the testimony [*marturia*] of Jesus Christ" (1:2). John's witness is to what he has seen and experienced: Jesus' inauguration of the kingdom and his death and resurrection. Jesus' testimony consists of both his witness to the coming of the kingdom of God and the giving of his life in faithfulness to his saving mission to the point of death as God's Messiah. This is made clearer in verse 5, where Jesus Christ is described as the witness who is "the faithful one" (*ho martus ho pistos*). The meaning here is akin to the Pauline references to "the faithfulness of Jesus Christ" (*pistos Iesou Christou*) (Rom. 3:22; Gal. 2:16) and to the references to Christ's obedience in the epistle to the Hebrews (Heb. 3:2).

The title which is here applied to Jesus, "the faithful witness," plays as significant role as any of the Christological titles for understanding the nature of Jesus' saving work. The New Testament presents Jesus maintaining his faithful witness to the coming of the kingdom of God even to the point of his death on the cross, to the point of becoming a curse (Gal. 3:13). Jesus is the authentic witness-martyr in both of these principal senses of the term. He witnessed to the coming of God's kingdom throughout his ministry, up to and including his crucifixion as a witness-martyr. In this text Jesus' witness is specificially linked to his death.

So here we are in the presence of an important image which the New Testament community used to understand the meaning of the saving work of Christ—that of witness-martyr. Jesus, the witness-martyr, is supreme: "the first-born of the dead, and the ruler of kings on earth ... [to whom] glory and dominion" are ascribed. But where are the roots of this image for understanding the work of Christ to be found and what are its implications for the community of the Messiah?

Martus in the Old Testament

In the Septuagint the *martus* family of terms is widely used in the legal sense of witness in a judicial procedure. This use of the term is no different from its popular non-biblical sense. However, in Isaiah 40ff. we come across the use of the term with a new shade of meaning. The prophet depicts Yahweh staging a kind of court trial before the nations in which it will be shown that Yahweh alone is truly God and that the gods of the Gentiles are not really gods. This is a contest between monotheism and polytheism, but it is much more than that. It will also be shown that Yahweh alone is able to save his people; he is more powerful than the gods of the nations. But the power of Yahweh differs from that of the gods of the nations who by the exercise of coercive power seek to control events. Yahweh alone is able to do "a new thing," to assure the continuity of the life of his people in keeping with his covenant promise. In spite of their bitter experience in exile Yahweh calls upon his people to serve as witnesses to his saving acts in the second of three courtroom scenes.[1]

> Bring forth the people who are blind, yet have eyes
>   who are deaf, yet have ears!
> Let all the nations gather together,
>   and let the peoples assemble.
> Who among them can declare this,
>   and show us the former things?
> Let them bring *their witnesses* to justify them,
>   and let them hear and say, It is true.
> "You are *my witnesses*," says the Lord,
>   "and my servant whom I have chosen,
> that you may know and believe me
>   and understand that I am He.
> Before me no god was formed,
>   nor shall there be any after me.
> I, I am the Lord,

and besides me there is no savior.
I declared and saved and proclaimed,
    when there was no strange god among you;
    and you are *my witnesses*," says the Lord.
"I am God, and also henceforth I am He;
    there is none who can deliver from my hand;
    I work and who can hinder it?"
                            (Isa. 43:8-13, emphasis mine)

The principal features of this picture are reproduced in Isaiah 44:6-9. Witnesses to the gods of the nations are summoned to speak from their experience (43:9; 44:9), but they are eventually "put to shame" (44:11). For all of their vaunted power to coerce their enemies and to take captives (Israel is in exile), neither the gods nor their witnesses have anything whereof to testify. They are impotent and are put to shame (44:9-11).

In contrast to the witnesses of the gods, Israel is told three times, "You are my witnesses" (43:10,12; 44:8). In the same context Israel is called Yahweh's servant (41:8-9; 43:10; 44:1,2,21). On the basis of its experience of Yahweh's covenant election and his saving deliverance and sustaining guidance, Israel, his servant, will declare to the nations the reality of God's saving activity and his power which stands in marked contrast to the ways of the nations. In this the people, or Israel, are God's witnesses. However, the character of their witness moves beyond the strictly literal sense of the term as attestation of externally demonstrable fact. Rather than being used in a strictly legal sense of law-court witness, the term here carries the meaning of confession, of the mission of God's witnessing community in the midst of the nations.

Just as Israel's witness is certainly not limited to verbal attestation of externally demonstrable facts about Yahweh, neither is its confession limited to a strictly verbal declaration of Yahweh's uniqueness. Throughout Scripture the witness of Israel is tied to Israel's substantial difference from the nations inasmuch as Israel is called to reflect faithfully the holiness of God. So the witness to which Isaiah refers is the proclamation of the living God whose saving activity is reflected in the conduct and very existence of Israel.[2]

The dual motifs of witness and servanthood are intensified in the Servant Songs (Isa. 42:1-6; 49:1-6; 50:4-9; 52:13-53:12). The identification of the servant moves from Israel as a people to a prophetic figure who is called "servant of Yahweh," and vicarious suffering becomes integral to his witness. His witness to the nations is pointed out in several passages (42:4,6; 49:1,6; 52:15; 53:11-12; 62:10; cf. 9:2; 11:9). These passages suggest that the prophet or the messianic figure must die for his witness. While one must be cautious not to read more into these texts than is there, to judge from the development in later Judaism and primitive Christianity, the seeds of a missionary prophetic martyr vision are to be found in Isaiah 40ff. (Strathmann, 1967:485).

The figure of the prophet in mission or the righteous person in pursuit of justice who suffers persecution and even death is familiar in the Old Testament. Elijah, the prophet who was hated by Jezebel, and Uriah, the prophet who was slaughtered by Jehoiakim are examples of this (1 Kings 19:10; Jer. 26:20ff.). These "troublers of Israel" (1 Kings 18:17) bore the consequences of faithfulness to their mission. The righteous among God's people also bore suffering and death (Pss. 69:8-10; 44:22). These experiences of witness and suffering reach a climax in the Syrian persecution described in the Maccabbean accounts. Faithful witness which takes the form of obedience unto death is the hallmark of these accounts.

The Old Testament, from the murder of Abel onward, is viewed as a history of God's people which illustrates the true spirit of martyrdom (4 Macc. 18:11ff.). Other intertestamental writings (Mart. Is. 5:14; En. 47:2) reflect a similar appreciation for this prophetic witness of suffering. This is the vision which spills over into the New Testament at a number of points (Heb. 11:35-38; Matt. 23:29-39; Luke 11:47-51), and the violent death of the righteous prophets almost appears to have been taken for granted in some circles in Jesus' time (Matt. 5:11f.; 23:37; Luke 13:33; Acts 7:52). So the ideal of the prophets and the righteous ones who are faithful to the point of suffering and death was a vital aspect of Judaism during and following the inter-testamental period. This vision lived on in Judaism until the Barchochba revolt in the second century.

However, a notable difference exists between Judaism's vision of martyrdom and that which is reflected in the writings of the New Testament. In Judaism the *martus* word group is not used to describe the faithfulness unto death of the prophets and the righteous ones. On the other hand, these terms are used in Isaiah 40ff., where witness, servanthood, and suffering are all brought into close relationship as well as in the many New Testament passages where the same juxtaposition of concepts is found.

Perhaps this difference can be explained by the two common elements found in witness as portrayed by Isaiah and the New Testament. First, in both cases the witness is borne to someone. In Isaiah 40ff. witness is to Yahweh and against the gods of the nations. In the New Testament witness is borne to Jesus Christ, the faithful witness against the powers. Second, in both cases the witness is given to the nations. Apparently both the personal and the missionary dimensions of this witness-suffering were missing in Judaism.

Martus in the New Testament

In the New Testament, too, the *martus* family of terms is used most often in the general sense of witness to ascertainable facts. However, use of the terms in the sense we have already noted in Isaiah 40ff., i.e., of witness-suffering to God's saving activity toward humanity, is substantial. Something of this meaning is observable in the "cloud of witnesses" *(marturon)* who watch the struggle in which the readers of the epistle to the Hebrews are engaged (12:1). They are those described throughout Hebrews 11 who have been faithful in their obedience in witness even to the point of suffering and death.

In Luke 24:48 *martures* is used in a way which combines witness to the facts of Jesus' life, death, and resurrection with witness in the sense of evangelistic confession which lies beyond the realm of observable facts and includes the living experience of the witness who has grasped the significance of Jesus. In Acts 1:8 Jesus reiterates the fact that his disciples are his witnesses. The early part of the book of Acts underscores the importance of a firsthand knowledge of the story of Jesus (1:22; 10:39; 2:32; 3:15; 5:31f; 10:41). Acts 13:31-32 may well reflect the transition between the two shades of meaning which the term *witness* carries. Eyewitnesses are "his witnesses to the people" (Israel in Palestine). And now Paul and his colleagues "bring . . . the good news" of God's saving activity in Jesus to the world outside of Palestine. There witness is confession based on their experience.

This development in the meaning of witness from the eyewitness declaration of observable facts to confession based on the experience of the witness is apparent in the latter part of Acts. Paul is a witness of Jesus (Acts 22:15; 26:16), and Stephen is referred to as Jesus' witness (Acts 22:20). Obviously, neither Paul nor Stephen were witnesses in the sense of Acts 1:22. In fact in Acts 22:15 Paul is called to be "a witness *for* him [Christ]" (emphasis mine), a phrase which appears in this passage alone in the New Testament. In the case of Stephen, he is referred to as "thy witness" (Acts 22:20). He is not called a witness *(martus)* because he dies; rather, he dies because he is a faithful witness. Stephen's suffering and death are the crowning evidence of the seriousness of his confessional witness.

So we also note in Acts the way in which the meaning of witness moves from its original literal sense of those who give eyewitness testimony to the fact of the incarnation (Acts 1:22) to confessional witness based on the witness' experience of the risen Christ (22:15). Finally the meaning of witness comes to include the elements of suffering and death as the crowning certification of that witness. In this development the meaning of the term has moved from testimony to saving facts, to confessing the experience of this reality, to a witness which is crowned by participation in the faithful witness of Jesus himself.

Peter gives fraternal counsel to his peers in the early church "as a fellow elder and a witness of the sufferings of Christ as well as a partaker in the glory that is to be revealed" (1 Pet. 5:1). He clearly refers to more than simply being an eyewitness of the crucifixion. Being a witness means bearing similar suffering for similar reasons—faithful witness to God's righteous reign. Witness here is personal participation in Christ's mission to the point of suffering. This is to "share Christ's sufferings" (1 Pet. 4:13). In fact this motif appears to have been widespread in the early church (cf. 2 Cor. 1:5; Col. 1:24; 1 Pet. 2:21; Matt. 10:38; 16:24).

In 1 Timothy 6:13 Jesus Christ is described in "his testimony before Pontius Pilate" as making "the good confession." An obvious parallel exists between this reference to Jesus' testimony and the call to Timothy to live up to his calling. However, the fact that Jesus' suffering under Pontius Pilate is referred to as his testimony *(martureo)* points to the fact that both witness and suffering were integral to the messianic mission in the understanding of the circle in the early church to which 1 Timothy was addressed.

The verb form *(martureo)* is used frequently in John's Gospel and first epistle, where the meaning is generally a witness to the nature and significance of the person of Jesus Christ. The sense in which the term is used here too moves from attestation to facts to the confession of experience. However, in Revelation the concept of witness leading to and including suffering becomes prominent. But before we consider the Apocalypse of John, it will be helpful to consider Jesus' own understanding of his role as witness-martyr as found in the synoptic Gospels.[3]

Jesus' Self-understanding as Witness-Martyr

The Gospels present Jesus as one who reckoned with the possibility of violent death. He was reproached for blasphemy (Matt. 9:3; 26:65; Mark 2:7; John 10:33-35; cf. 5:18) which carried the threat of stoning and subsequent hanging of the body on a cross. Deliberate Sabbath breaking was also punishable by death. The two Sabbath experiences reported in Mark 2:23—3:7a include a warning for the first offense (2:24), a counsel aimed at punishing him for the second offense (3:6), and Jesus' need to flee in order to save himself (3:7a). The Gospels report that Jesus repeatedly stood in danger of being stoned, and this appraisal of the situation must surely have been realistic (Luke 4:29; John 8:59; 10:31-36; 11:8; cf. Matt. 23:37; Luke 13:34).

In light of this historical situation it is perfectly reasonable to suppose that Jesus reckoned with the possibility of violent death. This is implied in identifying himself among the prophets; the expected fate of the prophets was martyrdom (Matt. 23:34-37; Luke 13:33). Both the New Testament and Jewish legend point to the notable degree in which martyrdom was considered to be an integral part of the prophetic calling (Matt. 21:35f.; 22:6; 23:30-37 and parallels; Luke 13:33; Acts 7:51f.; Rom. 11:3; 1 Thess. 2:15; Heb. 11:35-38; Rev. 11:7; 16:6; 18:24; cf. James 5:10).

Jesus referred to salvation history as a succession of the martyrdom of the righteous from Abel to Zechariah (Matt. 23:35). The fate of John the Baptist, the last of the prophets, foreshadowed for Jesus his own destiny (Mark 9:12f.; cf. 6:16; Luke 13:31).

If Jesus reckoned with the possibility of violent death, he must have also thought about its meaning, particularly since there was a contemporary Jewish doctrine of the expiatory efficacy of death. The fact that Isaiah 53 played such an important role in Jesus' own interpretation of his messianic mission, as well as in the primitive community's understanding offers valuable clues.

We have already noted the significance of Isaiah 40ff. for Jesus' self-understanding. The many allusions to Isaiah 53 in his message fit simply into this framework. While in late Judaism the expiatory vow of a condemned criminal ("May my death expiate all my sins," Zimmerli and Jeremias, 1957:102) was a formal part of the execution procedure, the Maccabean martyrs saw their death as having expiatory value for their people (4 Macc. 6:27-29; 2 Macc. 7:37f.). However, Jesus conceived his death as the transfer of expiatory value to his tormentors, who, as in Isaiah 53:10, are unwitting sinners (Luke 23:34, Zimmerli and Jeremias, 1957:99, n. 455).

Jesus' conviction that the prophecy that he be "reckoned with transgressors" (*anomon*, Luke 22:37; Isa. 53:7) may well imply that he anticipated being driven out of the community of Israel as an *anomos* (a lawless one). Furthermore, his disciples would be treated as *anomoi*—refused food and threatened for their lives (Luke 22:36).

The phrase, "for many," found in the eucharistic saying of Jesus (Mark 14:24 and parallels; cf. Mark 10:45) most probably comes from Isaiah 53. Jesus interpreted his impending death as a vicarious dying "for the many" who lay under the judgment of God (Mark 10:45; 14:45). Because Jesus went to his death innocently, voluntarily, patiently, and in absolute obedience to the will of God (Isa. 53), his dying has an unbounded expiating virtue.

The saying about the shepherd who is slain and the sheep who are scattered (Mark 14:27f.) is a reference to Zechariah 13:7-9. The death of the shepherd ushers in the eschatological tribulation of the flock, but it also points to the gathering of the remnant into the kingdom of God (cf. Zech. 14:9; Luke 22:35-38; John 10, Jeremias, 1965:47-48).

Early Church Understandings of Witness-Martyr

The source of the understanding of witness (*martus*) as witness-martyrdom was assigned to Jesus himself by the New Testament writers. The second of the five discourses included in Matthew's Gospel (10:5-42) is a key passage for understanding the writer's view of the meaning of the suffering and death of Jesus. We can assume that the early community's missionary vision (10:5-15) and its eschatological zeal (10:23) were essential components of their self-understanding. But to judge by the way in which the martyrdom motif found in Matthew 10:16-39 reappears in Jesus' repeated passion announcements (16:21; 17:22-23; 20:17-19; 26:2), it must have been of prime importance for understanding both the passion of Jesus and the suffering of his followers.

The fact that Jesus was "delivered up" to the Sanhedrin (Matt. 10:17) and taken before the "governor ... to bear testimony" (10:18) was consistent with what Jesus taught the twelve to do (10:22b,24-25,28,38) and what the readers of Matthew's Gospel were most certainly facing. Matthew makes it clear that Jesus' followers are likewise to be witnesses, confessors, and martyrs (10:26-39).

The lives and attitudes of these confessors and martyrs are described in the instructions of Matthew 5:3—7:27. The characteristics of meekness and mercy prevented the community from splintering into opposing camps of confessors and ordinary disciples, since even those who apostatized in the face of trial could be freely forgiven. This is the kind of suffering witness-martyrdom which would eventually break imperial persecution and bring the Roman emperors to their knees before a Lord and Savior at whose name "every knee should bow, in heaven and on earth and under the earth, and every tongue confess that Jesus Christ is Lord, to the glory of God the Father" (Phil. 2:10-11).

The important role of Matthew 10:16-42 for understanding the meaning of Jesus' death is clear. Jesus had indeed died for us, as the early tradition recognized (1 Cor. 15:3). But Matthew points out that Jesus also died to show those who confess him before the world (10:32-33; cf. Phil. 2:11) how to make this confession and how to die in their witness when necessary.

This understanding is by no means limited to Matthew. Paul's counsel in Philippians 2:5-8 serves, among other things, as instruction for Christian witness, in its broader sense, as both testimony and suffering. Paul's exhortation to "be imitators of me, as I am of Christ" (1 Cor. 11:1) surely pointed in the same direction during his lifetime. After his martyrdom, the same words encouraged his readers to think of the death of Jesus, as well as that of Paul and the other apostles, as examples for them. In fact, the answer to the question of whether the phrase "to be in Christ" implied a readiness to die like Christ evoked an affirmative response in the tradition of Ignatius, Polycarp, Irenaeus, and Origen, while the Gnostics generally responded negatively.

In this community of witnesses, confessors, and martyrs the Lord's Supper, shared on the night Jesus was handed over to the authorities, occupied a central place. The community was continually reminded that Jesus' body was broken for them and his blood was shed for them. In a community which was suffering for its witness these words carried special meaning. To drink from the Lord's cup would be to identify with their crucified and risen Lord. United by their participation in his death and resurrection and enduring to the end in their witness-martyrdom, according to Jesus' own promise, they would be saved (Matt. 10:22).[4]

As we observed at the beginning of this chapter, Jesus himself is emphatically referred to as "the witness the faithful one" (literal translation of Rev. 1:5 and 3:14). The phrase itself appears to have been inspired by Psalm 89 and Isaiah 55:34, where God is proclaimed to be absolutely faithful to his covenant promises and to set his anointed as a witness to the nations. Here the references are taken to be messianic, and this context sets the stage for understanding the meaning of the term in Revelation. Jesus' revelation of God's character and saving intention is the "witness of Jesus Christ" (1:2,9), and he has fulfilled this mission obediently. Jesus showed himself faithful to his mission to the point of shedding his blood (1:5). The same title is applied to Antipas, "the faithful witness" who was killed in Satan's realm at Pergamum (2:13). In line with his own interpretation of his mission (John 18:37), Jesus showed himself utterly faithful to his mission to the point of dying. The fact that the same title is applied to Antipas shows that the crucified Lord is model for Christian witness.

The phrase translated "the testimony [*marturia*] of Jesus" is a truly striking feature of the book of Revelation (1:2,9; 12:17; 19:10, twice; 20:4; cf. 6:9) and offers a clue to the meaning of the term in the book. The genitive case here is best understood as subjective—

Jesus' testimony or witness, rather than a witness to Jesus (Strathmann, 1967:500-501). Four times the phrase "the testimony of Jesus" accompanies the phrases "word of God" or "command-ments of God" (1:2,9; 12:17; 20:4); once it is the witness of martyrs who had been slain "for the word of God" (6:9). This should not be understood as a contrast between the Old Testament or Law on one hand and Jesus' message on the other. Rather they are comple-mentary expressions referring to one reality, God's saving revelation. So the phrase "the testimony (or witness) of Jesus" becomes a for-mula for gospel.

The development in the meaning of the *martus* terms which we noticed in earlier writings is completed in Revelation. The witness of Jesus is linked to his passion. Witness as attesting to facts and the confession of that which is experienced culminate in suffering and death which demonstrate the final faithfulness of the witness and his testimony. The book of Revelation takes its clue from the "witness of Jesus" for understanding martyrologically the witness of Jesus' servants.

This understanding of the term is made especially clear in Revelation 12:11. Satan is overcome "through the blood of the Lamb," the witness of Jesus unto death: "by the word of their testimony, for they loved not their lives even unto death." Suffering and death are integral parts of the "witness of Jesus" (Rev. 1:9). This relationship, which is explicit in texts such as Revelation 1:9, is im-plicit in Revelation 12:11 in order to complete the parallelism with the witness unto death of the "brethren."

The use of the *martus* family of terms in Revelation sheds light on both the biblical understanding of the meaning of Jesus' death and its view of the mission of his people. The revelatory-saving mis-sion of Messiah required a faithfulness to the Father, whose mission it was, even to the point of suffering and death at the hands of the enemies of God. For Messiah's people, faithfulness to their Lord in his mission in the world which has fallen under Satan's dominion calls for a witness of attestation and confession sealed by suffering and even death.

Understanding the saving work of Christ in terms of the Revelation's image of the faithful witness contributes to our under-standing of categories found in the writings of Paul and the epistle to the Hebrews. The Pauline concept of the "faith *of* the Messiah" *(pis-teos Iesou Christou;* cf. Rom. 3:22; Gal. 2:16)—but generally translated "faith *in* Christ"—is made more plausible by the Revelator's reference to Jesus (more emphatic in the Greek) as "the witness, the faithful one" who shed his blood as a final seal of his witness (e.g., 1:5; 2:15; 3:14). In light of this understanding of the meaning of Jesus' death it is possible to understand the Pauline perspective of justification through the "faithfulness of Christ" without the need to posit a theoretical requirement that a satisfaction be paid.[5] The emphasis in the epistle to the Hebrews on the fact that the Son needed to learn obedience and be faithful (3:2; 5:8) as "the pioneer of . . . salvation [made] perfect through suffering" (2:10) is compatible with the Pauline view of the faithfulness of the Messiah and the Revelator's vision of the faithful witness.

Historical Remnants of the Witness-Martyr Motif

During the second century the martyrological sense of the terms emerged so that by mid-century a fixed technical martyrological use of the terms spread from Asia Minor throughout the post-apostolic church. While extraneous ideas and implications eventually came to be associated with martyrdom (e.g., idea of merit), the basic elements of the church's vision of martyrdom can be traced to the New Testament and to Jesus himself.

Persecution for the sake of Christ can be expected in the messianic community (Matt. 5:11f.), but the Spirit will support the community in time of testing (Matt. 10:17ff.). The offering of life is seen as the way to life (Matt. 16:24ff.). Suffering for the "name" was occasion for rejoicing (Acts 5:41). Paul rejoices in suffering which he sees as completing "what is lacking in Christ's afflictions for the sake of his body" (Col. 1:24). The complementary nature of witness and suffering underlies Paul's understanding of mission. The characteristic relationship of suffering and joy is truly noteworthy (Rom. 5:3; 8:17; 1 Pet. 4:13). These elements build to a climax in Revelation, where Jesus Christ is the Lamb (servant) slain, the faithful witness, the original martyr among a martyr community (2:13; 6:9; 12:11).

Traditionally, the martyr motif has occupied a relatively minor role in the Christian church's understanding of the work of Christ.

But this fact really comes as no surprise when we recall the history of the church. From the beginning of the fourth century onward, the established church has found itself in a position of power in which suffering and martyrdom tend to become an anomaly. The Christian church, which was a persecuted minority during the first three centuries of its existence, became a persecuting church in the fourth century. The witness-martyr image then became largely irrelevant as a means for understanding the work of Christ and the mission of his followers. Rather than think of Jesus as the faithful witness-martyr to be faithfully followed, the confessors and martyrs of the earlier period were venerated. The church concentrated on other biblical images for understanding the work of Christ which were more consonant with its practice and thought and could be adapted more easily to conform with its stance in the world. The principal theories with which the church has traditionally sought to understand the meaning of the work of Christ depend only minimally on the martyr image.

Meanwhile throughout the history of the church, radical renewal movements, persecuted as they have been by the established church, have found themselves in situations akin to that of the pre-Constantinian Christian communities. In these circles the witness-martyr motif has again proved helpful in understanding the meaning of the work of Christ and has inspired them in their Christlike witness and suffering. Not surprisingly, these communities have also produced martyrologies with the same kind of spirit of witness and suffering which characterized the early church.

To share a concrete social and spiritual stance similar to that of the primitive Christian community is to find meaningful the same images for understanding the work of Christ which inspired the early church in its quest for understanding and meaning. Wherever the church finds itself living under the cross (In light of the New Testament, where else can the true church live?), it discovers in the witness-martyr motif a powerful image for understanding the meaning of the work of Christ, as well as orienting its own life and mission in the world.

7

Sacrifice Motif

Ancient Israel celebrated its covenant relationship with Yahweh by means of elaborate sacrificial ritual. The new covenant is not so much the abolishing of the old as it is a fulfillment. So it should come as no surprise that the New Testament writers understood the Christ-event in sacrificial language and imagery and that they applied the same kind of imagery to the Christian life itself. In the New Testament, particularly in the Pauline writings, the work of Christ is seen in sacrificial terms. Christians are perceived as the new temple. The life of Christians is understood in sacrificial images, not primarily in a ritualistic or liturgical sense, but above all in an ethical and practical way.

Nowhere in the Old Testament do we find a fully developed rational explanation for the practice of sacrifice. Perhaps a part of the essential nature of sacrifice is that it cannot be fully explained in purely rational categories. Ancient Hebrew sacrifice was complex, and modern attempts to identify its essential elements must be tentative at best. The most common suggestions include: a gift offered to the deity (Lev. 7:11-16); homage of a subject to the Lord (Gen. 12:6-8); the expiation of offenses (Lev. 4:5); communion with the deity, especially in sacrificial banquet (Daly, 1978:4).

The presence of these elements of meaning can be detected in several representative examples of sacrifice in ancient Israel.

Sacrifice could *protect* against evil and destruction. In the more ancient tradition of the Old Testament the blood of circumcision and of the Passover lamb were credited with power to ward off the destroyer (Ex. 4:24-26; 12:27). This idea may have continued to some degree to underlie subsequent sacrificial ritual in Israel.

Sacrifice was seen as a way of *interceding* with God. In fact, spilled blood speaks more loudly than the voice alone. Abel's blood cries out to God (Gen. 4:10). This is the image which is picked up in Hebrews. Christ's priestly ministry included intercession for his people offered up in "prayers and supplication, with loud cries and tears" (Heb. 5:7) and mediation by "sprinkled blood that speaks more graciously [better] than the blood of Abel" (Heb. 12:24). The power of a life of intercession unto death is augmented by the blood which seals it. This view of sacrifice as intercession is explicitly set forth by the prophets (Isa. 56:7; Jer. 7:10-11).

Sacrifice was used in the *establishment of covenant.* Blood is shed to seal covenant commitment. Examples of this from the Old Testament are the covenant with Abraham which was validated by means of an ancient sacrificial ceremony (Gen. 15) and the covenant made with Israel at Sinai which was sealed by "blood of the covenant" (Ex. 24:3-11). So also the new covenant established with "the many" (Gentiles a well as Jews) is made at the cost of Christ's blood (Matt. 26:28 and parallels; 1 Cor. 10:16; 11:25; Heb. 9:16-18).

Sacrifice was the *offering of life* to God. This offering of life, or shedding of blood, was a means of making atonement and receiving forgiveness (Lev. 17:11; Heb. 9:22). The sin offering described in Leviticus 4 and 5 fulfilled these functions.

Rather than viewing these theories as mutually exclusive, it is better to see them as complementary attempts to understand the biblical practice of sacrifice. Furthermore, in biblical sacrifice *what* is offered is not of primary importance, but rather the *disposition* with which sacrifice is offered. This emphasis on the importance of the attitude of the offerer is stressed heavily by the prophets during the critical periods of the Northern and Southern kingdoms in response to the magical uses being made of sacrifice (cf. Isa. 1; Jer. 7; Amos 4:5). The nature of biblical sacrifice is to emphasize the inner, spiritual, and ethical significance of cultic ritual as opposed to a merely material or external understanding.

Sacrifice in the Old Testament

Burnt Offering

Burnt offering appears to be the most important and the most frequently mentioned of ancient Israel's sacrifices. In this type of sacrifice, the animal (and sometimes grain) was completely consumed by fire on the altar (Lev. 1-2). This is distinguished from peace or covenant offerings or from sacrificial banquets in which only a part of the offering was burnt and the rest was consumed by the people (esp. Lev. 3), and sin and guilt offerings which were consumed by the priests alone (Lev. 4—5; 6:26-30; 7:6-10; 10:16-20). Some offerings, such as firstfruits and tithes, were not burned at all, but given for the support of the temple and priests.

While a theology of burnt offering is not explicitly set forth in the Old Testament, one can note three of the most common general theories of sacrifice present to some degree in this type of sacrifice: gift, communion, and expiation. The burnt-offering ritual appears in the Old Testament as follows: the daily burnt offering of a lamb (Num. 28:6); special sacrifices offered on feast days (Num. 28:1— 29:40); royal sacrifice (2 Kings 16:15); purification rites, e.g., following childbirth (Lev. 12); as a sacrifice of atonement (Lev. 4,5,16); as an expression of joy, thanksgiving, and praise (Ex. 32:6; Judg. 6:25-32; 11:29-40; 1 Sam. 6:14; 1 Kings 18:17-40); as a private sacrifice (Lev. 1:2-12; Num. 15:1-10; Ezek. 44:11; 2 Chron. 29:31-35; Ezra 3:1-6). The implication is that the purpose of the altar was to be the place where burnt offerings were sacrificed, and the fire which consumed the burnt offering was the symbol—and sometimes even the mode—of God's presence (2 Chron. 7:1-3; Ex. 19:16-24; 24:15-18; 40:34-38).

The value of all sacrifice was perceived as being dependent on its acceptance by Yahweh. The phrase translated "soothing odor," "pleasing fragrance," "odor of sweetness" was a technical term signifying that the offerer and the offering are acceptable to God. However, this acceptance of the sacrifice is a totally free act. On the other hand, sacrifice is somehow expected to have some effect on God. This apparent contradiction is similar to the implied paradox of prayer; even though we confess that God is transcendant, we believe that prayer is somehow efficacious. The prophets' warnings that Israel's sacrifices "are not acceptable" (Jer. 6:20; Hos. 9:4; Amos 5:22) are the negative counterparts of the priestly assurances that the sacrifices were properly offered and therefore acceptable to God. While the prophets assume the acceptability of sacrifice, they insist that it depends on the dispositions of the offerer, rather than on the size or nature of what is offered or the ritual correctness of the liturgical ceremony.

Sin Offering and Atonement

The concept of atonement is central in both Jewish and Christian self-understanding. In the Old Testament atonement is understood as "the process whereby the creature-creator relationship, after having been disturbed (by the creature), is restored by the creator to its proper harmony" (Daly, 1978:25). This process is particularly associated in the Old Testament with the sin offering and, specifically, the ritual manipulation of sacrificial blood.

The Hebrew verb *kipper* carries the basic meaning of carrying out an atoning action. In ancient Israel sin was an offense or disobedience against God and was, by nature, a social reality, not strictly a private one. Transgression, which would eventually lead to destruction among the people, needed to be neutralized by atonement. Likewise ritual impurity or contamination called for purification by atonement, lest the contagion and its consequences spread.

In a certain sense the epitome of sin in the Old Testament is viewed as violence. Sin and corruption are gathered up and summarized by the term *violence* (Gen. 6:11,13; cf. Ezek. 7:10-11; Jon. 3:8). In the prophetic writings lists of sins frequently culminate with some form of violence (Hos. 4:2; 12:1; Mic. 7:2). According to Isaiah, the sins which separate the people of Judah from God consist fundamentally in their violence (Isa. 59:2-7). In view of this, the thesis that an essential function of sacrifice is somehow to diffuse, absorb, contain, and arrest violence and its cumulative consequences in the human community takes on special meaning. Sacrifice, including the death of Jesus Christ, effectively serves to interrupt the spiral of human violence in all of its spiritual and social dimensions (Pries, 1983; cf. Schwager, 1978).

One notes a double function in the atonement process. The positive element is that of rendering persons or objects acceptable to Yahweh, thus making it possible for them to participate in Israel's life and worship. Negatively, atonement was understood as averting or interrupting the course of evil set in motion by transgression (Lev. 10:6; Num. 1:53; 17:11; 18:5).

Expiatory actions set in order the relationship between creature and Creator which has been disturbed by sin. In contrast to the concept of propitiation in which the action is understood as being directed to God by the creature in order to appease or placate God's anger, expiation is an action in which God alone is ultimately the subject or origin and the creatures are the objects of God's action. Leviticus 16 shows that both people and things can be objects of expiation. However, since the Old Testament is not always fully clear and explicit in viewing atonement as ultimately a creature-oriented action of God and since the church has inherited a long tradition of viewing atonement as a penitential act by which the creature earns or is made worthy of God's forgiveness, this has influenced even Protestantism's theories of the atonement (Daly, 1978:28).

The sin offering was characterized by a number of distinguishable elements.

1. An unblemished animal (if the offerer could afford it) was brought to the altar.

2. The hands of the offerer were laid on the animal sacrifice, probably signifying a certain connection or identification between the offerer and the animal victim. (Someone has suggested that the laying on of hands entered the sin-offering ritual via the scapegoat ritual of the Day of Atonement (Lev. 16:21-22). Through confession spoken by Aaron, as he laid his hands on the head of the goat, Israel's sins were transferred to the scapegoat who bore them away, rendering them harmless. However, this ritual was neither a sin offering nor a sacrifice. In the Day of Atonement liturgy the sin offering had already taken place (Lev. 16:15ff.). Furthermore, this rite does not in itself signify the penal substitution of the animal victim in place of the human offerer, although it is possible to understand why this interpretation might commend itself later on (Daly, 1978:28-29).

3. Confession, which in the Day of Atonement ritual was associated with the scapegoat ceremony, probably came eventually to be associated with the sin offering. In later Judaism the priest had to assure himself that any injury to one's neighbor was being adequately repaired before allowing the sacrifice to proceed (Daly, 1978:29).

4. The victim was then slaughtered by the offerer (and in later times by Levites or other cultic officials). The Old Testament attached little importance to the slaying of the victim, as such. Slaying

was necessary for obtaining the sacrificial blood and flesh.

5. The ritual manipulation of the blood was essential to atonement.

6. A declaration by the priest affirmed the validity and efficacy of the sacrifice, and on a deeper level this meant that Yahweh accepted the sacrifice and effected atonement.

7. The flesh was then eaten by the priests or burned in a "clean place" (Lev. 4:12).

Early rabbinic Judaism tended to attribute atoning value to any kind of sacrifice and to associate it so closely to the blood rite that the two were practically perceived as identical. This tendency is also visible in the New Testament. In Paul's letters and in Revelation the concept of being "redeemed by the blood of Christ" recurs, and Hebrews 9:22 quotes what was apparently a popular rabbinic saying, "Without the shedding of blood there is no forgiveness of sins." The use of sacrificial blood in ancient Israel is especially notable in four places: the Passover blood rite (Ex. 12), the covenant sacrifice (Ex. 24:3-8), directions for the use of blood (Lev. 17:11,14; Gen. 9:4), and the atonement rituals (Lev. 4:16).

The Passover

The Egyptian Passover was celebrated as a family feast. The blood of the original Passover lambs was the sign by which destruction was warded off and the firstborn sons in Israel were saved. Later laws about redeeming or consecrating the firstborn and the firstfruits commonly appear in a Passover context. This has tended to give rise to the ideas of substitution in connection with the Passover. However, no really firm evidence indicates that the Old Testament considered the sacrifice of the Passover lamb to be an atoning death in the sense of vicarious penal substitution, since it shows no interest whatsoever in the suffering and death of the sacrificial animal (Daly, 1978:33).

In the Passover the blood on the doorposts served to ward off the powers of destruction which otherwise would have struck the inhabitants of the house (Ex. 12:22-23). The blood does not merely exercise a justifying role or a sanctifying function, but also a protecting role. In this sense it covers or shields the offerer.

In Deuteronomy 16 the Passover becomes a corporate celebration which is joined to the Feast of Unleavened Bread and turned into a pilgrimage feast. By the time of Jesus it had become the Jewish Passover, begun with the lamb being slain by priests in the temple and accompanied by a blood rite in which blood tossed at the altar appears as an essential element.

Early Christians understood Christ's passion as a Passover event. This is the context which makes Paul's illustration in 1 Corinthians 5:7 meaningful: "Christ, our paschal lamb, has been sacrificed."[1] All four of the Gospels set the last supper in the context of the Passover feast which served as a memorial of the exodus, objectified Yahweh's saving action, and anticipated the awaited eschatological salvation (Isa. 31:5; Hos. 2:16; Jer. 23:7; 31:31-32; Isa. 40—45). This Passover context provides the background of the New Testament idea of Christ's vicarious ("for us") sacrificial death. However, this does not necessarily imply the ideas of vicarious punishment or penal satisfaction.

The Covenant Sacrifice

From the covenants with Noah (Gen. 8:20-9:17) and Abraham (Gen. 15), it is clear that the act of making (or "cutting") a covenant was a sacrificial ceremony. This is even clearer in the Mosaic covenant sacrifice (Ex. 24:3-11), which is a fundamental event in the history of Israel.

The participation of the people of God in the ritual of covenant sacrifice makes an important contribution to our understanding of the relationship of sacrifice to community. Sacrifice is performed representatively for the community. The community responds freely to the reading of "the book of the covenant": "All that the Lord has spoken we will do, and we will be obedient" (Ex. 24:7). The "blood of the covenant" then seals their commitment to live in fellowship with Yahweh in the context of community. "They beheld God, and ate and drank" (Ex. 24:11). In biblical perspective then, sacrifice carries a community creating and conserving function in consonance with God's original intention, expressed first of all in creation, and then again in the call of Abraham, i.e., in the creation of a people who bear his name.

Sacrifice in the Old Testament is rooted in the covenant order into which God, by his saving action, has integrated his people.

While the sacrificial practices of the Old Testament may have had varied origins, their characteristic distinctiveness is due to the way in which God has ordered relationship between himself and his people. Sacrifice may be a gift of humans offered to God, an expression of spiritual fellowship between God and his people, or a means of atonement. But in every case it is oriented by the presence of God in grace and judgment among his people.

Covenant sacrifice was perpetuated in Israel only as a part of the sacrifice of peace offerings (Lev. 3). The blood rite here, "throwing against the altar" (Lev. 3:2,8,13), is the same as in the burnt offering (Lev. 1:5,11), but distinct from the rites of the sin offering (Lev. 4:5-7).

Early rabbinic Judaism failed increasingly to distinguish between the ideas and technicalities associated with particular sacrificial rites. The blood rite of covenant sacrifice tended to become associated with those of other sacrifices, especially where there were similarities in the manipulation of the blood. This blending can be observed in the epistle to the Hebrews (ch. 9), where the writer combines images, ideas, and rites from the Day of Atonement (Lev. 16), the covenant sacrifice (Ex. 24:3-8), the rite of sprinkling with the water of purification (Num. 19), and the vicarious expiatory suffering of the suffering servant (Isa. 53).

Significance of Sacrificial Blood

Blood played a central role in sacrificial ritual in the Old Testament. However, we note a variety of meanings assigned to it. At the first Passover, the blood of the lamb warded off destruction from God's people. In the covenant ceremony at Sinai blood seems to have symbolized sharing in commitment. It also has power to atone because it is life and therefore stands in close relationship to the living God.

Three Old Testament texts, all of them prohibitions against eating blood, suggest a direct connection between sacrificial blood and atonement (Gen. 9:4; Deut. 12:23; Lev. 17:11,14). Leviticus 17:11 contains the fullest statement, "For the *life* of the flesh is in the blood; and I have given it to you upon the altar to make atonement for your *souls*; for it is the blood that makes atonement, by reason of the *life*." (The highlighted terms translate *nepesh*, which means simply "life" or "seat of life" or "person.")

Eating blood is prohibited because the life of the flesh is in the blood and only God has dominion over life. One legitimate use for blood is to make atonement upon the altar. Blood fulfills this function because life is contained in it. The text in itself and in the context means that "the blood of the sacrificial animal atones by means of and by power of the life contained in the sacrificial animal" (Daly, 1978:32).

While it has been common to read substitutionary meanings into this text, the concept is not explicit in this passage. It is true that the idea of substitution is present in the text in the general sense that the rites of atonement take the place of or substitute for the necessity of suffering the consequences of one's transgression. However, the idea of "penal satisfaction" can scarcely be based on the verse as it stands in the Hebrew text. (The Alexandrian version of the Septuagint translates Leviticus 17:11 *anti tes psuches* which could suggest that the sacrificial animal makes atonement in place of the life of the offerer, but it does not need to carry this meaning. In addition to being unsupported by the Hebrew text, this translation also tends to create a theological problem by implying that God is a wrathful, avenging Being.)

In Hebrews we read that "without the shedding of blood [i.e., sacrifice] there is no forgiveness of sins" (9:22). While in this form it may have been a popular rabbinic saying, it is an apparent allusion to Leviticus 17:11, "For it is the blood that makes atonement." In its context in Hebrews it refers to the shedding of blood in the Old Testament sacrificial ritual (9:18ff.). Does the writer of Hebrews mean by this that God is somehow captive of a need for retribution (as Anselm's line of reasoning would have us to believe)? Or does he mean that God himself has graciously provided animal sacrifice in the Old Testament as his initiative in providing a means for recurrent reconciliation?

God has provided what is needed, rather than being himself captive of that need. Since the provision for blood sacrifice in the Old Testament is already a matter of God's gracious initiative in making a way for reconciliation to occur which would otherwise not have been possible, then to understand the saving work of Christ as sacrifice is a natural and congenial step.

The Sacrifice of Isaac

The offering of Isaac (Gen. 22:9ff.) is in many ways important for understanding sacrifice in the Old Testament. In addition to being the rejection of human sacrifice and the identification of Mount Moriah with the site of the Jerusalem temple, the theological heart of the narrative is to be found in Abraham's faith-obedience relationship with God which brings God's blessing upon him and his descendants. Early rabbinic Judaism drew heavily upon this event for its soteriology, and the event plays an important role as background for the sacrificial soteriology of the New Testament.

By New Testament times the rabbinic tradition contained a sacrificial soteriology based on the offering of Isaac which included the following elements: (1) Isaac's oblation was regarded as a true sacrifice in its own right; (2) the effects of this offering were believed to be redemptive; (3) a causal relationship existed between this offering and the atoning efficacy of other sacrifices; (4) the offering of Isaac was liturgically commemorated in the Passover feast, and the slaying of the Passover lamb was related to it (Daly, 1978:49).

There are a number of New Testament references to the offering of Isaac. Hebrews 11:17-20 speaks as if the sacrifice actually occurred—in this it agrees with Jewish sources—and goes on to speak of God's ability "to raise men even from the dead." James 2:21 also refers to the sacrifice as accomplished. "He who did not spare his own Son but gave him up for us all" (Rom. 8:23) echoes the Septuagint version of Genesis 22:16. The phrase, "to give" or "to give up" (Gal. 1:4; 2:20, Eph. 5:2, 25), used to express Christ's act of self-giving, echos the portrayal of the offering of Isaac in the Targums.[2]

Sacrifice in the New Testament

On the surface the New Testament appears to be relatively less interested in covenant ritual and sacrifice and more oriented toward a prophetic interest in covenant law and righteousness. Evident exceptions to this generalization are Hebrews and Revelation. However, a careful reading of the New Testament will show a surprisingly widespread use of sacrificial imagery and concepts.

In the synoptic Gospels, for example, the gifts of the magi are described with technical sacrificial terms. Zechariah's vision of the birth of John came to him while he was occupied in temple ritual

(Luke 1:8-23). Jesus' teaching in Matthew 5:23-24 presupposes altar offerings, and his instructions to the cleansed leper recognize ritual sacrifice (Mark 1:44).

Other references to Jesus' teaching and activity imply criticism of sacrifice: his cleansing of the temple (Mark 11:15-19); the parable of the good Samaritan with its criticism of the priest and Levite (Luke 10:29-37); Jesus' superiority over the temple (Matt. 12:1-8).

If we include the servant-of-God or vicarious-suffering image as a sacrificial motif, then we find many more allusions. "To give life ... for many" (Mark 10:45) is based on Isaiah 53:10-12. Regardless of whether the Last Supper was an actual Passover meal, the evangelists all thought of it as a Passover event, and the command to "do this in memory of me" (Luke 22:19; 1 Cor. 11:24-25) seems to parallel the commemorative aspects of the Passover.

"My blood of the covenant" (Mark 14:24; Matt. 26:28) alludes to the covenant sacrifice in Exodus 24:3-8. The phrase "blood ... poured out for many for the forgiveness of sin" (Matt. 26:28) clearly points to the atoning function of sacrifice. However, at the deepest level the suffering-servant motif supplies the context of the words of the institution of the Supper. The phrases "shed for you [many]," "give up for many," and "on the night he was betrayed" are both verbal and thematic allusions to Isaiah 53.

The body and blood of the institution of the last supper depend essentially on the servant motif rather than corresponding primarily to the flesh and blood which resulted from the separation of these two elements in the slaughter involved in Israelite sacrificial ritual. Contrary to the crucifixion, the Old Testament never emphasized the dying of the sacrificial victim. Furthermore, instead of seeing himself as a victim, Jesus emphasized the free and voluntary character of his death as an act of self-giving. Body (soma) refers to a concrete living person (cf. Rom. 12:1) rather than sacrificial flesh. Here the reference is to Jesus as servant of God who gives himself in vicarious suffering and death. By giving his blood, Jesus gives himself unto death on behalf of the many. Jesus' death is the free, fully voluntary self-offering of Christ the servant. In this the Last Supper interpretation of the meaning of Christ's death is more akin to the rabbinic understandings of the offering of Isaac as "willing self-offering" than it is to the principal Hebrew rituals of sacrifice.

The best of the ideas contained in Isaiah 53, the Maccabean martyr-theology, and rabbinic understandings of the offering of Isaac all find their climax in Jesus' vicarious self-offering (Daly, 1978:56-58).

In Acts Jesus' mission is interpreted essentially in terms of the servant motif. The sacrificial motif, as such, receives no particular emphasis. The temple is viewed both positively and negatively. It is a place of prayer (2:46; 3:1—4:3; 21:26; 22:17), and it is an idolatrous human construction "made with hands" (7:41-50; cf. vv. 41,48). In the same passage Stephen associates the Hebrew practice of sacrifice with idolatry.

In Paul's letters and 1 Peter the sacrificial motif comes to the fore as a way of understanding the death of Christ. Proper participation in the Lord's Supper is enjoined by comparing it to Old Testament sacrificial practice (1 Cor. 10:14-22). Apparently Paul expected his readers to view the Lord's Supper and Jesus' passion in terms of sacrifice. The texts which refer to Christ's death, or "giving himself up for us," reflect a sacrificial understanding of one type or another (2 Cor. 5:14-15; Rom. 5:6-11; 8:23; Gal. 2:20; Eph. 5:2,25; Col. 1:24; 1 Tim. 2:5-6; Titus 2:13-14; 1 John 3:16).

The reference that "Christ, our paschal lamb, has been sacrificed" in the context of exhortation presupposes the fact that Paul's readers were familiar with this image (1 Cor. 5:7). In 2 Corinthians 5:21 Paul depicts Christ as a sin offering, "for our sake he [God] made him [Christ] to be sin [i.e., sin offering] who knew no sin, so that in him we might become the righteousness of God."[3] Romans 8:3 surely carries the same meaning; in Romans 3:25, expiation might be understood as "means of expiation" or "sin offering."[4] So Paul saw the death of Christ in terms of two particular Jewish sacrifices, the Passover and the sin offering. A suggestion is that these were the two rites which Jews of the New Testament period most closely associated with redemption and forgiveness (Daly, 1978:60).

But Paul also moves beyond the use of the sacrificial motif to understand the death of Christ. He spiritualizes both temple and sacrifice by applying these images to the Christian community and the life of believers. Both the community and individuals are called God's temple (1 Cor. 3:16-17; 6:15,19; 2 Cor. 6:16). Paul also calls the new humanity, created of Jews and Gentiles, a "holy temple in the Lord" and "a dwelling of God in the Spirit" (Eph. 2:19-22).

As for sacrifice, Paul compares the life and death of Christians with the sacrificial death of Christ in numerous texts scattered throughout his letters. Psalm 44:23, quoted by Paul in Romans 8:36, "For thy sake we are being killed all the day long, we are regarded as sheep to be slaughtered," was applied in Jewish tradition to the Maccabean martyrs (cf. 2 Cor. 4:10-11; Gal. 2:20; Col. 1:24). Paul saw his life and impending death as a continuation of Christ's—a personal self-offering (Phil. 2:17; 2 Tim. 4:6). Not only are the lives of Christians sacrifices, so are the monetary offerings they share with others (Rom. 15:31; Phil. 4:18).

Just as the body of Christ is given as sacrifice (1 Cor. 11:24), so the bodies, or persons, of the Romans are living sacrifices (Rom. 12:1). Paul saw his own life and mission as a "sacrificial service" (Rom. 15:15-16). In 2 Corinthians 2:14-17 he also underscores the idea that apostolic mission is sacrifice through the use of the terms "aroma" and "fragrance," which in the Septuagint express the acceptability of a sacrifice before God.

First Peter 2:4-10 underscores emphatically the spiritualization of temple and sacrifice. Here the community is the "spiritual house" in which "spiritual sacrifices acceptable to God" are offered. This passage reinforces the central message of Romans 12. True Christian sacrifice is to place oneself wholly at the service of both God and neighbor.

In the epistle to the Hebrews the idea of sacrifice is presented in two principal ways: The sacrifice of Christ is Christ's high-priestly self-offering, and the sacrifice of the Christian is praise to God and service and economic sharing toward others (Heb. 13:15-16).

Jesus, as high priest according to the order of Melchizedek, king of righteousness and peace (Heb. 6:20—7:3), is both the end and the fulfiller of Old Testament priesthood. In this new order Jesus is both priest and sin offering. Following the model of the Day of Atonement ritual, the writer of Hebrews pictures Jesus, the eternal high priest, entering the eternal sanctuary, once for all, with his own blood to make expiation through a single, perfect offering. Then, seated at the right hand of God, he has become our continuing intercessor—a function of sacrifice (7:25—8:7; 9:6-14, 23-28; 10:12-22; 12:18-24).

The difference between the sacrificial system of the old

covenant and the work of Christ in the new age is not merely quantitative. It is also qualitative. It is a free, personal act of self-giving which Christ accomplishes once for all (Heb. 10:11; 7:23ff.; 9:6f.,11f.,15f.). Christ, in contrast to all others, achieved eternal redemption (9:12; 10:14). Hebrews does not present an atoning Christ who is merely an improvement on the sacrificial system of the old order. The work of Christ is a radical departure from sacrifice as it developed in Israel and was perpetuated in Judaism. It was a radical return to the original purpose of sacrifice in the Old Testament, that is, a means of restoring personal relationship between God and humanity. In the personal, voluntary, and unique offering of his life, Christ fulfilled the original purpose. Cultic sacrifice was not merely transcended; it came to an end in him (10:18).

Just as in Paul's letters and 1 Peter, sacrifice in Hebrews is spiritualized in terms of Christian living. Since Christ offered himself for our sakes (Heb. 2:9; 5:1), we may all "draw near," a technical term signifying the priest approaching the altar of sacrifice. So in light of Jesus' sacrifice we are called to life as sacrifice (10:19-25). This is the same concept we have already noted in Romans 12:1; 15:15-16; and 1 Peter 2:4-10. Living the Christian life in the community of Christ takes on the reconciling function of sacrificial ritual. Hebrews 13:10-16 reiterates the idea that Christian living is sacrificial (cf. 12:28). Recurring ideas in chapters 10, 11, and 13 include the fact that Old Testament ritual is superseded by worship in the new covenant in which all believers participate by offering spiritualized sacrifice of praise, good works, and generous sharing (12:28; 13:15-16) by virtue of Christ's continuing high-priestly mediation.

These are the sacrifices of the new age in which there is no more sacrifice in a literal cultic sense. To bring ourselves, our wills, our actions wholly to God and to our brothers and sisters in the new community of the Spirit is the new meaning which the concept of sacrifice acquires in Hebrews as well as in the writings of Paul and Peter.

John's writings develop the idea that the Christian community is the new temple. "The Word . . . pitched his tent among us" (John 1:14, my translation) implies that the temple is replaced. That John places the cleansing of the temple in the Passover context (2:13-33) is also significant. Jesus' words, on the occasion of the Feast of

Tabernacles, with its traditional water ceremony, show that the feast has been superseded by Christ: "If any one thirst let him come to me and drink. He who believes in me, as the scripture has said, 'out of his heart shall flow rivers of living water' " (John 7:37-38).

The idea of sacrificial self-giving, based on the servant motif, which is reflected in the phrases "for us" and "for you" is prominent in John's writings (John 3:16; 10:11,15,17; 13:1-15; 11:49-52; 18:14; 15:13; 1 John 3:16; 4:10-11). First John 3:16 and 4:10-11 also show the same intimate association between the sacrifice of Christ and sacrificial self-giving of Christians which we have already noted in Paul's writing and in Hebrews.

The sin-offering motif is also present in 1 John where "Jesus Christ the righteous . . . is the expiation [sin offering] for our sins" (2:1-2; cf. 1:7; 4:10). But perhaps even more important in understanding this text is the fact that according to early rabbinic thought the concept of the sin offering of the Day of Atonement ritual was strongly influenced by the vicarious sufferings and death of the "righteous man" (Daly, 1978:78).

John, like Paul, saw Christ's death as a Paschal sacrifice and emphasized much more than the synoptic Gospels the idea that Christ's death is a Passover event. John organized his Gospel around three Passovers; Christ's death and resurrection occur on the third. He locates the time of Christ's death at the hour in which the Paschal lambs were slain (John 19:14,31). The reference to hyssop (19:29) recalls the Passover blood rite in Exodus 12:22. John's report that "not a bone of him shall be broken" (19:36) sets up a direct comparison between the crucifixion of Christ and the Paschal lamb (cf. Ex. 12:46; Num. 9:12; Ps. 34:20).

Toward an Understanding of Sacrifice in Our Time

Biblical Sacrifice

The use of the sacrifice motif in the New Testament in general corresponds to Paul's understanding: Christ's death is understood in sacrificial terms; Christians are the new temple; and Christian sacrifices are spiritualized in a way which makes them primarily ethical rather than ritual. This has consequences both for our understanding of the meaning of Christ's death as well as the meaning of

Christian worship as integral Christlike living.

The Old Testament background of sacrifice and the ways in which the New Testament writers apply the motif to the death of Jesus furnish insights into its meaning. Christ is depicted as a sin offering by which relationships—which have been disturbed by sin—between the creature and the Creator are put in order through expiatory action in which God alone is ultimately the subject, or agent. As the Day of Atonement ritual shows, people (as well as things) are objects of expiation. Subsequent concepts of penal substitution were not integral parts of this ritual.

Sacrifice on the occasion of the Egyptian Passover is related to the redemption of the firstborn as well as liberation from Egypt. This provides the background for understanding Christ's death as a vicarious (for us) sacrificial death. However, subsequent views of vicarious punishment and penal satisfaction are not necessarily to be found in this image.

Covenant sacrifice was a convenient way for early Christians to understand the reality of the new covenant which had come through the death and resurrection of Christ who is both priest and sacrifice of the new covenant.

The principal New Testament passages which speak of Christians' sacrifices are Romans 12:1-2; 15:15-16; 1 Peter 2:4-10; Hebrews 10:19-25; 12:18—13:16. All of these passages, either explicitly or implicitly (by virtue of the fact that they all occur in contexts of ethical exhortation), understand sacrifice as the living of a life of Christian conduct and mission. So the center of a specifically New Testament concept of Christian sacrifice is not ritual or liturgical, but practical and ethical.

Twentieth-Century Sacrifice

When they deal with the theme of sacrifice, contemporary theologians tend to fall into two broadly defined types. One group insists on the universal validity of sacrifice in human experience in all periods and places; however, the meaning of sacrifice is conceived in purely religious or theological categories. Another group recognizes the existence of the concept and practice of sacrifice in the ancient world (the biblical world included) and among primitive peoples of the modern era, but hastens to add that this category is meaningless to modern Westerners. So we are left with what has often seemed to be an impasse: Sacrifice is a purely religious or cultic phenomenon in the limited sense, and thoughtful people of the industrialized West simply cannot accept this seemingly archaic concept as having any validity.

Biblical scholars have been pointing out that the modern tendency to separate the religious realm from the social and political realm in ancient Israel is untenable from the biblical perspective. The practice of dividing ancient Hebrew law into civil and cere- monial categories does not stand up under a careful scrutiny of the nature of these biblical laws. In ancient Israel the areas of civil and ceremonial law, of politics and piety, of justice and liturgy, of eco- nomics and cult, overlap to such a degree that to separate them into neatly logical and distinct categories is really not possible.

In light of this global biblical vision of reality, the question arises, What if we moderns did not separate so sharply the sup- posedly religious and secular, or political, spheres? Might we find that the concept of sacrifice is not so alien to contemporary Westerners as some of us have often imagined?

In reality the amount of sacrificing done in the twentieth century among the so-called Christian nations of the West is im- pressive. One need not limit one's understanding of sacrifice to cultic acts, such as those practiced among ancient pagans which were destined to placate the anger of the gods, or in the later Anselmic sense of an offering needed to redress the wounded honor of God. Surely we have a sense in which sacrifice is something we're willing to offer or the price we're willing to pay in order to gain well-being (salvation), be it personal, corporate, or national.

The twentieth century has stood out as the century in which hundreds of thousands of victims have been sacrificed for causes which in one way or another are salvific: "to save democracy," "for the public welfare," "in the nation's best interests." Most Westerners have been able to believe that in some way these deaths were effica- cious for the salvation of the nation, and for others. In some cases it may be possible to establish a cause-and-effect relationship between the deaths of the sacrificial victims and the ends sought. But in other cases it is not possible. However, in all cases a quasi-religious value is attached to the cause which is pursued and to the necessary sacrifice offered on the altar of the fatherland. A remarkable thing about this sacrifice is that, while the ancient Hebrews offered selected animals, both ancient pagans and modern Western nations have offered human victims.

In ancient Israel the scapegoat was driven into the wilderness to stop the effects of sin and save the people from harm. In ancient Greece people were driven into exile for similar reasons (Hengel, 1981:24-27). In modern Western societies social offenders are driven out of society and isolated through imprisonment in order to preserve the social order. In some cases these human scapegoats are converted into sacrifices whose deaths are generally interpreted in one of two ways: Either it is for the welfare of society or it is to satisfy the just demands of a moral universe (cf. Anselm).

On another level human beings have generally been willing to offer sacrifices for personal benefit. In ancient times these sacrifices included human victims, animals, or the products of their labors. The case of their modern counterparts provides a striking similarity. The unborn are sometimes sacrificed in the interests of the well-being, self-realization, or honor of the offerers. Both people and things are sacrificed in the interest of self-realization in vocational achievement.

With sacrifice in all of these modern forms so deeply rooted in contemporary Western experience, it should not be so foreign for us to hear that God did not hold back his Son, but delivered him up "and sent him as an atoning sacrifice for our sins" (1 John 4:10, NIV). Furthermore, the conviction of the New Testament is that this is the ultimate sacrifice to end all sacrifice (with the exception of free self-sacrifice which expresses itself in praise to God and serving others). Since the sacrifice of Christ, humanity need no longer sacrifice at any of the many altars on which we are still prone to offer victims. Our well-being (salvation) depends on simply trusting obediently in God who provides for absolutely all of the needs of his people.

8

Expiation Motif
and the Wrath of God

As we noted in the previous chapter, one of the essential functions of sacrifice in the Old Testament was the expiation of sins. Since this particular element of sacrifice is accented in the New Testament references to the death of Christ, we will treat expiation as a motif in its own right for understanding the work of Christ.

Traditionally this image has been one of the principal categories for interpreting the death of Christ, even though relatively few specific references to the term appear in the New Testament. In only six New Testament texts do these terms appear: *hilaskomai, hilasterion,* and *hilasmos,* variously translated "be merciful" (Luke 18:13), "to make expiation" (Heb. 2:17), "expiation" (Rom. 3:25; 1 John 2:2; 4:10) and "mercy seat" (Heb. 9:5).[1] The most notable difference in translation in English versions occurs between the RSV and the KJV. In the RSV the substantive is regularly translated as "expiation" and in the KJV as "propitiation."

These English terms, of course, carry different shades of meaning. The English term "to expiate" requires as its object a sin or some impurity. The object of this action is impersonal. On the other hand, in the English language the verb "to propitiate" calls for a personal object. The traditional interpretations of these passages hold that the object of propitiation is God.

A related term, *hileos,* occurs in Hebrews 8:12 where the writer cites Jeremiah 31:34: "I will be merciful toward their iniquities." This term was used among the ancient Greeks with special reference to rulers and gods. In fact, to make the gods gracious was considered one of the tasks of cultic acts. In marked contrast to this use of the term, in the Septuagint *hileos* is used only as a predicate of God.

147

Ancient Understandings of Expiation

To understand the use of this family of terms in the New Testament, we must note the meanings which their Old Testament equivalents carried.

Ancient Hebrew Understanding

Among the ancient Hebrews the term *kipper* (literally, "to rub off" or "to rub on") appears to have carried two basic meanings: (1) to purge, to purify, to cleanse; and (2) to cover (Herrmann, 1965:305-10). Expiation was both cultic and non-cultic. In the case of the latter, expiation could be made through the payment of money, thus covering the hurt which had been committed and releasing the guilty party from obligation (Ex. 21:30). In other cases expiation appears to be accomplished through the forfeiting of a life (Num. 35:31f.; 2 Sam. 21:3-6). This life thus substituted was a sort of representative or ransom payment (cf. Num. 8:19; Ex. 30:16). Ancient Israel's conviction was that the merciful God is accustomed to expiating guilt. If God does not atone, or does not make or grant expiation, or does not forgive, then sinful people must die (Jer. 18:23; Isa. 22:14). If God atones, people may live (Ps. 78:38) and be saved (Ps. 79:9).

About three fourths of the occurrences of *kipper* in the Old Testament are in connection with specific sacrifices, so expiation was primarily cultic. Leviticus 17:11 reports that expiation is made with the blood that Yahweh has given for the altar, and this is brought about by the fact that in the blood is the life. In its cultic use expiation is linked with the manipulation of the blood of animals. This is reflected in the fourfold ritual of the sin offering reported in Leviticus 4, where the manipulation of the blood seems to be the climax of the action which results in expiation and forgiveness (Lev. 4:20,26,31,35). In the case of economic adversity a cereal offering also results in expiation and forgiveness (Lev. 5:11-13). In the ritual of the great Day of Atonement the central place of the manipulation of blood in the expiation and forgiveness of sin is certainly evident. Atonement is made for the priest and his house (Lev. 16:6,11,17) and for the entire congregation (16:5,17).

Among the people of God is the possibility of expiation and forgiveness of all transgressions of the commandments of Yahweh (Lev.

4:2; Num. 15:22ff.) and for all injuries caused by offenses (Lev. 5:16), as long as these are committed unintentionally and unwittingly (Num. 15:30). Sins committed deliberately and with evil intent ("with a high hand") result in being cut off from God's people and bearing one's iniquity alone (Num. 15:30-31). The community of God's people is the context in which expiation and forgiveness take place. The consequences of sin are collective, and the restoration of the sinner also has social dimensions.

When the biblical material on expiation (both cultic and non-cultic) in ancient Israel is assembled, it becomes clear that in the community of Yahweh nothing which needs expiation is to be left unexpiated. The possibility is that those who transgress the commands of Yahweh with evil intent and show themselves to be unrepentant may be cut off from the people of God wherein atonement is possible. But in the community of God's people disturbed relationships can be restored through the provisions for expiation which Yahweh has provided for his people.

The intimate relationship between a holy God and holy people calls for all sin and uncleanness to be expiated. It is not merely a matter of averting the destructive consequences of unexpiated sin, although this is certainly true. The character of God must be reflected in the relationships which characterize his people. The call to holiness among God's people is based on the fact of God's holiness. As we have noted, expiation is effected by Israel's merciful God, be it through the cultic means of manipulating the blood of sacrificial animals or by means of the various non-cultic forms of expiation.

The theological interpretations of ancient Israel's atonement rituals have probably often been influenced by confessional doctrinal considerations. Rather than attempting to force all of the Old Testament material into a rational theory of atonement, we do well to recognize the variety of ideas and motifs in the provisions for making expiation and forgiveness concrete in the experience of God's people. Among the cultic forms ordained by Yahweh as a means for atonement, the blood of sacrificial animals occupies a prominent place. Blood is both suitable and effective by virtue of the life which is contained in it. But in no case are sacrifices ever considered valid irrespective of the attitude of the offerer. *Kipper* was not inherently efficacious. This set its practice in Israel radically apart from contemporary ancient Near Eastern understandings. Covenant relationships form the context in which true repentance can take place and expiation can effectively occur.

Ancient Greek Understanding

Among the ancient Greeks two terms were required to express the reality contained in the Hebrew concept of *kipper* (Büchsel, 1965:310-12). In ancient Greece *katharismos* meant purification from both cultic and moral defects. On the other hand, *hilasmos* referred to the propitiation of supernatural beings (gods, demons, or the departed) whose favor was sought or whose wrath had supposedly been provoked. These were seen as two aspects of the same process: the purification of people and the propitiation of supernatural beings. The cleansing was viewed as essential to restoration of relationship with the deity. This cleansing might consist of the removal of physically conceived stains by washings in water or blood, rubbings with clay, or fumigations. For some sacrifices, both animal and human, guilt was conceived of as transferred to the victim.

A wide variety of sacrifices and actions were available in order to propitiate angry deities, but they also were to expiate guilt and to cleanse from moral stain. While some practices and beliefs were undoubtedly crude in their attempts to appease the gods, more enlightened Greeks were probably convinced that what really mattered was moral disposition and conduct. Both aspects were present in the Greek world and characterized understandings of expiation and propitiation.

Hilaskomai was employed quite commonly in ancient Greece with people as subject and a god or a deceased person as object. Used in this sense the term meant "to make gracious" or "to placate," "to propitiate," or "to make propitious." This was the cultic use of the term. It was also employed to denote the placating of the emperor in his anger, and on the secular level it was used in the sense of a bribe by which appeasement was effected in relationships among people. In the New Testament usage of *hilaskomai* we discover a truly remarkable reversal of meaning. Instead of referring to people's actions in relation to God, the verb refers to God's action in relation to humanity.

Later Hebrew Understanding

In later Judaism, the rabbis taught that all sin destroys fellowship with God (Büchsel, 1965:312-14). Furthermore, God's wrath is provoked by sin alone. Therefore, cleansing from sin, or expiation, is of fundamental importance. This expiation is accomplished by cultic means on one hand, and by personal achievements and experiences on the other. The rites of the Day of Atonement were preeminent as a cultic means of expiation which leads to reconciliation, but other sacrifices were also significant. Among the personal experiences which achieved atonement were penitence, suffering, death, works of charity, restitution, study of the Torah, fasting, and prayer. When blood sacrifices were no longer possible due to the destruction of the temple, Jewish piety found in these good works a substitute for the temple cult. These were achieved by a punctilious fulfillment of the provisions of the law.

People also had the idea that the innocent suffering of the righteous carried an atoning value. An example of this attitude is found in references to the death of Jewish martyrs. "They become as it were a ransom for our nation's sins, and through the blood of these righteous ones and their propitiatory death, the divine Providence preserved Israel which before was evil entreated" (4 Macc. 17:22).

Among the Jews of the dispersion one finds the same attitudes concerning the expiation of sins. They saw themselves as a part of the people of God for whom the rites of the Day of Atonement were effectual and for whom the keeping of the Torah was a practical path to expiation.

New Testament View of Expiation

When we come to the New Testament, we are impressed more by the differences which distinguish these documents from the ideas of expiation and propitiation found in the ancient world than by the similarities. In the New Testament *hilaskomai* occurs only twice. In Luke 18:13 the term is used in a cry to God for mercy. This use of the term was also found in the Old Testament, as well as among the ancient Greeks. In Hebrews 2:17 the task of Jesus as "a merciful and faithful high priest in the service of God" is to expiate the sins of the people. By Jesus' ministry, Old Testament sacrifices are robbed of their ongoing significance (Heb. 10:11-18).

The expiation motif does not stand alone here as a way of understanding Jesus' suffering and death. In this particular context the conflict-victory image appears to be even more prominent than the idea of expiation (Heb. 2:14-17). Furthermore, this text has no explicit reference to propitiating God, in a sense needing to render God gracious toward us.

Hilaskomai: *God's Action*

Probably the most striking change we note in the New Testament use of *hilaskomai* is that alongside the common Jewish and Greek sense of (1) "to propitiate," we now find the term used in the sense of (2) "to purge or cleanse from sin" and (3) "to cover" or "to expiate." In the first of these three senses, the person propitiated appears in the accusative case in the sentence structure. In the case of God, this would mean in the active mood that people seek to propitiate God, and in the passive mood that God allows himself to be propitiated and thus become gracious. In the second of these senses the person or object which is purged appears in the accusative case. An example of this usage is found in the text which we have just examined (Heb. 2:17) where "the sins" of the people appear in the accusative case in the Greek text. In the third sense the guilt or sin which is expiated appears in the accusative case, or as the object of a preposition such as *peri* or *apo*, generally translated "from."

Examples of the first of these senses are found everywhere in ancient literature: pagan Greek, the Septuagint, Philo, and the New Testament (Luke 18:13). But a notable difference exists between the Septuagint and the New Testament where *hilaskomai* appears only in the aorist passive. It is used in the New Testament in Luke 18:13 where the sinner's prayer is that God will be merciful or gracious to him.

Someone has suggested that the term originally carried the first meaning, to propitiate, and that the second and third meanings were later expansions of the meaning of the term. According to this view, there is an effect on God as well as on people and their sin so that there is simultaneous propitiation and expiation. Be this as it may, what is really striking about the supposed development of this term is that a word which in the ancient world was originally used to denote people's action in relation to God has ceased to be used in this way in the New Testament. Here the term refers to God's action in relation to people (Büchsel, 1965:316-17).

Hilasmos: *Related to the Total Person and Work of Jesus*

Hilasmos, though seldom used in ancient Greece, meant both cultic propitiation of the gods and expiatory action in general. In the Septuagint *hilasmos* usually refers to the cultic expiation by which sin is made ineffective. In the Greek Old Testament, God is not the object of *hilasmos*; the objects are rather people or their sins. According to Psalm 49:7 people cannot offer God an *exhilasma*. In Psalm 130:4 *hilasmos* is God's forgiveness.

In the New Testament *hilasmos* occurs only in 1 John 2:2 and 4:10. The construction here corresponds to that found in the Septuagint, which John apparently follows. Rather than implying the propitiation of God, *hilasmos* refers to the purpose which God has fulfilled by sending his Son. Therefore, it rests on the fact that God is gracious, i.e., on his love (cf. 4:10), and its meaning is the setting aside, or covering, of sin. The context (1:9) indicates that forgiveness and cleansing are parallels of *hilasmos*.

According to the context of 1 John 4:10 *hilasmos* begets love for others. So, overcoming sin as guilt cannot really be separated from overcoming sin as disobedience or transgression, which for John is the lack of love. Apart from the reference to the blood of Jesus (1:7) and God's sending of his Son (4:10), John does not emphasize the death of Christ as the means of *hilasmos*. The question of how *hilasmos* is achieved is not answered. In fact, John seems to refer to a specific function of the risen Lord as advocate-intercessor (2:1) and to the total mission of Jesus as an expression of love (4:10).

So in these texts we find no warrant to link *hilasmos* exclusively with the death of Jesus. It is rather related to the total person and work of Jesus, of which his death is an indissoluble and climactic part (cf. 1 John 5:6; 3:16-17). For John, *hilasmos* is more than a mere concept of Christian doctrine, if indeed it is that. It is rather the reality by which the messianic community lives.

God's Hilasterion: *Jesus Christ*

In the space above the *hilasterion*, or mercy seat on the ark of the covenant, the presence of Yahweh was actualized among his people (Ex. 25:17-22; Lev. 16:2). There Yahweh met his people during the ritual of the Day of Atonement (Lev. 16:14). In the Septuagint the term also came to be used in a general sense for "that which makes expiation."

In Hebrews 9:5 the term is clearly used in the specific sense of the place of God's presence over the ark. However, in Romans 3:25 it is difficult to determine in which of the two senses Paul used the term: the mercy seat in particular, or a means of expiation in general. In either case, it most certainly denotes that which expiates sins. Throughout the context of this passage, God is the subject, not the object. Therefore *hilasterion* should not be read as meaning "to propitiate" as though God were the object. God has made the *hilasterion* what it is, a place of mercy.

In the New Testament only people or the sins of people are the objects of the verb *hilaskomai*. Since Paul's writings contain no uses of the verb form, this statement cannot be supported by other instances of Pauline usage. But this interpretation is in line with other aspects of Paul's thought. For example, it is in keeping with Paul's teaching about reconciliation. Paul states that it is God who reconciles, and it is people who are reconciled (2 Cor. 5:18).

The center of earlier expiation in Israel had been the Day of Atonement with the sprinkling of blood on the *hilasterion*, or mercy seat, in order to mediate the remission of sins. In this text Paul assumes a church acquainted with the Mosaic practice (cf. Rom. 7:1). In this context Paul quite naturally depicts Jesus as a higher mercy seat which is efficacious through a relationship of faith rather than merely through external observance (cf. 2:28-29) and whose death was a public affair in contrast to the Old Testament rite carried out in the confines of the holy of holies. *Hilasterion* can well be understood in a concrete, or plastic, sense here and be no more out of place than, for example, designating the Christian community as a "temple," or Jesus as "the door." Paul possibly used the term abstractly as a reference to something that cleanses from sin. But since Paul's writings are saturated with references and allusions to the Septuagint, one need not be surprised to find this the case here with *hilasterion*.[2]

To join the images of mercy seat and expiation in this way will most probably seem contradictory to many modern readers. Mercy seat conveys the idea of a throne from which a merciful God grants mercy or forgiveness. On the other hand, expiation has often been understood as a performance rendered by a guilty person, or some sort of suffering inflicted on the offender, or some kind of payment in order to make restitution for the evil caused. Therefore mercy seat and expiation are anything but synonymous in their traditional sense. However, when we realize that *hilasterion* in Romans 3:25 can be translated as mercy seat just as naturally as expiation, we discover a basic commonality of meaning in the two terms.

Humankind, not God's attitude, needs to be changed. God may be said to hate sin, but at the same time God loves the sinner (Rom. 5:6-8). The highest expression of God's love was Jesus Christ and his self-sacrifice on behalf of sinful humanity. In fact, Jesus Christ in his death for us has become God's mercy seat for humanity.

For Paul, *hilasterion* is not something which makes God gracious, since the provision of a *hilasterion* for human sin presupposes a gracious God. Jesus, as *hilasterion*, reveals and expresses most fully God and his covenant righteousness (Rom. 3:21,25,26). In Christ (God's *hilasterion*), sinners and their sin are distinguished. Sinners are separated from their sin. They are brought to faith which involves repentance, i.e., self-judgment, and conversion. The work of Christ is not merely a declaration of a transcendent attitude on the part of God. The experience of grace and judgment really happens in the human race. Jesus Christ is God's *hilasterion* which genuinely frees humans to experience a new reality variously called in the New Testament redemption, reconciliation, adoption, justification, communion, and peace.

The Wrath of God

Of all the human characteristics applied to God in the Bible, wrath is probably the most difficult for people of a modern mentality to understand. However, in a number of New Testament passages we observe a close association between the saving work of Christ and the wrath of God (John 3:36; Rom. 5:9; cf. Rom. 1:18; Eph. 2:3ff.; 1 Thess. 1:10). It is therefore all the more important that we seek to understand the concept of the wrath of God in its biblical sense.

The biblical understanding of God's wrath is deeply rooted in the loving covenant relationship which God has established with his people. The salvific relationship is the center around which the biblical view of the wrath of God is oriented. It is fundamentally the response of God to covenant violation on the part of his people in the interests of protecting this merciful, loving relationship with his people. In this the biblical understanding of wrath stands in sharp contrast to contemporary concepts in the ancient Near East.

In ancient Greece wrath was one of the most prominent characteristics of the gods. In fact the wrath of the gods appears to have been a basic ingredient in ancient religions. The anger of the gods was directed against their own kind, as well as against humans. Their anger was generally provoked by violation of a fundamental demand of life, morals, or law. And the results of this wrath could be healed particularly through cultic means including vows, prayers, ministerial acts, and rites of expiation and dedication (Kleinknecht, 1967:385-87; Hahn, 1975:107).

The ancient Romans held similar ideas about the wrath of the gods. Punitive judgments, especially against religious guilt, took concrete historical form in natural disasters, famine, sickness, plague, and hostile armies. These expressions of divine wrath called for appeasing the gods by means of cultic actions such as expiatory rites (Kleinknecht, 1967:389-92).

Old Testament: Wrath of a Covenant-Love God

When we compare the Old Testament understanding of the wrath of God with other concepts held in the ancient world, the differences are more noteworthy than are the similarities. In the Old Testament there is a consistent linking of nouns for wrath with Yahweh, the covenant God (Fichtner, 1967:396). (In fact, Genesis contains no term for the wrath of God [Fichtner, 1967:396, n. 101].) This is a fact of great theological importance, since it shows that the biblical idea of wrath is essentially bound to the reality of the covenant. This serves to set the concept of the wrath of God in context. If indeed wrath is an important Old Testament theme (nouns for wrath are used 375 times in the Old Testament with reference to God [Fichtner, 1967:395, n. 92]), covenant love, or tender mercy (*hesed*), is more important by far, since it is both the love which is shown in covenant, and the love on which the covenant relationship itself is based (McKenzie, 1968:752-53).

So the source of wrath in ancient Israel was not some mysterious and distant deity. It was Yahweh whose electing, covenant-establishing love had formed Israel into a people of his own possession. Far from the irrational, unmotivated wrath of the gods, the wrath of Yahweh is associated with the justice which characterized covenant relationship.

In a truly remarkable way the Old Testament writers relate God's wrath to his jealousy (Ex. 20:5; 34:14; Deut. 32:16, 21; Pss. 78:58; 79:5; Ezek. 16:23ff., 38, 42). God's wrath can also be understood as jealousy, as the response of the wounded love of the Lover of Israel. Wrath, like covenant love, was an intensely personal characteristic in ancient Israel, based in God's saving activity on behalf of his people.

For this reason in the Old Testament God's anger is primarily directed against Israel itself. God has given his salvific covenant to his people. And by his jealous wrath God sought to protect them from their unfaithfulness and apostasy (Deut. 4:25; 9:7,8,18,19). In God's exercise of wrath in his concern for his people, the collective solidarity of the individual within the totality of the community is clear. When God's wrath is directed against individuals—Moses (Ex. 4:14,24), Aaron (Deut. 9:20), Miriam (Num. 12:9), and kings and prophets (Jer. 21:1-7)—their function within the people of God is in view (Fichtner, 1967:398).

Among the pre-exilic prophets the wrath of God against his unfaithful people is one of the central themes of their message. Their struggle was fundamentally against the false assurance of the people grounded in their misconceived sense of election and the security which they imagined was guaranteed by God's promises (Isa. 5:18f.; 28:14-22; Hos. 13:9-11; Amos 3:2; 5:18; Mic. 3:11). Post-exilic prophets looked back upon the exile as the outworking of God's wrath upon his people (Isa. 42:25; 47:6; 51:17; 54:8; 60:10; Zech. 1:2,12). But they recognized that there was still occasion for the wrath of God to manifest itself among his people (Isa. 64:8; Joel; Hag. 1:5-11; Zech. 1:3,12).

Of course, God's wrath is not limited to his people. Although the nations may serve as instruments of God's wrath against his chosen people, they in turn will feel its effects as a result of their own rebellion and violence (Isa. 13:3,5,9,13; Jer. 50:13,15; Jon. 3:9). In the post-exilic period, especially in later Judaism, the eschatological visitation of God's wrath came to be seen as coming primarily on the nations (Pss. 9:16f.; 56:7; 79:6-9) and on the ungodly in Israel (Pss. 7:6; 11:5f.), while God's forgiveness would protect the righteous among God's people from the wrath to come (Pss. 30:5; 65:3ff.; 103:3; Fichtner, 1967:401).

In the earlier strata of the Old Testament the wrath of God is sometimes seen in unpredictable and catastrophic events. It appears at times in ways which appear almost arbitrary and capricious (e.g., Gen. 32:23-33; Ex. 4:24-25) (Fichtner, 1967:402). Increasingly, people came to recognize that God's wrath was a response to Israel's violation of his covenant. God's gracious election and guidance, his covenant love, is the background against which the prophets bring their warnings of the wrath of God. Underlying every prophetic denunciation, be it against the prostitution of cultic practice (Isa. 9:11; Hos. 5:10), social injustice (Isa. 1:10-17; Amos 5:21-27), trust in armaments and alliances rather than in God's providence (Isa. 30:1-5; Jer. 2:35-37; Hos. 5:13), the worship of other gods (or the supposed worship of Yahweh through alien cultic forms), we find the continual lament that the people have turned away from Yahweh and despised his covenant love (Hos. 11:1-6; Amos 2:9-11) (Fichtner, 1967:403).

In the Old Testament divine wrath is viewed as a personal activity of the covenant-establishing God. It is the form which God's wounded covenant love takes. It is the divine response to Israel's repeated faithlessness, in spite of God's constant faithfulness, rather than being primarily a response to the transgressions of certain legal statutes. It was more fundamentally a question of personal covenant relationship than the mere infraction of laws, serious as this might be. It was sometimes experienced in specific, mysterious, and unpredictable ways. But more often it came in ways which bore some relation to the form of Israel's infidelity and rebellion. So we can observe a certain degree of cause-and-effect relationship in the way in which unfaithfulness to the covenant called forth the response of God's wrath.

This is especially clear in the book of Judges (2:11-19). Yahweh redeemed his people from Egyptian bondage and gave them his gracious covenant at Sinai. However, this faithless people repeatedly forsook Yahweh and worshiped foreign gods. In his wrath Yahweh delivered Israel into the hands of their enemies (and their gods). Eventually, in their suffering and oppression, Israel cried out to Yahweh in repentance, and he delivered his people from their enemies. This is the cycle which recurred time after time. Finally, in the Old Testament this cycle culminated in the exile.

Judges 10:6-9 offers a concrete example of the form which God's wrath took in one of these cycles. Through worship of the gods of the Philistines and the Ammonites, Israel placed themselves under their sphere of influence. By their action Israel indicated that their preference was for the ways and values of these gods over and above those of Yahweh. So Yahweh finally let them have their preference, and Israel came fully under those forces which they had been worshiping. So while divine wrath was the personal activity of Israel's covenant-making God, it was carried out by abandoning his people to the inevitable consequences of their unfaithful ways (Finger, 1983).

The wrath of God toward Israel is the reverse side of his covenant love. The wrath and covenant love of Yahweh are not like the precarious balance of anger and pity traditionally found in Oriental monarchs. Isaiah 54:8-10 offers a clear view of the way in which the compassion and steadfast love of a covenant-making God cause mercy finally to triumph over wrath (cf. Jer. 31:18-20).

While Israel shared with their neighbors of the ancient Near East a concept of divine wrath, it was filled with meaning which set it distinctively apart. It was the personal response of the covenant-making God to the faithlessness of his people. Its aim was not so much the destruction of his rebellious people as it was their restoration. It was a way of taking the sin of his people seriously while remaining steadfast in his love for Israel. It was a jealous anger whose last word was the mercy of covenant love.

New Testament: Messianic Deliverance from God's Wrath

The New Testament understanding of the wrath of God is basically a continuation of that which is found in the Old Testament. While one may discern some development in the concept of divine wrath, the Old Testament offers the best background for understanding the wrath of God in the New Testament.

Wrath continues to be understood in the context of God's covenant-making love. In contrast to the contemporary pagan world in which divine wrath takes the form of eternal hostility between gods and humans, in the New Testament God's mercy stands alongside and above his wrath. Just as relationships in the old covenant were characterized by covenant love, wrath in the face of infidelity, and everlasting mercy, so also in the new covenant all of these elements are present. In contrast to the earlier strata of the Old Testament, the enigmatic, irrational expressions of God's anger are fully superseded in the New Testament by a theological concept of wrath similar to that which was already present in the Old Testament, especially with the prophets. The wrath of God is exercised in history in the interest of protecting covenant relationships with God's people. And, as we shall note, the scope of this wrath reaches beyond history.

We find at the beginning of the New Testament the concepts of wrath, repentance, gospel, and kingdom set in fundamental relationship (Matt. 3:2,7-12; 4:17-25; Mark 1:4-8, 14-15; Luke 3:2-18; 4:14-21, 43). For Paul and John, too, an essential relationship exists between the gospel and the wrath of God (Rom. 1:16-18; John 3:36). In the New Testament God's covenant-establishing love manifests itself in wrath in the face of unfaithfulness and rejection, just as it had in the Old Testament. In both Testaments the God who saves his people will also be their judge. Likewise the same God, who in infinite love has given both the new and old covenants, manifests his wrath against all forms of unfaithfulness.

The wrath of which the New Testament speaks has both eschatological and historical dimensions. The eschatological character of wrath is designated by terms such as "the wrath to come" (1 Thess. 1:10) and "the day of wrath" (Rom. 2:5). Among the images for the wrath of God which appear to be especially eschatological in their thrust are fire (Matt. 3:10-12), the cup (Rev. 14:10), and the winepress (Rev. 19:15) (Stählin, 1967:430). This dimension of wrath is significant in the New Testament, as seen from the fact that the New Testament opens with this message (Matt. 3:7) and also closes on the same note (Rev. 19:15). Furthermore, the New Testament writers unanimously proclaim that Jesus liberates from this ultimate manifestation of wrath.

However, God's wrath is also a present historical reality. Although Paul also speaks of wrath as a future event (Rom. 2:5; Eph. 5:6; Col. 3:6), in a fundamental sense the saving work of Jesus Christ frees us from wrath in the present (Rom. 1:16—3:20; Eph. 2:3 [Hahn, 1975:111-12]). We have already noted that in the Old Testament while the wrath of God was fully personal, it could normally be carried out by abandoning his people to the inevitable consequences of their unfaithful ways. Romans 1:18-32 appears to describe precisely this type of manifestation of God's wrath in which the horrible consequences of disobedience to God come down upon the heads of the evildoers. Three times Paul repeats the phrase "God gave them up" to the evil which they had chosen (Rom. 1:24,26,28). In a similar way, Paul refers to a present manifestation of wrath in Ephesians 2:3. We are concretely saved from wrath by the work of Christ and raised up to a new life in a different realm in the present (Eph. 2:4-6).

So God's wrath is clearly both future (Rom. 2:5,8; 9:22) and present (Rom. 3:5; 4:15; 1 Thess. 2:16). However, present historical manifestations of God's wrath are certainly harbingers of the eschatological wrath to come. In a sense, the future manifestation of God's wrath is already anticipated in the forms which wrath takes in the present (Stählin, 1967:432).

As in the Old Testament, God's wrath is understood in the New Testament in relation to its objects. Wrath is not a mere aspect of the divine essence (Stählin, 1967:438). In the Old Testament the first object of God's wrath was his ancient covenant people in their unfaithfulness. This is the same note with which the New Testament begins. Both John the Baptist and Jesus warned of God's wrath, or his concern over the unfaithfulness of his people (Matt. 3:7; Luke 3:7; 21:23). Paul also views God's people, the objects of God's steadfast covenant love, as objects of God's wrath in their faithlessness (Rom. 2:5; 4:13ff.; 1 Thess. 2:16).

But just as the biblical vision called for the blessing of the nations through the family of Abraham, and God's house was to be a house of prayer for all nations (Gen. 12:3; Isa. 56:7), so also people share a certain solidarity in disobedience, and all humanity is the object of God's wrath, as well as being called to experience his mercy (Eph. 2:3-4; Rom. 9:22-26).

As in the Old Testament, so also in the New Testament divine wrath comes upon people not so much for individual infractions of the divine will as it does for rejection of covenant love and the despising of God's saving intention as this has been made known. This may be made known through God's covenant, by other means (Rom. 1:19-21a), or through the giving of the new covenant (Rom. 2:4).

In the New Testament, as well as in the Old, we observe a certain relationship between cause and effect in the operation of God's wrath. While God's wrath is indeed personal and the expression of his wounded covenant love, it appears to operate through the inexorable consequences of disobedience so that the sinners' acts come down upon their own heads (Stählin, 1967:443). This is the phenomenon which we observed in Romans 1:18-32. This is probably also the meaning of texts such as Romans 9:22 and 1 Peter 2:8. It also gives us insight into the meaning of texts such as Matthew 26:52b and 27:25. Just as in the case of Pharaoh, violence has a way of falling upon the heads of the violent; this is concretely one of the manifestations of the wrath of God from which Jesus has come to save us.

A universal desire is to escape from wrath, both in its present historical forms as well as in its eschatological manifestation. In the Old Testament, therefore, is a call to repentance, a return to covenant relationships of faithfulness, obedience, and righteousness. In the New Testament the message is a similar one: return in repentance or conversion (Matt. 3:7-12; Luke 3:7-14) to the covenant-establishing God who has most fully revealed himself in his Messiah.

The New Testament relates deliverance from wrath, both in the present (1 Thess. 2:16), as well as from the wrath to come (Rom. 5:9), to the person and the saving work of Jesus Christ. Through his vicarious self-offering unto death we can be both set right and made righteous (i.e., restored to covenant relationship with God and his people). In God's reconciling initiative in Jesus, his Messiah, his wrath is breached, his wounded covenant love is healed, and the new possibility of covenant relationship in the kingdom of God is opened to all who receive it.

9

Redemption-Purchase Motif

The redemption image used in the New Testament to understand the work of Christ has its roots in the Old Testament. The divine act of redemption from Egyptian bondage became a paradigm for understanding God's future acts of salvation in behalf of people (Ex. 6:6; 15:13; Deut. 9:26; 21:8).

The redemption of Israel from Egypt was a fundamental historical reality in the life of God's people. The same is true of the term as it is applied to the manumission of slaves. Precisely this reality gives the image its metaphorical strength when it is applied to the work of Christ in freeing us from sin.

We can readily understand, then, that the writers of the New Testament would have appropriated this image in order to describe the saving work of Christ. The experience of the primitive community was that Jesus Christ had indeed freed this new people of God from bondage to sin, to Satan, and to the evil powers. Therefore this image was especially appropriate in its primary corporate sense as referring to the redemption of God's people.

Furthermore, the redemption-purchase image could also be applied personally in an especially meaningful way. In the ancient world the manumission of slaves was carried out through the payment of a ransom, or purchase price. This was a reality with which Christians of a Greco-Roman background, where enforced servitude in the mines and galleys was a terrifying reality, would have been especially familiar. So it is quite natural that they would have understood the saving work of Christ as a ransom payment or purchase out of slavery to sin in order to live in the freedom of sonship and service to God.

Therefore the family of related biblical terms translated "to ransom," "to redeem," and "to buy," together with their corresponding nouns, constitute an important word group in the New Testament for understanding the saving work of Christ.[1] Since the roots of this usage are to be found primarily in the earlier experience of God's covenant people, a brief review of Old Testament backgrounds will be helpful for our understanding of the New Testament meanings.

Redemption in the Old Testament

The term translated "ransom" *(lutron)* is used in several different ways in the Old Testament with different shades of meaning (Procksch, 1967:329-35). In one of its uses *lutron* refers primarily to the *means* of the redemption. As the translation for the Hebrew term *kipper, lutron* always denotes a vicarious gift whose value covers a fault, not merely to cancel indebtedness but to make representative reparation. The *lutron* in these cases generally appears to be money given in lieu of human life (Ex. 21:30; 30:12; Num. 35:31-32; Prov. 6:35; 13:8).

In another Old Testament usage of the term, *lutron* seems to underscore the *practice* of redeeming, as well as the *subject* of the redemption. It refers to the way in which the family or clan ransomed people or goods which had fallen into bondage (Lev. 25:25, 48ff.; Jer. 32:7). This concept is applied to God who redeems his chosen, be they the forefather Jacob (Gen. 48:16) or God's people, Israel. The title Redeemer, applied to God in this context, is one of the favorites of the prophet Isaiah. God is called Redeemer of his people at least thirteen times in Isaiah 40-65.[2] God is depicted here as the responsible relative of Israel by adoption. In this usage the idea of the payment of a ransom price is excluded (Isa. 45:13; 52:3). So the prophet contributes to the freeing of the concept of redemption from the need to make ransom payment. Israel's redemption is a free act of God's grace which embraces the Gentiles as well.

Understood in this light, the term leads us to the heart of the biblical understanding of the relationship between God and his people. God will be Israel's Redeemer just as surely as he was their Creator (Isa. 41:14; 54:5). Israel's redemption rests on the sure foundation of God's covenant faithfulness.

In a third Old Testament usage of *lutron* the emphasis falls on the redeeming action more than on the subject, as such. Therefore the role of grace becomes prominent. The term is widely used with reference to Yahweh's deliverance of Israel from Egyptian bondage (Ex. 6:6; 15:13; Deut. 7:8; 9:26; 15:15; 21:8; 24:18; Mic. 6:4). In this usage of the term the thought of paying a ransom price is again absent. In the redemption of Israel from Egypt, God does not pay a ransom price. Rather, by his power he redeems them (Deut. 7:8; 9:26). Yahweh owns both Israel and the nations (Deut. 4:32ff.), so all payment of ransom would be out of order.[2]

In contrast to the concept of atonement, which is a sacral act in which sacrifice is the means of expiation, the cultic element does not appear to be essential to the biblical idea of redemption in its primary sense. Its roots are found in the bond of covenant relationship in which God commits himself to redemptive activity on behalf of his people. As we have noted, this idea is dominant in Isaiah 40-65. Since the Creator of the world and the Ruler of Israel also reveals himself as Redeemer, this assures Israel's redemption from Babylonian captivity.

This redemption is primarily collective. God redeems his people. However, by natural extension, this redemption came to include deliverance of God's people from all sorts of trouble, as well as individuals in their troubles (Ps. 25:22; Hos. 13:14). This personal dimension of redemption is especially prominent in the Psalms (144:10; 34:22; 49:15; 55:18; 71:23).

In the Old Testament God is pictured as redeeming people from the hostile forces which seek to ruin them. Far from being a strictly commercial transaction involving payment of a ransom price, redemption is an act of salvation and grace and presupposes that all hostile powers are ultimately subject to God.

Greek Ransom

In ancient Greece and in Judaism we find other concepts of ransom (Büchsel, 1967:340-41). Among the Greeks *lutron* was applied specifically to the money paid to ransom prisoners of war, as well as slaves, and to the release from a bond. Occasionally the term was used in a cultic sense for payment made to cover indebtedness to a deity. It sometimes carried the idea of expiation or compensation.

In Judaism the same general views of *lutron* appear to have prevailed. Since the rabbis held the principle that a ransom is an expiation, this led to a transition from the idea of ransom to that of expiation. For the Jews ransom could easily carry the thought of expiation by the vicarious suffering of a righteous person, so that finally the ransom idea led to a belief in the atoning power of righteous suffering. In this view, martyr suffering could be redemptive.

In rabbinic Judaism the verb *lutron* meant "to free by ransom," "to buy by ransom," or "to set free." This understanding of the term is reflected in Hebrews 11:35. In later Jewish usage it always refers to the redemption of Israel from the domination of Gentile nations. Quite commonly it was understood as the final redemption which will be achieved in the last age by God through the Messiah. Echos of these ideas are found in certain New Testament passages (Luke 1:68; 2:38; 21:28, 24:21).

Redemption in the New Testament

Role of a Redeemer

In the New Testament God's deliverance of Israel from Egyptian bondage became a type for understanding his saving acts in their ongoing history. In Luke this vision of redemption is especially evident. The hope expressed by Jesus' disciples in Luke 24:21 is based on this vision. God redeems people by delivering them from the hand of their enemies so that they may serve him in holiness and righteousness. But this redemption is not purely material. It also includes experience of salvation and forgiveness of sins (Luke 1:68-77).

Similarly, Simeon and Anna were among those devout Jews "who were looking for the redemption of Jerusalem" (Luke 2:38). This hope is referred to in the same passage as a "looking for the consolation of Israel" (2:25). Both phrases apparently find their inspiration in Isaiah 52:9-10: "For the Lord has comforted his people, he has redeemed Jerusalem. The Lord has bared his holy arm before the eyes of all the nations; and all the ends of the earth shall see the salvation of our God." The dependence of both passages upon the exodus paradigm is evident. In the case of Luke, this dependence becomes even clearer when we note that this redemption is linked to the Messiah: "a horn of salvation . . . in the house of his servant David" (Luke 1:69).

In Acts 7:35 Moses is called a deliverer *(lutrotes)*. Just as the first Exodus from Egypt and the first covenant required a deliverer, so also the new exodus from the bondage of sin and the new covenant call for a redeemer, the Messiah (Jeremias, 1967:857-73). The role of redeemer, which was ascribed to God alone in the Old Testament, is now transferred to Jesus. For Luke this hope for redemption has been fulfilled in the coming of Jesus.[4]

In addition to the four passages already noted, Luke uses redemption *(apolutrosis)* once more (Luke 21:28). Here the reference is to the deliverance of God's people from the tribulation and suffering of the last days by the coming of the Son of man. In the same way in which Yahweh delivered people from tribulation, Jesus will bring about final redemption. The passage simply reflects the terminology of Old Testament piety with no particular thought as to the means of this redemption.

Belonging to a New Master

In other parts of the New Testament, and particularly in Paul, the redemption-purchase motif is used more concretely to understand the meaning of the work of Christ. Two terms of special importance are *exagorazo*, "to redeem" (Gal. 3:13; 4:5), and *agorazo*, "to buy," "to ransom," or "to redeem" (1 Cor. 6:20; 7:23; 2 Pet. 2:1; Rev. 5:9; 14:3-4).

These terms were used in the ancient world to refer to the sacral manumission of slaves in which a god buys the freedom of a slave from the former owner. In reality the participation of the god is a fiction since the money for the purchase is supplied by the slave and deposited with the priests for securing the slave's freedom. The invocation of the god in the process was merely a formal legal structure provided to guarantee the seriousness of the venture. In addition to these sacral manumissions, freedom could be purchased with purely secular forms. Although there is no evidence of sacral manumissions in the Jewish temple, the Jews living in the Greco-Roman world were familiar with this pagan religious application of the concept of redemption from slavery (Büchsel, 1964:124-25).

Paul borrowed this terminology from the contemporary practice of release from a state of slavery to describe the action of Christ in redeeming believers (Gal. 3:13; 4:5). The fact that the term is used only here in the New Testament and has no background in Septuagint usage appears to indicate that Paul must have had special reasons for using it (Marshall, 1974:154). While there is a remarkable correspondence to the practice of sacral manumission, there is also an essential difference. In contemporary practice the god paid the purchase price only in appearance, while in reality the price was deposited by the interested slave. However, in the Pauline metaphor, Christ pays the purchase price, not only in appearance, but in costly reality. In this the role of Christ does not correspond to that of the Delphic god of contemporary pagan practice who merely makes a fictitious payment.

The Pauline picture is one of release from a condition of slavery from the curse of the law, of relying "on works of the law" (Gal. 3:10); from slavery to the "elemental spirits of the universe," which exercise control over those who rely on works of the law for their salvation, in order that they may be adopted as children and heirs of God (Gal. 4:3-7). The cost of this deliverance was Christ's having become a curse in our behalf *(huper)* in submitting to crucifixion, the sign of standing under the curse of the law (Gal. 3:10,13).[5] While the cost of this deliverance from bondage is the death by crucifixion of Messiah, these texts do not specifically speak of a price or of a recipient of a ransom payment.

The result of this act is "being made righteous" (Gal. 3:8,11), receiving the gift of the Spirit (Gal. 3:14; 4:6), and being set free from slavery in order to become the free children of God (Gal. 4:5-7). Therefore, the emphasis of this metaphor of ransom of slaves falls on the fact of deliverance of sinners and their entrance into a new life of freedom.

The phrase "You were bought with a price" (1 Cor. 6:20; 7:23) must have been almost a slogan for Paul, if we judge from the almost verbal repetition of the phrase and the abruptness with which it is introduced in both cases. The phrase was undoubtedly so familiar to readers that this brief allusion was adequate to communicate its meaning. The implication is that previously they had served themselves or other persons like themselves. To be "bought with a price" is probably not intended to emphasize the magnitude of the price paid, but simply to point out the fact that the purchase has been completed (Barrett, 1968:152). The consequence of this purchase is that they now belong to God. Paradoxically, this manumission converts us into slaves of God (1 Cor. 7:22).

The emphasis here is on purchase which leads to slavery to God. In sacral manumission slaves who were purchased from an earthly master became the fictitious property of the god in whose name they were purchased. However, here again the Pauline metaphor differs from contemporary pagan practice. The Christian becomes the slave of God in a real sense, rather than in a mere fictitious one.

The main point in both texts is that Christians are not their own (1 Cor. 6:19), but are the possession of Christ (1 Cor. 7:23). Paul apparently was not concerned with questions about from whom they had been purchased, or for what price. Paul's reference is simply to the fact of their redemption. Paul's understanding of salvation is being bound in slavery to Christ and to God. The alternative to being a slave to sin is to be redeemed in order to become a slave of Christ. This is salvation as Paul understood it.

The fundamental element stressed in these texts is the fact that the Christian, as a result of redemption by Christ, now belongs to a new Master. The stress is on change of ownership, rather than simply setting slaves free.

This is the same concept we find in 2 Peter 2:1 where Christ is described as the slave master *(despotes)* who has purchased Christians for himself (cf. Jude 4). This view of possession and divine ownership is consistent with Peter's view of the people of God. One of the images he used to describe the new people of God is "God's own people" (1 Pet. 2:9), an image drawn from the Old Testament where Israel is declared to be God's "own possession among all peoples" (Ex. 19:5). Peter shares with Paul the vision of a people who have been bought by a new Master.

In the book of Revelation a series of references takes up the same idea: service under God's exclusive ownership (5:9; 14:3-4). In his death Christ has purchased a kingdom of priests out of "every tribe and tongue and people and nation" (5:9) who are "firstfruits for God and the Lamb" (14:4). In the Old Testament the firstfruits are especially dedicated to God for use in his service. And, in all probability, that is the sense in which the figure is used here. Again, the emphasis of this metaphor is not so much on the question from whom Christians have been purchased, nor on the process or conditions of purchase, but on the destination of the new people who have been purchased by the blood of the Lamb: to the exclusive service of God or his Messiah. In fact, we do not normally expect the language of worship to yield a rationally satisfying statement about the work of Christ in all of its details.

In 1 Peter 1:18-19 redemption is described as being "from the futile ways [lit., empty conduct] inherited from your fathers" with "the precious blood of Christ, like that of a lamb without blemish or spot." From the context we note that this redemption is from a past of captivity to passions and futility (1:14-18) for the obedience of sonship (1:14) and service as God's own people (2:5,9). Without doubt, the background for understanding this text is to be found in the Exodus experience. The verb here translated "ransomed" (*lutroo*) is applied specifically to redemption from Egypt in the Old Testament (Ex. 6:6, 15:13; Deut. 7:8; 9:26), and Christ is here undoubtedly compared to the Passover lamb, judging by the presence of other exodus terminology in this context. The comparison between silver and gold and the "precious blood of Christ" is a reference to the cost of redemption. But rather than merely accentuating the price, the more fundamental contrast is between monetary payment and divine provision (cf. Acts 3:6).

A similar emphasis upon the church becoming the possession of God through redemption is found in Acts 20:28. Here we read of "the church of God which he acquired [*peripoieomai*] with the blood of his Own (RSV, alternative rendering)." In the Septuagint the corresponding noun and adjective are used in an almost stereotyped way to refer to Israel as Yahweh's special possession (Ex. 19:5; Deut. 7:6; 14:2; 26:18; Mal. 3:17). The implications of this are clear. Just as Israel became God's special people at the Exodus, so also God has acquired the church to be his people through the redeeming work of Christ. The repetition of this motif in the New Testament (1 Pet. 2:9; Titus 2:14) seems to indicate a well-established tradition of viewing redemption as God's way of acquiring for himself a new covenant people (cf. Isa. 43:20-21) (Marshall, 1974:161).

This thrust probably offers the best clue for the interpretation of Ephesians 1:14. A common view, including that of the RSV, understands the text to be speaking of the way in which the Spirit is a foretaste of the inheritance which will become the full possession of believers at the future day of full redemption (Eph. 4:30). However, in view of the biblical understanding of possession (*peripoiesis*) which we have just noted, it seems better to understand the text as a reference to the way in which the body of believers is sealed with the Spirit (1:13) as a sign that God will one day come into full possession of the property which is already his. The context also seems to favor this interpretation since it speaks of the saints as God's chosen inheritance (1:11), those whom he proposes to make holy (1:4) for the "praise of his glory" (1:14). These are all peoplehood concepts rooted in Old Testament covenant relationship. Rather than seeing the Spirit as a foretaste of the believers' full redemption, in this particular text the Spirit appears to be the sign that God's redeemed people will become fully his possession at the day of full redemption (Marshall, 1974:161).

In Romans 8:23 those who already experience the firstfruits of the Spirit look forward to the redemption of the body. Here, too, redemption is viewed as the completion of an act already begun by God's giving his Spirit to believers. While in Galatians 4:4-7 redemption from the curse of the law leads to sonship, in this text future redemption will mean deliverance of the body from corruption and pain into the glorious freedom of the children of God (Rom. 8:18-22). Therefore, here, too, full redemption will mean, for God, the completion of the process whereby his people become his full possession.

The Redeeming Work of Christ

Romans 3:24 is a key passage for understanding the work of Christ from several perspectives since the context deals with expiation, justification, and redemption. The context of Romans 3 is one of universal sinfulness and liability to judgment. This includes both Jews and Greeks (3:9). The motif of slavery to sin appears in Romans 6:15-23; 7:14. The need to be set right and made righteous (justified) is supplied by God as a free gift of grace "through the redemption which is in Christ Jesus whom God put forth as an expiation by his blood" (3:24b-25a).[6] The redemption image here points powerfully to God's gracious initiative in freeing from bondage by means of the vicarious expiatory suffering of Christ who was faithful to the point of shedding his blood. So while the cost of redemption here is the death of Christ, the principal thrust of the image is not so much on the price paid as it is on the reality of redemption from bondage to sin and to death and the new possibility of being set right with God and made righteous. This is possible through the redeeming work of Christ alone.[7]

In Colossians 1:14 the emphasis again falls on redemption as the effective deliverance from bondage to "the dominion of darkness" and entrance into the "kingdom of his beloved Son" (1:13). The verb form in the phrase "in whom we have (*echomen*) redemption" shows that the reference is more to a continuous condition of life and relationship than it is to the act of redemption. However, the means of redemption is present in the phrase "by the blood of his cross," which appears at the end of the hymn which follows (1:15-20). Sharing in "the inheritance of the saints" reminds us of the exodus-covenant imagery in which the redemption motif is rooted. So redemption is essentially a reality which is made possible by God's saving initiative in the work of Christ.

The text in Ephesians 1:7 similarly refers to redemption in terms of the sphere of sonship in which the people of God live after being freed from bondage (1:5). However, the means of this redemption, "through his blood," is more specifically set forth.

Hebrews 9:11-15 shows that eternal redemption comes through the blood of Christ. The imagery is sacrificial with reference to the Day of Atonement ritual as well as covenant and exodus motifs. This is a prime example of the tendency in the New Testament to overlap images and mix metaphors for understanding the work of Christ.

The simple wording of Mark 10:45 and Matthew 20:28 surely points to the fact that these words of Jesus, "The Son of man came . . . to give his life as a ransom for many," underlie the early community's reflection on the meaning of the death of Christ as a ransom which we have reviewed in the preceding pages (Büchsel, 1967:341). This expression, most certainly based on Isaiah 53:10-12, illuminates Jesus' view of his messianic mission as being ultimately the offering of his life to God as an expiation for all humanity.

The noun "ransom" (*lutron* and *antilutron*) appears only twice in the New Testament. The first is used by Jesus in the parallel passages, Matthew 20:28 and Mark 10:45, and the second appears in

1 Timothy 2:6. The fact that *lutron* is used only by Jesus in the New Testament points to the fact that the concept is deeply embedded in the New Testament tradition. It goes back to Jesus' understanding of his mission rooted in the prophetic suffering-servant vision and should certainly not be attributed to the primitive community or to Paul as a later accretion (Marshall, 1974:169).

The context in Mark 10:35-45 (as well as Matt. 20:28) is clearly messianic. The meaning of Jesus' messianic work is service or servanthood, which flies in the face of the world's criteria for leadership and authority. Jesus' messianic mission, which culminated in his death, was characterized by voluntary obedience to the will of God to the point of self-sacrifice (cf. John 10:11,15,17). The death of Christ was more than merely a matter of succumbing to the treachery of the Pharisees and the Sanhedrin. It was the outcome of a life lived in utter obedience to the will of God which proved to be redemptive, not merely in behalf of the nation, but for many. (The term denotes an indefinite multitude.)

The preposition "for" (*anti*) carries several meanings in the New Testament. It may carry the sense of "in place of" or "in exchange for" (Rom. 12:17; 1 Thess. 5:15; 1 Pet. 3:9). It may also mean "on behalf of" or "to the account of" (Matt. 17:27). It may mean "for the sake of" or "for this cause" or simply "because" (Eph. 5:31; 1 Thess. 2:10). A suggestion is that here *anti* must be taken in the first sense and therefore Jesus' death is seen as a substitute for the lives of many. While in a certain sense Jesus' death, as a ransom, was certainly substitutionary, it is not necessary to understand this as simply being instead of many. Jesus' death may be seen as vicarious expiatory suffering in behalf of many. In fact, this meaning is suggested by 1 Timothy 2:6 where the preposition *huper* (in behalf of) is used.

According to the context of this passage, Jesus' life of obedience and service, even unto death, functions as a model for his followers. The reason we do not lord it over others, living instead as servants of God and of others, is because Jesus lived and died that way (cf. 1 John 3:16-17). The preposition *anti* in this context does not carry the idea of substitution in the sense of "instead of," but rather in the sense of "face to face"; that is, his life, given as a ransom, is a model for our lives. In other words, our lives (and deaths) of servanthood are to match his. He is the prototype of what we should be.[8]

Questions concerning the need for and the destination of the ransom payment are simply not addressed in this passage. The emphasis falls on Jesus' complete subjection to God's will. The life and death of Jesus is a service to God, and it is a vicarious expiatory death for many in virtue of which they may be forgiven and freed from sin.

The saying of Jesus reported in Matthew 20:28 and Mark 10:45 is undoubtedly the basis of what became a kind of formula in the early church for understanding the death of Christ (1 Tim. 2:6; Titus 2:14).[9] In 1 Timothy 2:6 Christ's mediatorial role between God and people is carried out by his giving "himself as a ransom for *(huper)* all." In Titus 2:14 Christ is described as the one "who gave himself for *(huper)* us to redeem *(lutroo)* us from all iniquity *(anomia)* and to purify for himself a people of his own who are zealous for good deeds." The language of the verse echos strongly Psalm 130:8 where God is the one who "will redeem Israel from all his iniquities." We are ransomed from lawlessness and cleansed in order to become the people of God's possession.

Free Slaves of God: Obedient and Faithful

Redemption means being ransomed in order to become the possession of God. This is stated in terms highly reminiscent of the exodus-redemption paradigm. Furthermore, the fact that all this is achieved by Christ who is described specifically in the text as Savior links the biblical concept of redemption to that of salvation. The fundamental thrust of this ransom saying is that of coming into peoplehood under God, without giving any particular attention to the details of the act of ransoming.

When the redemption-purchase metaphor is applied in a strictly logical way to the work of Christ, then the question of cost or price surfaces. In fact, the term "ransom" can be understood as practically a synonym for price, as in Psalm 49:7a. However, the New Testament use of this image indicates more concern for the fact that ransom results in a redeemed people who are God's own possession than for the precise way in which this redemption has been achieved (Marshall, 1974:169). The New Testament writers refrain from drawing out the dimensions of commercial transaction which can be logically deduced from the redemption-purchase metaphor.

In the Exodus experience of the Old Testament, redemption is achieved by the matchless power of God's saving activity. In the New Testament, redemption from bondage to sin is achieved supremely through the work of Christ. As we have observed, in a number of texts, redemption is explicitly associated with the blood of Christ or with his death. However, the use of this image to understand the meaning of the death of Christ does not necessarily require us to draw out rationally logical conclusions in terms of cost and price. The primary concern of the New Testament, it seems, is to show that Christ's blood, i. e., his faithfulness unto death, is the *means* of redemption and the *result* is the formation of a people who bear God's name and who faithfully reflect his nature in the world.

The tradition of the Christian church has widely held that the redemption-purchase image found in the New Testament supports the Anselmic view of the atonement, according to which Christ paid a ransom debt, which humankind was unable to pay, in order to satisfy God's offended honor. However, our study of the image in its biblical usage has shown that this is simply not the case. In the New Testament ransom-purchase does not free from indebtedness; it is, rather, purchase from slavery—from slavery to sin in order to become the free slaves of God.

So the question of satisfying God's offended honor is not the real concern of the New Testament. The primary concern of God in redemption is acquiring an obedient and faithful people characterized by righteousness and holiness (Rom. 6:17-22; 1 Cor. 6:20; 7:23). Understood in the biblical perspective, the redemption-purchase metaphor greatly enriches our understanding of the saving work of Christ.

10

Reconciliation

To reconcile means literally to bring people into council again, and this calls for restoring broken relationships. All five of the New Testament passages in which the reconciliation motif occurs contain some reference to real restoration of relationships among humans as well as with God.[1] Reconciliation is used in a figurative way, as an image, in the sense that restored relationship with God may be conceived of as a mystery not fully accessible to the sphere of human observation. Reconciliation, however, whether between God and humans, or humans among themselves, is both an image and a literal reality.

A Change in Order

The terms translated "to reconcile" and "reconciliation" in the New Testament belong to a family of Greek words which carry the basic meaning of "to alter," "to change," or even "to exchange" (Büchsel, 1964:251-54). In the New Testament the terms refer to the act of establishing friendship and peace by removing enmity. The resulting state is a relationship of oneness. In fact, the King James Version translates *katallage* as "at-one-ment" in Romans 5:11.

However, in view of the meaning which atonement has taken on in modern secular usage, the term is hardly acceptable as an equivalent of reconciliation in trying to understand the meaning of the saving work of Christ. To reconcile is to return to a council, to bring people back together. Although to atone meant to reconcile originally, it has come to mean to expiate, or even to propitiate, in current English usage. To atone for something carries the idea of making a wrong right by suffering, by laying on oneself a penalty. This is certainly not the biblical meaning of the term which is generally translated "to reconcile."

In their primary use in the New Testament the terms refer to restored relationship with God and others, i.e., Jews and Gentiles reconciled to God and to each other in one body (Eph. 2:16), achieved through the work of Christ. And although the use of the terms in the New Testament is relatively infrequent (twelve times in five passages), it is a fundamental category for understanding the saving work of Christ. In fact, during the past century it has become almost a catchword under which soteriology has come to be subsumed.

The terms *katallasso, apokatallasso,* and *katallage* played no essential part in the Greek or Hellenistic pagan religious scene, not even in relation to rites designed to propitiate deities or to expiate sins (Büchsel 1964:254). This was, no doubt, due to the fact that the relationship between deity and humans was not characterized with the degree of personal nearness that these terms convey.[2]

In Greek-speaking Judaism the term translated "to be reconciled" does occur, but its use is infrequent. If, as a result of prayers, or confession, or conversion from disobedience on the part of humankind, God renounces his wrath and is gracious again, it is said that God becomes reconciled (Büchsel, 1964:254). In 2 Maccabees 1:5 we read, "He might hear your request and be reconciled to you." Further on we read, "If He has been wroth for a time, He will again be reconciled to His servants" (2 Macc. 7:33; cf. 5:20; 8:28-29). This verb also appears in the works of Josephus and in the writings of the rabbis in both the active and passive forms, meaning to reconcile or to placate or to appease. These terms are applied both to relations between people and between God and people (Büchsel, 1964:254).

In the New Testament these terms are used only in Paul's writings to refer to the relationship between God and humankind. The active form of the verb "to reconcile" is used only of God, while the passive form is applied exclusively to humankind (Büchsel, 1964:255).[3] God reconciles us or the world to himself (2 Cor. 5:18f.; Eph. 2:17; Col. 1:20,22). Strictly speaking, God is not reconciled, nor does he reconcile himself to us or to the world. God (or Christ, in the case of *apokatallasso* in Ephesians 2:16 and Colossiam 1:22) is the subject of reconciliation. Humankind, as well as the world, is the object of reconciliation. We are said to be reconciled to God (Rom. 5:10) or to receive reconciliation (Rom. 5:11). In a sense we reconcile ourselves to God (2 Cor. 5:20). Reconciliation is not viewed as a mutually reciprocal process in which both parties become friends, whereas they were formerly enemies. God's supremacy and initiative in this process is everywhere presupposed.

Katallassein does not refer to a relationship which is either amoral or a legal fiction. It denotes a substantial transformation or renewal of the relationship between God and people, and therefore, of people's own state. The context for understanding concretely what it means to be reconciled from the perspective of the New Testament is the new creation, that is, the new social reality of peoplehood in God's new order (2 Cor. 5:17-18). Only in the context of this new reality is reconciliation authentically experienced.

In Romans 5:10 we also note that reconciliation denotes a substantial, incisive change. Humankind, which is described as enemies (5:10), weak, ungodly (5:6), and sinners (5:8), has been radically changed "because God's love has been poured into our hearts through the Holy Spirit" (5:5). So reconciliation is not merely a matter of change in people's inner disposition nor of their so-called legal standing before God. It has to do with a concrete change in the order or realm in which they live, as well as changes in them personally. Furthermore, since God from Old Testament times has been revealed as gracious, we cannot maintain that reconciliation involves a change of mind on the part of God (Büchsel, 1964:255).

The Work of Christ: Reestablishment of Relationships

The contexts in which the reconciliation metaphor occurs are characterized by the presence of vicarious suffering and sacrificial images making it clear that it is an essential category for understanding the work of Christ. "We were reconciled to God by the death of his Son" (Rom. 5:10). "For our sake he made him to be sin [a sin offering or sacrifice][4] who knew no sin" (2 Cor. 5:21). "You who once were far off have been brought near in the blood of Christ" (Eph. 2:13). Reconciliation of "both to God in one body" is "through the cross" (Eph. 2:16). In Colossians 1:20 Paul says that reconciliation is peace achieved "by the blood of his cross."

Clearly in these texts justification, a legal term of primary importance for understanding the atonement, and reconciliation are in reality parallel concepts (Büchsel, 1964:255). "For our sake he made him to be sin . . . so that in him we might become the righteousness of God," i.e., be justified (2 Cor. 5:21). This statement is parallel to being "reconciled to God" in verse 20. In Romans 5 the same parallelism appears in verses 9 and 10. The verb translated "to reckon," which plays such an important role in the articulation of Paul's view of justification (Rom. 4:3,4,5,6, 8,9,10,11,23,24), is also used in 2 Corinthians 5:19 ("not counting their trespasses") in relation to reconciliation. So in light of the insights which the contexts and parallels contribute to our understanding of the terms, we conclude that reconciliation—and justification as well—is much more than a mere removal of guilt. Through the revelation of the superabundant love of God, who did not find the sacrifice of the Son too great and who still does not regard it as too humiliating to plead with humankind through his ambassadors, we can be radically renewed within the context of God's new creation.

The love of Christ becomes a compelling force *(sunechei)* in those who are reconciled (2 Cor. 5:14). The death and resurrection of Christ transfers people's orientation or focus from themselves to him (5:15). By this reconciliation our sinful self-seeking is overcome and the fellowship with God is created in which egotism is replaced by living for Christ. Paul understands that the "for-all-ness" of Christ's death reorients the lives of the reconciled in the direction of "forness." This reconciliation is by no means a legal fiction or a purely inner psychological or spiritual state. It is a present and concrete social reality which can be pointed to in answer to Paul's opponents (2 Cor. 5:11-15). Reconciliation is not a mere projection of faith, but the social reality of a community in which love for one another is motivated by the love of God.

This new reality (the reconciled community) is both basically and continuously brought about by God's action toward humankind. This is particularly clear in Romans 5:6-11. Four parallel present participles underscore the human predicament: being weak, ungodly, sinners, and enemies (5:6,8,10). Reconciliation is the new reality in which those transformed by the self-sacrificing love of God in Christ are brought to the new possibility of walking together "according to the Spirit" (Rom. 8:4). "God's love has been poured into our hearts through the Holy Spirit which has been given to us" (Rom. 5:5) "in order that the just requirements of the law might be fulfilled in us, who walk not according to the flesh but according to the Spirit . . . , who live according to the Spirit" (Rom. 8:4-5).

Does humankind play an active or a passive role in reconciliation? In a sense both appear to be the case. Perhaps the best answer is that people are *made* active. Certainly the passive use of the verbs in Romans 5:10-11 shows that God, through the death of the Son, is the acting agent. In Ephesians 2 reconciliation is described as the act of Christ. In Colossians 1 God reconciles through Christ. In 2 Corinthians 5:18a,19a God through Christ is the reconciler.

But by the very nature of the case reconciliation is not unilateral. The ministry of reconciliation (2 Cor. 5:18b) and the message of reconciliation (v. 19c) are given to the church, and finally the appeal is stated in the imperative, "be reconciled to God" (v. 20b). The fact that Paul speaks of reconciliation as a request excludes the possibility of regarding persons as merely passive in reconciliation. In reconciliation, as in all of God's relationships with humankind, we are treated as people. As such, we can be invited to accept a gift. The analogy between the imperative "be reconciled" (v. 20) and the similar form, "should be reconciled" (lit. "let her to her husband be reconciled," 1 Cor. 7:11), which is applied to a married couple, is instructive. Even if the woman does not attempt reconciliation in taking the initiative, she must at least agree to the attempt of her husband. If she were to remain purely passive, there could not be any new fellowship. Authentic reconciliation excludes mere passivity on the part of humankind. To speak of reconciliation as being either objective or subjective, as if it must by definition be one or the other, is not really helpful. In a certain sense it is both (Büchsel, 1964:256).

Paul speaks of reconciliation in terms of personal confession. "We were reconciled to God by the death of his Son" (Rom. 5:10), and "God, . . . through Christ reconciled us to himself" (2 Cor. 5:18). When he speaks of the reconciliation of the world (2 Cor. 5:19-20) and of all things (Col. 1:20), he is not setting it up against the "we," but representing precisely the same thing in its widest possible range. We and the world are here both objects of a reconciliation which is intended for all without restriction.

In a sense Paul did not see reconciliation as a transaction concluded in the death and resurrection of Jesus in such a way that the reconciling ministry of the church no longer forms a part of it. Obviously, there can be no question of a continuation or a repetition of that which underlies reconciliation, i.e., the death and resurrection of Jesus. But the ministry and message of the reconciled community is seen as the ongoing realization of reconciliation. Our reconciliation is concluded. This is implied in Paul's use of the aorist tense in Romans 5:9-11 and 2 Corinthians 5:18. But a remarkable relationship exists between God's reconciling work through Christ and through the reconciled community. "God . . . reconciled us to himself and gave us the ministry of reconciliation; . . . God was in Christ reconciling the world to himself, . . . and entrusting to us the message of reconciliation" (2 Cor. 5:18-19). The verbs in verse 19 do not denote a concluded work. Reconciliation is an ongoing process.

Paul does not conceive of reconcilation as consisting exclusively (or primarily) in the removal of people's guilt. The primary concern appears to be the reestablishment of relationship. Clearly, reconciliation among alienated segments of humanity, elsewhere described as the creation of a new humanity (Eph. 2:15), is a fundamental objective of the work of Christ. The reconciliation of the world is perceived by Paul in Romans 11:15 as an ongoing action of God in the world. So reconciliation is not seen merely as an action which occurred at a particular time in the past. Reconciliation began in the cross of Christ and depends on the free response to the ongoing ministry and message of reconciliation for its fulfillment. According to 2 Corinthians 5:19-20 the church's continuing mission of reconciliation is both witness (message) and representative (ambassador) in its character.

Reconciliation: a New Creation

The nature of the hostility which calls for reconciliation has been the subject of debate in the Christian church. Does reconciliation imply a change in people's hostility, in God's attitude, or in both? Another way in which the question is sometimes posed is to ask if atonement is objective or subjective or both?

Clearly hostility on the part of humankind calls for change if reconciliation is to take place. The problem of humankind takes the form of disobedience to God (Eph. 2:2) and hostility toward each other (Eph. 2:14,16). This hostility toward God is seen fundamentally as disobedience to God's covenant intention expressed in the law (Rom. 8:7). In 2 Corinthians 5:15 the problem which reconciliation overcomes is called living to oneself. This self-centered, self-seeking orientation, which is everywhere discarded as an unacceptable and idolatrous alternative in interpersonal relationships in the New Testament (Acts 4:32; Phil. 2:4), is simply incapable of fulfilling the divine love command (Rom. 8:7c). The context of the reconciliation passage in Romans 5:10-11 shows that humankind requires changing. We are weak, ungodly, sinners, and enemies (5:6-10). In Colossians 1:22 alienation, enmity, and evil deeds are the prelude to reconciliation. In Ephesians 2:16-17 the problems which reconciliation overcomes are also identified as enmity and alienation from God and his gracious covenant community.

God's response to the unfaithfulness of humanity (of which the descriptive terms in the foregoing paragraph are all expressions) is wrath. However, in the biblical perspective the wrath of God is not an abstract law of cause and effect in a moral universe to which somehow even God must subject himself. Biblical wrath is an intensely personal response of God to the unfaithfulness of his people with a view to protecting the salvific covenant relationship which he has established in the Old Testament and the New.

But neither is wrath a mere aspect of the divine essence so that God, like the pagan deities of the ancient world, somehow needs to be appeased or placated so that he will renounce the effects of his wrathfulness. Inasmuch as God's wrath is his wounded covenant love, it is in reality more salvific than punitive in its intention. The appropriate response to God's wrath is repentance and conversion, i.e., return to God and to relationship in the community of his covenant. In the sense that God's saving covenant concern, expressed in wrath, now becomes reconciling mercy, we may say that there is also change in God, and therefore, in this limited sense, reconciliation is objective and subjective.

Reconciliation is achieved through the death of God's Son (Rom. 5:10-11). In 2 Corinthians 5:18 God is reported as having reconciled us supremely through Christ. Reconciliation happens through the cross (Eph. 2:16), and cosmic reconciliation is achieved through Christ (Col. 1:20). But how does the death of Christ reconcile God's enemies? For one thing, Christ's death is a demonstration of God's love (Rom. 5:8). The life, death, and resurrection of Jesus—

but even more specifically, the cross—bring together and present in a dramatic demonstration (*sunistemi*) the love of God.

The relationship between being justified (Rom. 5:9) and becoming the righteousness of God (2 Cor. 5:21) to reconciliation through the death of Christ is also evident in these passages. Righteousness, in addition to describing the nature of Yahweh, is also a fundamental characteristic of God's covenant community. The wrath of God, directed toward his unfaithful people, is his call to return to right relationship with him in the community of his gracious covenant. Therefore, to be reconciled is to be set right and to be made righteous, i.e., to be justified, in the context of God's covenant community of salvation.

The prominent role of the preposition *huper* ("for" or "in behalf of") in these texts points to the fact that the "for-us-ness" of Christ's death is that which reconciles. In reconciliation, as with other metaphors used to express the reality of Christ's saving death, Christ's suffering is understood as a vicarious sacrifice. The Righteous One, faithful and obedient to the Father even to the point of death itself at the hands of the enemies of God, gave his life for the unrighteous in order that we might be set right and made righteous. This means, concretely, the restoration to relationships of peace and friendship (i.e., reconciliation) in God's covenant community in which we are saved from both present and future threats of wrath (Rom. 5:9-11). Reconciliation is personal, but this does not mean that its effect is essentially individual and inward, as much of Protestant theology has traditionally held.

The translation of 2 Corinthians 5:17 in the *Living Bible* is an example of the way in which modern Protestant Christians impose our Western individualism and almost exclusive preoccupation with personal guilt upon the task of biblical interpretation. "When someone becomes a Christian he becomes a brand-new person inside. He is not the same anymore. A new life has begun!" This has been a classic text for expounding a widespread modern Protestant view of conversion. It also lends support to the traditional view of reconciliation as having been achieved essentially between God and people and only secondarily and nonessentially among those in the community of God's new people.

However, this translation does not have real basis in the text itself (Yoder, 1980:129-33). First of all, the pronoun *he* is not in the text. And when it is supplied, the meaning is changed.[5] Second, the noun *ktisis* generally refers in the New Testament to creation or the act of creation. Nowhere in the New Testament is it used to refer to individuals. When this noun is used to denote people, the reference is to categories of people or human institutions. Furthermore, the context seems to indicate that Paul here has in mind a new social order. In verse 16 Paul says that he no longer evaluates people according to carnal criteria or by the world's values. For him the ethnic identities of Jews or Gentiles are no longer important. What really matters is the new people they have become in Christ. So a more accurate translation of 2 Corinthians 5:17 might go something like this: "So when any one is in Christ there is a new creation, the old order has lost its force, the new one has been created." (*The New English Bible* gives a similar translation.) This new social reality, says Paul, is the result of God's reconciling initiative carried out through Christ (5:18).

This interpretation does not stand or fall by itself. It is, in fact, supported by all of the parallel passages in the New Testament. The only other use of *kaine ktisis* (new creation) in the New Testament is found in Galatians 6:15 where it also refers specifically to the reconciliation of Jews and Gentiles. According to another parallel (Eph. 2:15), to create a new humanity is to reconcile Jews and Gentiles. And in Ephesians 4:24 the call to "put on the new nature [lit. man, or humanity], created after the likeness of God" is the unfolding of the apostle's call to unity (4:1-16). The life of this new community is concretely characterized by the communal virtues of truth telling because "we are members one of another" (4:25), working in order to be able to share with those in need (4:28), edifying one another (4:29), and being kind to one another and forgiving one another like God forgives in Christ (4:32). Another parallel (Col. 3:9-11) speaks in similar terms of the creation of the "new man" where communal practices reflect the values of God's kingdom, God's new creation.

All of the parallel passages cited confirm our interpretation of 2 Corinthians 5:17f. Without denying the personal dimensions of reconciliation, we should recognize that the reconciliation of Jew and Gentile in the new humanity is first of all a community event which cannot happen to an individual alone.

The reconciling work of Christ draws the estranged and the hostile into the new community of salvation characterized by holiness and blamelessness (Col. 1:21-22). Rather than being merely individual attributes, this is more properly a description of the church (Eph. 1:4; 5:25b-27). Reconciliation includes the cessation of hostilities and the incorporation into the new community of God's Messiah.

The context of the reconciliation passage in Colossians 1:20-22 is that of a new people, of God's new humanity made up of those who have been "delivered . . . from the dominion of darkness and transferred . . . to the kingdom of his beloved Son" (1:13), who have come "to share in the inheritance of the saints in light" (1:12). Reconciled by Christ, they have entered into the heritage of God's ancient covenant people as elect ones (3:12). All religious and racial disadvantages and distinctions have been overcome (3:10-11). Reconciliation is to share in the inheritance of the family of God (1:12,22). The language employed in this passage is highly reminiscent of the experience of deliverance from Egyptian bondage in order to become a holy people of God's own possession (Ex. 6:6; 15:13).

Reconciliation refers to more than the mere removal of a person's guilt. As we have seen, it is called the making of peace (Eph. 2:14-17; Col. 1:20; cf. Rom. 5:1), a new creation (2 Cor. 5:17), and the creation of a new humanity (Eph. 2:10,15). In reconciling humankind to himself, God has created a new order of human relationships. In Colossians 1:20 reconciling and making peace are really parallel concepts. This offers us a valuable clue to understanding the biblical view of reconciliation. The goal of Christ's reconciling work is the establishment of God's *shalom* intention for people. This peace leaves no part of our common life untouched by God's grace, and it will finally transcend the limitations of our historical existence in its ultimate fulfillment.

11

Justification

Justification has traditionally been used as a prime category for understanding the work of Christ. But in spite of the importance of the concept in the history of Christian doctrine, the New Testament has no common technical term which corresponds to the meaning which in traditional theological debate has been assigned to justification: the act in which God declared the individual to be righteous. In order to understand justification biblically, we will need to review the various forms of the term as they appear in the New Testament and attempt to understand the meanings assigned to them there (Schrenk, 1964:198-225).

Justification in the New Testament

The noun *dikaiosune* occurs ninety-six times in the New Testament. Over half of these are in Pauline writings, and in Romans and Galatians alone the word appears forty times. In the Septuagint this is the term usually used to translate the Hebrew, *tsedaqa*. It is usually translated in English versions as "righteousness." The term can refer to human character as well as God's. Depending on the context it can be translated "piety" (Matt. 6:1), "justice" (Acts 24:25), "justification" (Gal. 2:21), "right" (1 John 2:29), "what is right" (Eph. 5:9), "justified" (Rom. 10:4,10).

The adjective *dikaios* occurs 76 times in the New Testament and is usually translated "righteous" or "just." The term usually refers to human moral character, but depending on the context it can also be translated "right" (Titus 1:8) or "justly" (Col. 4:1).

The verb *dikaioo* appears forty times in the New Testament. The most common English translation of the term is "to justify." But depending on the context it may mean "show to be righteous" (Matt. 11:19), "pronounce righteous" (Luke 7:29), "to make righteous," or "to make just." This term is especially important for Paul, since 21 of the forty times it is used are in Romans and Galatians.

Other related terms are used with less frequency in the New Testament. The noun *dikaioma* appears ten times and signifies a concrete expression of righteousness, either in act or in command. It can, according to the context, be translated "just requirement" (Rom. 8:4), "decree" (Rom. 1:32), "justification" (Rom. 5:16), "acts of righteousness" (Rom. 5:18), God's "judgment" (Rom. 15:4), or "righteous deeds" of the saints (Rev. 19:8).

Dikaiosis signifies the act of pronouncing or making righteous or justifying. It is used only twice in the New Testament. Jesus was "raised for our justification" (Rom. 4:25); Jesus' act of righteousness leads to "acquittal and life for all men" (Rom. 5:18).

Dikaios, an adverb which occurs five times in the New Testament, signifies "righteously" or "justly" (1 Pet. 2:23; Luke 23:41). It can also be translated "upright" (Titus 2:12). In 1 Corinthians 15:34 the term is translated "come to your *right mind* and sin no more." *Dikaiokrisia* occurs just once signifying "righteous judgment" (Rom. 2:5).

The corresponding series of negative terms used in the New Testament also throws light on the meaning of the word group just reviewed. *Adikia* is a noun translated variously as "unrighteousness" (1 John 1:9; 5:17), "injustice" (Rom. 9:14), "iniquity" (2 Tim. 2:19),[1] or "wickedness" (Rom. 1:18). The term occurs 25 times in the New Testament. The adjective *adikos*, which appears eleven times, is translated "unrighteous" (Luke 16:11) or "unjust" (Matt. 5:45) where it is used in direct contrast to *dikaios*. The verb *adikeo* occurs 27 times and means "to do harm or injury" or "to act unjustly." The noun *adikema* (used three times) refers to an "unrighteous or unjust act." The adverb *adikos*, "unjustly," is used only in 1 Peter 2:19.

Historical Understandings of Justification

The emphasis which contemporary Protestantism places on justification as an image for understanding the work of Christ has not come about in an ideological vacuum. Therefore a review of some of the historical background behind the justification debate may be useful.[2]

During the Middle Ages justification, as a theological term, generally came to mean the act whereby God pronounced an individual righteous. Since medieval Catholicism was interested in the maturity and holiness of Christians, a tendency was to view justification as happening at the end of the sanctification process.

But since God was perceived as a distant and angry judge in much of medieval piety, many religious people were terrified at the prospects of purgatory and hell. They were anxious for assurance that God, indeed, regarded them as righteous—justified, and thereby exempt from punishment. This led to redoubled efforts to attain to justification: prayer, fasting, works of charity, frequent participation in the sacraments, and ascetic practices of various kinds. To a sensitive, introspective person the process was agonizing and the goal seemed hopeless. The church's theology insisted that only as such acts were enabled by God's grace did they contribute to justification. But to those who became Protestants, all this seemed to be an attempt at salvation through works.

Furthermore, the debate about justification dealt largely with the individual aspects of salvation. It was fundamentally a question of *when* and *how* the individual was justified. The story of Martin Luther's personal search for a gracious God is well known. When he finally realized that God's righteousness was not that of a severe and angry judge, but of one who "through grace and sheer mercy" justifies through faith, Luther felt himself "to be reborn and to have gone through open doors into paradise."

In reality, justification by faith meant for Luther and for others that justification comes at the *beginning* of the sanctification process rather than at the *end*. So the good works of righteousness are seen as the fruit which grows out of God's justifying love. The Reformers laid stress on the all-important primacy of God's justifying action as something distinct from human response. Justification is first of all something that God does apart from us for our salvation; that is, it is objective. Of course, people do not benefit from justification unless they respond in faith. Faith, then, is subjective. So justification came to be seen fundamentally as a forensic, or legally valid, declaration of God's acceptance.

Medieval Catholicism recognized that the biblical terms *dikaiosune* and *dikaios* usually refer to character or activity which is righteous. Therefore the church held that God's justification has something to do with producing actual righteousness of character. To justify, they held, meant actively to make righteous.

Subsequently, Protestant orthodoxy responded by defining its view of justification more precisely and distinguishing it more sharply from medieval Catholicism's understanding. Orthodox theologians, in order to stress the primacy of God's righteousness and to disallow any tendency toward a salvation by works, began to emphasize the imputed nature of humankind's righteousness. God declares us to be righteous, not because we actually are, but because Christ's merits are imputed to us.

In Protestant orthodoxy sin is understood as transgression of the law, and Jesus' death is viewed largely in terms of meeting the resulting legal demands of a divine moral law. In justification God declares us to be legally innocent on the basis of Christ's substitutionary death. Christ's righteousness is "all he became, did and suffered to satisfy the demands of divine justice, and merit for his people the forgiveness of sin and the gift of eternal life" (Hodge, 1898.142). Since God accepts this righteousness as a substitute for human righteousness, then when he looks at those who are in Christ, he sees Christ's righteousness instead of their unrighteousness. In other words, Christ's righteousness is imputed to them. Although Christians are not subjectively righteous, they are treated by God *as if they were* righteous. By trusting in Christ through faith, individuals are declared righteous; they are justified in a legal or forensic sense (Hodge, 1898:144-45).

Reformation and post-Reformation theology, of course, had a great deal to say about the forensic character of justification. The term "forensic" was used only in a restricted sense to indicate that God's righteousness was fully credited to humanity's account, thus avoiding any notion of real righteousness in humankind. The Reformers and their successors made a distinction between *declaring* that a person is righteous and *making* that person righteous. They intended to rule out any possibility of claiming human merit. Justification meant that humankind was looked upon by God as if people had fulfilled what the obedient Son of God, Jesus Christ, had done. So God simply gave righteousness to the evildoer forensically by declaration, in spite of people's being dead in sin. According to this view, justification is a legal fiction, i.e., it exists only in abstract formulation—it is not concretely real (Sanday and Headlam, 1902:367).[3]

Western Christianity has generally placed far more weight on the legal metaphor of justification than did Paul, for instance, who is the chief articulator of this image in the New Testament. Alongside the juridical metaphor, the apostle Paul used imagery from political, cultic, social, familial, biological, technological, and athletic realms. These include liberation from Egypt (or the ransoming of slaves), conflict and victory of Christ over his enemies, reconciliation, adoption, and formation of the body. But in the church, while the doctrine of justification has even been made a test of orthodoxy, other images have fallen into disuse.

The extraordinary development and popularity of the juridical image for understanding the work of Christ in Christendom probably owes more to the Roman Empire and the legal practices of the Justinian Code than it does to Paul and the source—the Old Testament—from which he drew the juridical imagery which he used. The Western church has poured content into its understanding of the juridical metaphor from the familiar spheres of Roman law (guilt, punishment, satisfaction, acquittal) and Greek philosophy (abstract concept of universal moral law), while the apostles used the juridical metaphor with Old Testament covenant concepts in mind.

The sacramental-penitential practice of medieval Catholicism as well as the solafideism of Protestant orthodoxy have both found the juridical metaphor especially compatible for explaining the work of Christ. This is not so much because of their biblicism, but because both were Constantinian in their view of the church, and each in its own way offered a solution to the problem which occurs when the church and society in general become coterminous.

As frequently happens in a bipolar debate, many have perceived only two alternatives for understanding justification. Either it is God's declaration of acceptance after a long process of sanctification, or it is a forensic declaration of people's righteousness *as if* they were righteous—which in reality is a legal fiction, since they are not.

Inasmuch as we are able to take a fresh look at the biblical material, we will discover another way to understand these terms and consequently the possiblity of enriching our understanding of the saving work of Christ by way of the justification image. One way to throw light on the meaning of justification is to reexamine the biblical meaning of *dikaiosune* in the light of its Old Testament predecessor, *tsedaqa*.[4]

The Character of Biblical Justice

Micah 6:1-8 contains two Hebrew terms ordinarily translated "justice" or "righteousness," *tsedaqa* (6:5) and *mishpat* (6:8). According to this passage, three fundamental things can be said about justice: Covenant community is the context for the practice of biblical justice; God's saving (righteous) acts are the foundation of biblical justice; and the only adequate response to God's righteous acts is to act according to God's revealed way of justice—covenant law.

Covenant Community

Biblical justice (or righteousness) is to be understood within the context of the covenant, in which the relationship between God and God's people is gracious, personal, and direct, i.e., an "I-Thou" relationship. In this relationship God redeemed his people from bondage. God's saving acts are called *tsedaqa* (Mic. 6:5). Israel is expected to respond to this redemption by doing justice, loving mercy, and walking humbly with God (6:8). This structure of covenant relationship sets biblical justice off from all other forms of justice.

"I-Thou" covenant relationship is the context of biblical law. The Decalogue presupposes God's gracious redemption and describes relationships which should characterize God's covenant people (Ex. 19:4-6; 20:2). This covenant context of biblical law stands in sharp contrast to all other ancient Near Eastern codes. These are set forth in the impersonal structure of kingship and carry with them the threat of coercion. Biblical law reaches its highest expression in the Sermon on the Mount. It is addressed to a redeemed people and depends on that redemption to elicit obedience in the community.

In Israel the authority of the king was not to be based on military or economic power, nor worldly wisdom, but on God's law (Deut. 17:14-20). The king's prime duty was to uphold covenant law and thus establish justice; he was faithful to God's intention when he did covenant justice. Acts 13:26-41 shows how Israel's rulers failed to fulfill this function and then proclaims that Jesus is the king who responds fully to God's intention for a righteous reign.

God's Righteous Acts

God's righteous acts are the foundation of biblical justice. Micah 6:4-5 lists the liberation from Egypt, protection in the wilderness, and the occupation of Canaan as God's *tsedaqa*. Similarly in the New Testament God's saving acts come to a climax in the gift of God's Son for the world's salvation. This act forms the basis for righteousness in the new covenant.

The fact that the God who brought Israel out of Egyptian bondage is the one who establishes justice means two things: Israel's laws reflect God's righteous character, and God's saving initiative is the motivation for obedience in the covenant community. Obedience to God's covenant intention is the only proper response to God's grace. According to Micah 6:6-8, the response is not burnt offering or sacrifice, but comparable acts of justice and steadfast love on the part of God's people—a humble walk along with their God.

This pattern comes to its climax in the New Testament where the good news of the saving act of God in Christ is the foundation of God's new law expressed in the Sermon on the Mount, as well as throughout the Epistles and the Gospels. In Romans, for example, Paul sets forth the way of salvation on which directions for righteous living among God's people are grounded (Rom. 12). So the message of both Testaments is that God's saving acts of righteousness for his people are the foundation of justice for his people.

Response to God's Acts

People's response to God's righteous acts is "to do justice (*mishpat*) and to love kindness and to walk humbly with . . . God" (Mic. 6:8). "To walk humbly with . . . God" means to walk along with him, to accompany God in his saving righteous acts. This salvation, climaxing in the giving of God's Son, becomes the model for the acts of God's people. God does great deeds of righteousness or justice (*tsedaqa*) so we can accompany him in deeds of justice (*mishpat*).

Among other things, this means relationships characterized by genuine love in the context of brotherhood. In ancient Israel this meant freeing from bondage and from the results of economic adversity; concern for the welfare of the weak—the poor, the orphan, the widow, the foreigner; generosity; relationships characterized by fraternal transparency (Deut. 15:1-11; 19:18-19). The same vision for righteousness among the people of God's new covenant is found in the New Testament (Acts 2:42-47; 4:32-35; Eph. 4:25-29).

The righteousness of God

Throughout the Old Testament Yahweh is proclaimed to be righteous (2 Chron. 1:6; Neh. 9:8; Pss. 7:8; 103:17; 111:3; 116:5; Jer. 9:24; Dan. 9:14; Zeph. 3:5; Zech. 8:8). This is one of the major motifs in the witness to God's person, as he reveals himself in his actions. This righteousness is not primarily God's inner nature, nor works which correspond to some external standard, nor merely a retributive justice which rewards good and punishes evil as these are defined legally. Yahweh's righteousness is fundamentally his fulfillment of the demands of the covenant relationship which exists between him and his people, Israel.

Yahweh is also described as righteous in his function as "Judge of all the earth" (Pss. 9:4,8; 50:6; 96:13; 99:4; Isa. 5:16; 58:2; Jer. 11:20). The purpose of God's judgment is the preservation of community, of his covenant with Israel (Pss. 89; 94). Therefore Israel continually appeals to Yahweh's righteousness for deliverance from trouble (Pss. 31:1; 88:12; 143:11), from enemies (Pss. 5:8; 143:1), from the wicked (Pss. 36; 71:2), for the vindication of its own cause (Ps. 35:24). Yahweh's righteous judgments are really saving judgments (Ps. 36:6). Yahweh is called a righteous God and a Savior (Isa. 45:21). Yahweh's salvation of Israel is his righteousness, the fulfillment of his covenant with that people. Righteousness is often placed parallel to salvation in describing God's relationship to his people (Pss. 40:10; 51:14; Isa. 61:10).

So *tsedaqa* is understood basically as God's saving activity on behalf of his people, as well as his people's appropriate response of obedience and love. God's faithfulness to his covenant commitments is presupposed. Biblical justice must be understood from this perspective.

The coming Messiah is expected to establish righteousness (Isa.

9:7; 16:4-5; 32:1ff.). This is the function of the servant, as Isaiah 42:1-4 emphatically states: "He will bring forth justice (*mishpat*) to the nations" (v. 1); "faithfully bring forth justice" (v. 3); "he will not fail ... till he has established justice in the earth" (v. 4). While the term *mishpat* may have a number of meanings, here it is most certainly an aspect of God's rule (cf. Isa. 51:4-5). Kingly characteristics are central to the task of Yahweh's servant and are in direct competition with the kingly reigns of rulers such as Cyrus. It is no wonder that the servant met opposition, persecution, and death. The Servant Poems reach their climax in Israel 52:13—53:12 where the servant is elevated to kingly rule. The main point of the poem is that the servant is one who exercises kingly rule. The life of this king-servant is offered in vicarious suffering and expiation.

In the light of the Old Testament understanding of justice, there is really no basis for understanding justification as essentially a juridical (forensic) pronouncement on the part of God. Rather, it has to do with the establishment of a new situation characterized concretely by God's righteousness.

Faith: Vital to Covenant Partnership

The Old Testament background of the term translated "faith" is also fundamental to our search for the biblical meaning of justification, since in the New Testament justification is by definition justification by faith (cf. Barth, 1971:65-68). The Hebrew noun *emunah* does not refer to a momentary or merely intellectual belief in something or someone. Its root means lasting, continual, or firm. When used of persons it points to characteristics such as consistency, reliability, and steadfastness. It has to do with both inner attitudes and the conduct which they produce.

The Old Testament refers frequently to the *emunah* of God, praising it as something essential to God's character. In fact it is extolled along with yahweh's *tsedaqa* (Pss. 36:5-6; 89:1,2,14-16; 143:1). When the term is applied to humans it denotes an enduring and constant steadfastness which is in line with the enduring qualities of God's purposes, actions, and character.

Faith, like justice or righteousness, takes on its meaning from the covenant context in which it is exercised. It is the mark of a faithful covenant partner. To accept God's covenant promises and justice as right, to stand unshakably on this foundation, to act, suffer, hope, and serve on this foundation is to believe. The faith of the Old Testament is that steady compliance with the conditions of covenant and loyalty to God and the brothers and sisters which is most properly called *faithfulness*. In this context faith is the response of obedience and commitment to God who has proved himself absolutely faithful.

The fact that Paul used Old Testament examples (Gen. 15:6; Isa. 28:16; Hab. 2:4) repeatedly (Rom. 4; Gal. 3; Rom. 10) indicates that he did not have a different kind of faith in mind from that which characterized covenant relationships in the Old Testament. Although the relationship between the Old and New Testaments may be characterized as promise and fulfillment, and the splendor of the New greatly surpasses that of the Old (2 Cor. 3:10), this does not mean that the mode of justification was unknown or contrary to the things "attested by the law and the prophets" (Rom. 3:21).

Faithfulness: the Obedience of Faith

Paul's epistle to the Romans (and Galatians to a certain extent) is essential to our understanding of the New Testament view of justification and the work of Christ. The three key passages which follow all deal with this theme and complement one another in a remarkable way. Although the translation is not the usual one, it is based on a solid grammatical foundation and enjoys increasingly widespread acceptance among biblical scholars.[5]

> For I am not ashamed of the gospel. For it is the power of God unto salvation to everyone who believes, to the Jew first, also to the Greek. For in it the righteousness *(dikaiosune)* of God is revealed from [his] faithfulness unto [our] faith. As it is written: The righteous one *(dikaios)* shall live by [his] faithfulness. For the wrath of God is revealed from heaven against all ungodliness and unrighteousness *(adikian)* of men (Rom. 1:16-18a).
>
> But now apart from the law the righteousness *(dikaiosune)* of God has been manifested, being witnessed to by the law and the prophets. The righteousness *(dikaiosune)* of God through the faithfulness of Jesus Christ unto all who believe, for there is no difference. For all have sinned and come short of the glory of God, being made righteous *(dikaioumenoi)* freely by his grace through the redemption which is in Christ Jesus, whom God set forth as a mercy seat *(hilasterion)*[6] [or a means of expiation] through faithfulness [in

shedding] his blood, in order to show his righteousness
(dikaiosunes) by passing over previously committed sins in the for-
bearance of God in order to show forth his righteousness
(dikaiosunes) in the present time in order to be righteous *(dikaion)*
himself and the one who makes righteous *(dikaiounta)* through the
faithfulness of Jesus (Rom. 3:21-26).

Then as one man's trespass led to condemnation for all men, so
also one man's righteous action *(dikaiomatos)* leads to righteousness
(dikaiosin) of life. For as through one man's disobedience many
were made sinners, so also through the obedience of one man many
will be made righteous *(dikaioi)* (Rom. 5:18-19, my translation).

Paul is saying that God's righteousness (saving activity) has
been publicly and visibly manifested through the history of Jesus the
Messiah. The substance and meaning of "righteousness/ right-wizing" (i.e., setting right and making righteous) is determined by
God's own nature and acts and has been concretely revealed in Jesus,
i.e., in his life, death, and resurrection, but especially in his faithful
obedience to the point of his self-offering unto death. Romans 3:21-
26 is a key text because it is Paul's point of departure for understanding the meaning of the justification, or righteousness/right-wizing,
motif.

A common way in which the Old Testament prophets
denounced Israel's disobedience and called to repentance and
obedience was to use legal court trial or lawsuit imagery. Micah 6:1-
8 is an example of this practice. In this way the prophet presents
God's indictments against his faithless people.

Paul seems to take a similar course in Romans. In light of Israel's history of disobedience, Paul charges that the possession of the
Old Testament law, rather than making Israel more righteous, has
simply made Israel's sin all the more obvious (Rom. 3:10-20; 5:20; cf.
7:7-24). "Whatever the law says it speaks to those who are under the
law, so that every mouth may be stopped, and the whole world may
be held accountable to God" (Rom. 3:19). In this lawsuit some ac-
cuse God of being faithless (3:3) and of unjustly inflicting wrath on
humanity (3:5). Paul responds that human faithlessness *(apistia)* can
never nullify God's faithfulness *(pistin)* (3:3). Paul's conclusion is,
"Let God be true though every man be false, as it is written, 'That
thou mayest be justified in thy words, and prevail when thou art
judged' " (3:4). God's lawsuit with the world has taken place, and his

righteousness and his faithfulness have been vindicated.

Negatively, wickedness has been condemned. The world is found guilty and left speechless before divine judgment. God's judgment is already being revealed (Rom. 1:18) and will be finally and fully revealed at the day of judgment (2:5,16; 5:9). The wicked are already being punished (1:18-32), anticipating the final judgment when wrath will be accomplished.

Positively, God's righteousness is already experienced as salvation (Rom. 5:9). "Now that we are reconciled, we shall be saved by his life" (5:10). God's people are already freed from condemnation (5:1; 8:33-34), and their future and final salvation is also assured (5:9).

Paul speaks of the reality of this new life as righteousness. Just like its meaning in the Old Testament, it refers to the active saving power of God which underlies and pervades the new life of his people. Therefore, Christians should not yield their "members to sin . . . but . . . to God as instruments of righteousness" (Rom. 6:13). And "just as you once yielded your members to impurity and to greater and greater iniquity (*anomian*), so now yield your members to righteousness for sanctification" (6:19; cf. 6:22). The life of Christians is characterized by "obedience [which in this text is the opposite of sin] which leads to righteousness" (6:16). "Your spirits are alive because of righteousness" (8:10). The sphere in which the life of the new order is lived, the kingdom of God, is "righteousness and joy and peace in the Holy Spirit" (14:17). Just as sin reigned in the sphere of death, "so grace reigns through righteousness to eternal life through Jesus Christ" (5:21).

So for Paul righteousness appears to be a quality of life, of action and relationship which characterizes life in the kingdom. And this righteousness of God was supremely manifested through Jesus Christ. This is a central theme for Paul (cf. Rom. 3:21-26). But in order to understand how this setting right and making righteous takes place (5:1), we must first look at Paul's understanding of faith.

Traditional Protestantism, in order to distinguish clearly between salvation by faith and salvation by works, hesitated to call faith a human activity or process. It was generally seen as a passive and punctiliar acceptance of a substitutionary atonement wrought by Christ. To believe generally meant to accept the fact that one is a sinner and that Christ has died in one's place. On the basis of this passive acceptance, one is declared legally righteous by God. Christ's righteousness is imputed to the sinner in a forensic or legal sense, even though one does not yet display righteousness or holiness of character. This has been an orthodox Protestant view of justification.

But this is not the meaning that Paul ascribes to faith. For Paul, Abraham is the classic example of faith. In Romans 4 (cf. Heb. 11:8-19) Abraham's faith is described as a continuing attitude of trust in the face of seemingly insurmountable difficulties and temptations to despair. Faith is not a matter of believing the unbelievable, but of undertaking the apparently impossible because God can be counted on. So like the Old Testament concept of *emunah*, Abraham's faith was a matter of attitude *and* conduct. Despite moments of doubt, wavering, and sin, it was a matter of being faithful to the faithfulness of God. Biblically speaking, faith's opposite is not doubt, but disobedience (Barth, 1971:66-67).

Paul frequently writes of the obedience of faith (Rom. 1:5; 10:6; 16:26). Faith is neither momentary nor passive. Abraham "grew strong in his faith" (4:20; cf. 4:19a). Some are weaker than others (14:1). Paul characterizes the Christian life as "faith working *(energoumene)* through love" (Gal. 5:6). And he sums up the case of his message with the quotation from Habakkuk, "The righteous shall live by faith [faithfulness]" (Rom. 1:17; Gal. 3:11).[7]

When we understand faith as primarily an attitude of faithfulness and those activities which grow out of it, then we can understand how Paul is able to ascribe faith or faithfulness *(pistis)* to God as well as to humankind. This is the case in Romans 3:3. The oracles of God were entrusted to Israel (3:2). That is, Israel was called to live in the reality of God's kingdom and spread its light to all nations. In the light of the failure of many, Paul says they were unfaithful (3:3). Their activity is called faithlessness *(apistia)* (3:3; 11:20,23). Paul contrasts the faithfulness *(pistin)* of God with the unfaithfulness *(apistia)* of Israel. This is the triumph of God. Israel's faithlessness cannot nullify the faithfulness of God (3:3).

In Galatians Paul writes about the faithfulness of Jesus Christ. Paul says that he lives "by the faithfulness of the Son of God who loved me and gave himself for me" (2:20). This verse is often translated as if Paul were saying that he lives by faith *in* the Son of God

(RSV, NIV). But Paul speaks of himself as being crucified with Christ and of his life coming from outside of himself. More likely Paul means that he lives "by means of the faithfulness of the Son of God." And of what does that faithfulness consist? In that Christ "loved me and gave himself for me" (2:20). A similar instance is found in Galatians 2:16 where being justified "through the faithfulness of Jesus Christ" is a parallel to the phrase "be justified in Christ" in verse 17. So the emphasis is not on human faithfulness which responds to Christ, but on the faithfulness of Christ himself who is the source of our being set right and made righteous. The same interpretation can be made of the text in Galatians 3:22. In fact, this interpretation of Galatians 2:20 and 3:22 is much in line with texts such as "so by one man's obedience many will be made righteous" (Rom. 5:19b).[8]

In Romans 3:21-26 *pistis* makes most sense when it is translated as "the faithfulness of Jesus Christ" (v. 22), "faithfulness in shedding his blood" (v. 24), and "the faithfulness of Jesus" (v. 26). This paragraph sums up the preceding discussion of the open revelation of God's righteousness through Jesus Christ (1:17). God's righteousness has now been manifested apart from the law (although it had been manifested there too) (3:21). How has this revelation of the righteousness of God taken place? Essentially through "Jesus Christ, whom God put forward as an expiation (*hilasterion*, lit. mercy seat, or the place where the faithful and merciful covenant God met his repentant people). This shows two things: that God has "passed over" the sins of the past and that God is, in fact, righteous and the one who sets right and makes righteous through the faithfulness of Jesus (3:26).

The Revised Standard Version translates Romans 3:26b as "he justifies him who has faith in Jesus." However, the thrust of the argument to this point shows that despite the universal sin and faithlessness of humanity (3:23), God on his part remains righteous and faithful. Humanity has totally failed, and God alone has stepped in and set things right again. The main point appears to be the righteous nature and acts of a right-wizing God who has revealed himself and his activity in the life and death and resurrection of Jesus Christ. Of course it is also true that we are set right and made righteous through our faith and obedience in Christ. But here the faithfulness of Christ appears to be primary.

This does not mean that in every Pauline usage of *pistis* the idea of the faithfulness of God, or of Christ, is in view. Certainly *pistis* and its adjective form *pistos*, and especially the verb *pisteuo*, often signify human trust and commitment (Rom. 4:14,16; 1 Cor. 15:14,17; 1 Cor. 1:24). Precisely in those Pauline texts where the traditional translations have created a certain redundancy (Rom. 3:22; Gal. 2:16; 3:22; Phil. 3:9) we see most clearly the dual role that faith/faithfulness plays in Paul's writings.

Romans 3:22 alludes to both the faithfulness of Jesus Christ and to the faith of believers.[9] Galatians 2:16 also makes it clear that two kinds of faith are in view. It may be translated thusly: "But knowing that man is not justified out of the works of the law, but through the faithfulness of Jesus Christ. But we in Christ Jesus believed in order that we might be justified out of the faithfulness of Christ and not out of the works of the law, because out of the works of the law no flesh shall be justified." These two kinds of faith include the faithfulness *of* Jesus and believers' faith *in* Jesus. In Galatians 3:22 Paul speaks of the faithfulness of Jesus Christ as being "given to those who believe [i.e., who have faith *in* Jesus Christ]." Justification is the righteousness of God "through the faithfulness of Christ," in whom we believe (Phil. 3:9). Clearly in this text, however, the establishment of God's righteousness depends on Christ's faithfulness rather than on our faith.[10]

We must keep in mind that the presuppositions of Paul's statements about the righteousness of God and his right-wizing actions are the Old Testament conception of God's righteousness. Yahweh is the absolutely faithful covenant-keeping God who redeems his people, who reveals his will for life and relationships within the covenant community, who empowers, protects, and sustains his people. This saving activity is the background for understanding Paul's thinking about God's righteousness and the justification of humankind. Justification, in this context, becomes a restoration into covenant relationship with God and his people. To be justified is to be restored to the relationships and attitudes and actions which correspond to a God who is just and to his community characterized by God's justice.

Romans 3:21-22 is generally translated, "But now the

righteousness of God has been manifested apart from law . . . through faith in Jesus Christ for all who believe." However, in this translation human faith is set forth in a rather redundant manner (*pisteos—pisteuontas*).[11] To understand it as a reference to both divine and human faithfulness, i.e., "the righteousness of God . . . manifested . . . through the faithfulness of Jesus Christ to all who believe," would seem to be more in keeping with Paul's logic.

Although these translations are by no means generally accepted, they do correspond to the overall thrust of Paul's thought. Romans 1 to 3 points primarily to the righteousness of God, rather than to human faith. Humanity stands condemned before the divine court. Only that divine act called "the righteousness of God" has changed things. Jesus' death is the point at which the revelation of this righteousness comes into clearest focus. Jesus' death was not an accident, nor merely a predetermined event designed to pay a legal penalty. The cross was the consistent result of Jesus' reversal of things in his kingdom proclamation and living. Opposition reaches its climax at the cross. As such it was the severest test of Jesus' continuing faithfulness to God. When the New Testament writers refer to the cross, the death, or the blood of Christ, they recall (at least implicitly) Jesus' life, the significance of which was most clearly displayed in his obedience unto death (cf. Rom. 5:19). So the cross is the supreme act of faithfulness: God's remarkable and undeserved faithfulness toward faithless humanity and Jesus' utter faithfulness to his Father and his mission.

Other passages in Romans point to the covenant faithfulness and righteousness of God as the source of human faithfulness and righteousness. The Revised Standard Version translates Romans 1:17, "through faith for faith," understanding that in both cases human faith is in view. In reality it would be more in accord with Paul's theocentric emphasis to translate the phrase, "from (God's) faithfulness to (our human) faith." In other words, God's righteousness is revealed in his faithfulness in Jesus, and this loving faithfulness is offered to us as an object of trust and a source of strength.

God's Righteousness: Saving Activity

How does this righteousness/right-wizing image correspond to the traditional orthodox Protestant understanding of justification by faith? First of all, it affirms the Protestant position in recognizing that our justification results from a divine act performed apart from our acts and in spite of our rebellion against God. God alone has proven himself faithful to us, as well as to himself as a convenant-keeping God, while we have been utterly unfaithful.

However, at other points this vision departs notably from traditional Protestantism. We do not conceive of God's act of justification primarily as one of declaring humankind to be just, i.e., of imputing legal righteousness in a purely formal sense. While legal metaphors are used occasionally in describing the death of Christ, this image, as it has been used in the church's tradition, has not taken human sin and God's holiness with sufficient seriousness. Sin involves our transferring ultimate allegiance from God to created things, faithless disobedience to the covenant-keeping God, and deceitful self-centeredness and self-aggrandizement.

In these attitudes and actions we have become enslaved to fallen structures from which we cannot escape. Orthodoxy has tended to reduce this state of affairs to a legal transgression; righteousness, God's struggle to defeat the powers and establish his new creation (we saw that *tsedaqa* in the Old Testament was God's saving acts), tends to be reduced to a forensic declaration. While the traditional view is not altogether inadequate, it provides the framework for reducing justification to the private transaction between the individual and God, while overlooking the social and cosmic dimensions of sin and righteousness. (Luther's intense personal struggle has left its indelible mark on Protestantism.)

The matter is not one of denying the validity of the personal aspects of justification. It is a question of getting a vision of the fuller biblical perspective of righteousness. The entire life, death, and resurrection of Jesus answers the question of whether God creates a people for himself, caring for them, keeping his promises to them, in short, whether he is the God of the Bible. God's righteousness is not merely the declaration which pardons the individual, but that power which establishes a whole new world, the force which brought the kingdom of God into being. So when Paul writes in Romans of the revelation of God's righteousness, his focus is on the historic saving acts of God in Jesus Christ.[12] This vindicates God in the face of human doubt and rebellion.

Protestantism's fundamental claim that human efforts can in no way earn the righteousness of God may be wholeheartedly affirmed. It comes to us as a gift. It is a matter of accepting the fact that God accepts us. But in spite of this, we may still question the value of justification as the major technical term to understand the work of Christ. The verb *dikaioo* can just as well be translated "to make righteous" as "to justify." Its relationship to *dikaiosune* (righteousness) and *dikaios* (righteous) is evident. However, the verb has nearly always been translated "to justify," and *dikaiosis* has been translated "justification." In doing this, Protestant theologians have often lost sight of the vital, subjective implications of making righteous or right-wizing. They have undervalued the social and cosmic implications of God's righteous saving acts. Traditional Protestantism has been able, relatively easily, to divorce faith from the rest of life and action.

As long as God's initiative and primacy in humankind's salvation remains clear, it might be better to speak of "right-wizing," that is "setting right" and "making righteous." God's righteousness is not merely a moral attribute or a legal standard or a forensic declaration. It is primarily saving activity. It includes the life and death and resurrection of Jesus Christ through which the powers were defeated and new life was bestowed. The kind of faith which makes us righteous is the covenant faithfulness of God "who raised from the dead Jesus our Lord" (Rom. 4:24; cf. 10:9-10). To be made righteous is to live in obedient submission to the righteous God (Rom. 6:13). In the biblical perspective, justification and sanctification are inseparable realities, and their separation in the interests of pastoral care or doctrinal logic in the church's tradition may well be challenged on the authority of the biblical witness.

12

Adoption-Family Image

The Greek term for adoption *(huiothesia)* occurs five times in the New Testament. It is translated in the Revised Standard Version as "sonship" (Rom. 8:15; 9:14), "adoption as sons" (Rom. 8:23; Gal. 4:5), and "to be his sons" (Eph. 1:5). Adoption has not generally been considered an image which helps us to understand the nature of the atonement. But while this category of thought is less clearly linked to the meaning of the death of Christ, it does provide a clear description of what God does for our salvation.

In fact, in three of the five occurrences of the term, the concept of redemption appears in one or another of its meanings in the immediate context. In Romans 8:23 Paul employs this image as a parallel to the eschatological dimension of redemption: "We wait for adoption as sons, the redemption of our bodies." In Galatians 4:4-5 adoption is related to both the incarnation and redemption: 'God sent forth his Son ... to redeem those who were under the law, so that we might receive adoption as sons." In Ephesians 1:5-7 the relationship between adoption and Christ's death is explicit: 'He destined us in love to be his sons through Jesus Christ.... In him we have redemption through his blood, the forgiveness of our trespasses according to the riches of his grace."

While the term translated "adoption" is limited in the New Testament to five Pauline occurrences, the concept is related to the family metaphor which is of prime importance in biblical literature as a description of the people of God (Moule, 1962:48-49). "Children" or "sons of God" is an important designation for God's people of both covenants. "Brothers" and "sisters" is the most common designation for God's people in the New Testament. "Being born anew" (John 3:3,7; 1 Pet. 1:3; 2:2) or "born of the Spirit" (John

3:5,6,8) is a related image which describes the reality achieved through the work of Christ. So the adoption metaphor would appear to be a useful image for understanding the work of Christ.

Old Covenant Understanding of Adoption-Family Image

With considerable frequency the father-son image is used in the Old Testament to denote the relationship of Yahweh to Israel. Yahweh is called the Father of Israel in a number of passages (Deut. 32:6,18; Jer. 3:4; cf. Num. 11:12). Yahweh speaks of Israel as his firstborn son (Ex. 4:22; Jer. 31:9), his dear child (Jer. 31:20). Yahweh has called his son out of Egypt (Hos. 11:1) and given him a special place among the nations (Jer. 3:19). Israel, understood in a corporate sense, consists of Yahweh's sons and daughters (Deut. 14:1; 32:5,19; Isa. 43:6; 45:11; Hos. 2:1). The Israelites, too, speak of God as "our Father" (Isa. 63:16; 64:7; Mal. 2:10). It is equally possible to speak of Israel as the son, or Israelites as the sons, of Yahweh. Some passages use both expressions (Deut. 32:5f.,18f.). In other passages "my people" and "sons" are used as parallels (Isa. 63:8; Jer. 4:22). And in the Old Testament Yahweh pities, bears with, and comforts his children like a parent (Deut. 1:31; 8:5; Pss. 27:10; 68:6; 103:13; Isa. 66:13; Mal. 3:17).

This father-child image does not express a relationship which has arisen naturally and therefore is, by the nature of the case, indissoluble. Israel and the Israelites are not children of God in a physical or quasi-physical sense, as was the case in the understanding prevalent among other ancient peoples. In fact, by unfaithfulness and disobedience they can become children of false gods (Jer. 2:26f.; cf. Mal. 2:11). So in ancient Israel this relationship was spiritual and moral in its nature.

The father-son metaphor also serves to denote two special aspects of the relationship between Yahweh and Israel. The first of these is the distance between them. Israel is subject to Yahweh. This is stressed when the father's dominion, possession, and control, together with the corresponding subordination of the son, are evident. The parallel between father and son and master and servant in Malachi 1:6 emphasizes this aspect. Deuteronomy 8:5 points to the same idea when it compares God's visitations on his people with parental discipline. Yahweh's legal claim on Israel which he has created, his care for them, and the duties of Israel toward him are often mentioned in relation to the father-son image (Ex. 4:22f.; Num. 11:12; Deut. 14:1; 32:6,18; Isa. 1:2; 30:1,9; 45:9-11; 64:7; Mal. 1:6; 2:10).

The second use of the father-son metaphor serves to express the kindness and love of Yahweh, since it is everywhere presupposed that this is the responsible paternal attitude (Ps. 103:13). This image of the father supplements the idea transmitted by the metaphors of husband, shepherd, and redeemer. The image stresses the fact that Yahweh is committed to his people and they may appeal to his mercy (Isa. 63:15f.). He has called his son out of Egypt and preferred him over other peoples as a favorite son (Hos. 11:1; Jer. 3:19; 31:20). Even in the face of rebellion and disobedience they are invited to return to their loving Father (Jer. 3:14,22), and he promises to receive them again as sons (Hos. 2:1).

New Covenant Development of Adoption-Family Image

The spiritual and moral content of the father-son relationship, as opposed to a quasi-physical dimension of sonship, is further developed in the New Testament. While there may be a sense in which God is Father of all, this does not mean that all people are God's children. In fact, only those of faith are "sons of Abraham" (Gal. 3:7ff.). The use of the term "son" for Israel is now transferred to the "Israel of God" (Rom. 9:7-8,25-26).

Jesus described as sons of the Father those who take the love of the Father in heaven as the model for their relationships (Matt. 5:45-48). Here, too, sonship is not given by nature. It is grounded in the fatherly love of God which first, by his grace, grants the possibility of obedience, and with it sonship. The parallel in Luke 6:35-36 also points to the fact that sonship implies participation, by God's grace, in the same kind of loving and merciful attitudes and actions which characterize God. Matthew 5:9 points in the same direction. God's children are *shalom*-makers, just as their Father is.

In the writings of Paul the sonship of believers is grounded theologically in the unique sonship of Jesus. While Paul does not speak about being born anew, he does say that "all who are led by the Spirit of God are sons of God" (Rom. 8:14). The reference to Hosea 2:1 in Romans 9:26 shows that Paul understood that the eschatological promises of sonship are already being fulfilled in the community of Christ. The alternative to slavery to the evil powers manifest in the universe is the Spirit who makes sonship a reality (Rom. 8:14-17; Gal. 4:3-7). To break the power and curse of law, as an attempt to establish relationship with God, and in order that life and peace might be found in the new community of the Messiah, God has sent his Son (Gal. 4:4; Rom. 8:3f.).

What Paul calls the "Spirit of sonship" (Rom. 8:15) is referred to as the "Spirit of the Son" (Gal. 4:6). By their sonship Christians are freed from slavery (Gal. 4:7a; Rom. 8:15a) to become heirs of God as co-heirs of Christ (Rom. 8:17; Gal. 4:7b). The reality of this sonship, which in its fullness is eschatological (Rom. 8:19), is already experienced in the family of God gathered by Messiah. The fact that Christ is God's image (Col. 1:15) underlies the possibility that, as members of his community, we may "be conformed (*summorphous*, literally, formed together) to the image of His Son" (Rom. 8:29). An alternate paraphrase of this text might be "to have a share in the form of His Son."

A similar vision is found in the Johannine epistles. Sonship is a gift of God's grace to us. This sonship is a present existential reality (1 John 3:1) which is at the time the object of our hope for the future (3:2). A prime evidence of this divine sonship is the concrete practice of the righteousness which characterizes God (3:7,10). Just as obedience was an essential characteristic of the Son, is also is a mark of sonship within the community of the Son (5:2).

The writings of both Paul and John contain a configuration of concepts which also relate to sonship and which are closely associated with the atoning work of Christ. These concepts include righteousness and justification, being freed from slavery to the powers of evil, redemption, cleansing, and purification (Phil. 2:17; cf. Deut. 32:5). This supports our thesis that adoption is another New Testament image useful for understanding the work of Christ.

In its New Testament usage the term generally translated "adoption" (*huiothesia*) is used exclusively for a relationship of sonship toward God. The choice of this word to describe the new relationships which are the result of the work of Christ shows that this sonship is not a natural one, but is conferred by God's act (Schweizer, 1972:399). As we have already noted, Israel's sonship rested on God's covenants and promises (Rom. 9:4). The main point of the context which follows is that sonship is not understood as a relationship of natural descent or based on merit, but as a sonship which is always dependent on God's free grace, to be received in faith.

In Galatians 4:5 reception of sonship is identical to liberation from the law as a principle of justification. This adoption is achieved through the work of Christ (Gal. 4:4). It is the transforming act of Christ, the Son, which changes our bondage into sonship. The use of the term "redeem" *(exagorazo)* as a parallel to adoption points to the fact that we are here confronted with another image to describe the atoning work of Christ. Paul in Ephesians 1:5 underscores the gracious character of God's initiative with the phrase, "He destined us in love . . . through Jesus Christ."

The use of the term *Abba* in two of these five passages (Rom. 8:15-16; Gal. 4:6) adds to our understanding of the character of the atoning work of Christ. It underscores the depth of intimate relationship with God which results from the work of Christ. While the Old Testament writers recognized God as Father (1 Chron. 17:13; Ps. 89:26; Isa. 63:16; 64:8; Jer. 3:18; 31:9; Mal. 1:6; 2:10), the image was not employed with great frequency. In fact Joachim Jeremias finds no evidence that *Abba* was used as a personal address to God in early Palestinian Judaism. Thus Jesus' use of this familiar form must have certainly been an innovation which astonished his contemporaries. The fact that this term was adopted in the common usage of the primitive Christian community (Gal. 4:6; Rom. 8:15b-16) indicates that the spirituality of the early church finds its roots in Jesus' own spirituality.

More importantly for our purposes, the use of *Abba* communicates in these contexts the depth and intimacy of the filial relationship with God that is achieved through the atoning work of Christ. This image speaks with a depth and clarity which has often not been possible in the case of the other images with which the church has understood the atonement. It was a relationship proclaimed and lived out by Jesus in the midst of his community. But now it is a relationship achieved through his messianic work and actualized by the presence of his Spirit in his community (Rom. 8:23; Gal. 4:5).

CONTEMPORARY
IMPLICATIONS

13

The Work of Christ and the Messianic Community

In Ephesians Paul gathers up and focuses in a truly remarkable way the various strands of thought about the work of Christ found in the New Testament. We find here direct references or allusions to all ten of the New Testament images with which the apostolic community sought to understand the death and resurrection of Christ which we have reviewed in the foregoing chapters.[1] In fact, as we shall note in more detail, all ten of these motifs are present in one way or another in the key passage in Ephesians 2:11-22.

Mature Pauline reflection on the significance of Christ's death and resurrection in the face of human relationships based on domination and exploitation (Gal. 3:25-29; Col. 3:9-11) and alienation from God (Col. 1:13) point to the creation of a new messianic community, the church, which is at the center of God's purpose for humanity as well as for all creation (Eph. 3:3-11; cf. Col. 1:13-14). In light of this we can point to Ephesians 2:11-22 as the key and high point of Ephesians and as a fundamental capstone to Pauline reflection on the meaning of the saving work of Christ (Barth, 1974:275).

Ephesians 2:11-22 can be divided logically into three parts:

1. First we note the fragmentation of humankind into two clearly distinguishable and seemingly irreconcilable segments (vv. 11-12). These differences between Jew and Gentile are, of course, cultic (v. 11), but more fundamentally they are Christological, sociological, and theological.

2. Next is a hymn in praise of Christ's reconciling work (vv. 13-18). This hymn on the death of Christ points to the purpose and the effects of the work of Christ—a new creation characterized by peace, reconciliation, and common access to God.

3. The creation of a concrete community is described by a series

213

of images—a people, a family, and a spiritual temple (vv. 19-22). These metaphors all describe a new social reality, a community in which Gentiles as well as Jews are essential members and which God has chosen as his residence—the church.

Creation of a New Humanity

The animosity which characterized Jew-Gentile relationships described in Ephesians 2:11-12 was one of the facts of life in the first century. Apparently the continual struggle of Israel against contamination from their Gentile neighbors led to a hardened and exclusive attitude toward other nations. This situation flourished especially following the return from exile when policies of isolation and separation gradually led to a posture of outright intolerance (see Ezra and Nehemiah). For a Jew of the first century to stigmatize a fellow Jew as a Gentile and a tax collector was an offense of the highest degree. In Judaism the hatred toward those who were obviously the enemies of God was held to be justifiable and even, to a certain degree, encouraged (cf. Matt. 5:43). On the other hand the Gentiles reciprocated with expressions of intense hatred against the Jews for their attitudes of privilege and superiority.

However, another current in the Old Testament served to soften this spirit of intolerance and mutual hatred. The book of Ruth served as a reminder that a pious Moabitess was among the ancestors of King David and Jesus (Matt. 1:5).[2] The book of Jonah was a constant reminder of God's merciful disposition toward even the most hated of Israel's enemies and of Israel's fundamental missionary vocation to the nations.

Prophetic Vision

But even more remarkable is the prophetic vision of the coming messianic era in which the salvation of the nations was envisioned. This is the same prophetic strand which served to inspire Jesus' own messianic self-understanding, as well as that of the apostolic community. This vision furnishes us with a background for understanding Ephesians 2:11-22.

According to this prophetic vision, Yahweh will be King of the whole world and the city of God shall be established prominently in the center of his purposes for all humanity. This perspective is offered in a variety of images by Isaiah (2:1-4), Micah (4:1-4), and Zechariah (14:6-11; 8:20-22):

> . . . in the latter days
> . . . the mountain of the house of the Lord
> shall be established as the highest of the mountains
> . . . and all nations shall flow to it
> and many people shall come and say:
> "Come, let us go up to the mountain of the Lord,
> . . . that he may teach us his ways
> and that we may walk in his paths."
> For out of Zion shall go forth the law,
> and the word of the Lord from Jerusalem.
> He shall judge between the nations,
> . . . and they shall beat their swords into plowshares,
> . . . nation shall not lift up sword against nation,
> neither shall they learn war anymore.
>
> Isaiah 2:1-4

> But they shall sit every man under his
> vine and under his fig tree,
> and none shall make them afraid;
> for the mouth of the Lord of hosts has spoken.
>
> —Micah 4:4

> And the Lord will become king over all the earth;
> on that day the Lord will be one and his name one.
>
> —Zechariah 14:9

The judgment referred to in these passages does not mean simply punishment or prosecution. It is rather a matter of establishing an order of right relationships and righteous deeds among humankind and with God which the Bible refers to variously as peace or righteousness or salvation.

The prophetic vision of the messianic "latter days" offers several clues as to what this messianic peace concretely includes (cf. Yoder, 1982:2-12). First, it apparently will call for economic conversion. Beating swords into plowshares and spears into pruning hooks calls for a reorientation of technological skills rather than their suppression. The call of the prophet is not to primitivism, but to the conversion of economic and technological resources in the service of humanity's needs.

Second, warfare is renounced as a means for the solution of interpersonal and international conflict. The prophets do not conceive of the suppression of nationhood and its interests, but rather dependence on God as arbiter of differences. This overcoming of warfare envisioned by the prophet will be the work of God's "servant [who] . . . will faithfully bring forth justice . . . in the earth" (Isa. 42:1-4). According to the prophet, it will be a matter of knowing and doing God's law and the ministry of a new kind of Judge.

Third, in his version of the vision, Micah calls for economic renewal. All will have the opportunity to work meaningfully and productively. This vision is not capitalistic, nor does it call for centralized control. It appears to be a kind of fresh start which the sabbatical and Jubilee provisions were designed to make possible (Lev. 25; Deut. 15). Messianic peace includes a jubilee economy.

Fourth, this vision of peace and righteousness and salvation for the nations calls for freedom from fear (Mic. 4:4). While this absence of fear is not defined in the text, its context makes clear that it is experienced concretely in a transformed human existence with economic and social dimensions. It is not just a psychological or spiritual condition to be experienced solely in the invisible sphere of feeling, or in the timelessness of eternity.

This relationship, in the prophetic vision, of the mission of the Messiah and the coming reign of God with the ingathering of the nations offers a remarkable contrast to the exclusivism and outright hostility which came to characterize Jew-Gentile relationships especially following the exile. In addition to those texts already noted, the Servant Songs of Isaiah refer to the anointing of the servant by the Spirit of God "to bring forth justice to the nations" and to offer "a covenant to the people, a light to the nations" in order that God's "salvation may reach to the end of the earth" (Isa. 42:1,6; 49:6). "And many nations shall join themselves to the Lord in that day, and shall be my people; and I will dwell in the midst of you." God "shall command peace to the nations; his dominion shall be from sea to sea" (Zech. 2:11; 9:10). God's universal reign of peace and righteousness and salvation which will be established by his Messiah among all nations is a theme which echoes throughout the Psalms (Pss. 2:8; 18:49; 22:27-28; 33:12; 46:10; 47:3,8; 67:2,4; 72:11,17; 86:9; 96:3,10; 98:2; 113:4; 117:1; 126:2).

The same prophetic references to God's saving intention for all nations are among the principal expressions—which Jesus drew from the Old Testament—of God's intention for his Messiah. This is the perspective from which the evangelists interpreted Jesus' messianic ministry. Simeon's testimony in the temple is, in effect, the affirmation that the prophetic vision of Isaiah 42:6; 49:6; 52:10 is coming to fruition in the mission of Jesus and that God's salvation is to be revealed for Gentiles as well as Jews.

Messianic Mission

Someone has suggested that Luke 4:17-30 is in reality a summary preview of Jesus' messianic mission. The use of the quotation from Isaiah 61:1-2 indicates that God's sabbatical and Jubilee provisions for establishing righteousness among his people are a paradigm for messianic salvation. The remainder of the Gospel of Luke shows that Jesus did, in fact, carry out his ministry of proclamation and service in line with this vision.

Furthermore, Jesus' references to the inclusion of Gentiles within the saving purposes of God (Luke 4:24-27) proved to be too much for the synagogue-goers of Nazareth to accept, and they attempted to put him to death. In this passage we are confronted with a microcosm of the work of Christ: God's gracious offering of his peace, righteousness, and salvation to all peoples, even at the cost of the life of Messiah himself.

The evangelists' reports of Jesus' messianic mission show that Luke's synthetic preview was right on target. Matthew reports that Jesus' ministry to all who were in need was the fulfillment of Isaiah 42:1-4. But even more notably, he underscores the fact that the messianic mission is to the Gentiles. Even within Israel, the fundamental thrust of Jesus' ministry was to the poor, the outcasts, those without hope, those for whom, according to the religious convictions of the time, the door to salvation was closed.

Apparently, in the official view, Jesus' messianic activity was so unpredictable that at one point the question was seriously raised as to whether Jesus might defect to the Gentiles (John 7:35). In Mark's version of the event, which may well have served to trigger the chain of events which ended in the crucifixion, the Gentile motif is again prominent—God's house "shall be called a house of prayer for all nations" (Mark 11:17-18; cf. Isa. 56:7).

The evidence in the Gospels makes the Pauline conclusion in Ephesians 2:11-22 fully plausible. The creation of the new humanity characterized by peace and righteousness in which Gentiles as well as Jews participate fully was achieved through the sacrifice of Messiah. The book of Acts and the Epistles report the fact that soon Gentiles and Jews were incorporated together in a new people of God. That such a logically unlikely thing would occur so quickly (Rom. 1:16; Col. 3:11) in the face of such pressure to the contrary is certainly due to the life, death, and resurrection of Jesus Christ and to the powerful presence of his Spirit within his body.

Paul refers four times in the early chapters of Ephesians to a mystery (1:9; 3:3,4,9; cf. Col. 1:26-27). This mystery has become an open secret since Jesus Christ has revealed it. This is in contrast to the common understanding in the first century that it had to do with some esoteric secret which could become known only to certain privileged devotees especially initiated into its realm. It had indeed been hidden in the sense that humankind had been incapable of understanding God's plan for the salvation of humanity. But what was humanly inconceivable has been manifest in the mission of God's Messiah. "The Gentiles are fellow heirs, members of the same body, and partakers of the promise in Christ Jesus through the gospel" (Eph. 3:6). From eternity, God was and is determined to draw Gentiles into his house, and now he has carried out this plan through Jesus Christ (Eph. 1:10; 3:9). The gospel is, in effect, the manner in which this good word is passed along (Eph. 6:19).

This mystery is, in a sense, the battle plan of salvation history. Previously it has been hidden from the public eye, although all along it has been in the mind of the Strategist. However, now in its enactment in the messianic community, it has become visible for all to see. The church is charged to make known everywhere (Eph. 3:10) this concrete enactment of God's mystery described in Ephesians 2:11-22.

The problem of the Gentile world was fundamentally one of being out of relationship. Their situation is described as being "in the flesh" and "in the world" (Eph. 2:11-12) in contrast to being "in Christ Jesus" (v. 13), "in one new humanity" (v. 15), "in one Spirit" (v. 18), "in the Lord" (v. 21), and "in the Spirit" (v. 22). It is a matter of two distinct realms and a question of being outside or inside. In reality the Gentiles are not the only ones with a problem. The fact that circumcision is here described as "made in the flesh by hand" may well indicate that many first-century Jews were in reality in the same realm in which the Gentiles found themselves.[3] Because of their role as outsiders before their incorporation into the new humanity, the Gentiles were without a messiah. They were excluded from citizenship in God's people. They were oblivious to the covenants founded in God's gracious promises. Although they were "in the world"—in the realm of the flesh or the sphere of unreconciled humanity—they were without roots in salvation history. And they who have no past are without hope for the future. In sum, they were without God (*atheos*).[4] In a real sense, those who have no people have no God.

Messianic Peace

The passage contained in Ephesians 2:13-18 is held together by a series of terms which describe through whom, how, and the means or price by which peace has been made between Jews and Gentiles, as well as with God. This peace is messianic. Peace is found exclusively "in Christ Jesus," "in his person," "in one body," "through him" (2:13,15,16,18). This fact is so fundamental that Jesus the Messiah is the personification of peace: "he is our peace" (2:14). Another series of phrases refers to the way in which Christ achieved this peace: "in the blood of Christ," "in his flesh," "through the cross" (2:13,15,16). Still another series of phrases describes the means of achieving peace—his messianic activity. He "came," "made us both one," "has broken down the dividing wall of hostility," "abolished the law of commandments and ordinances," "created one new man," "reconciled us both to God," "brings hostility to an end," and "preached peace" (2:14-17).

A New Social Order

This messianic peace is, first of all, a social event. Christ is praised here, not primarily for the peace which he brings to individual souls, although this may well be an important side effect. The peace he brings is a social, or ecclesial reality. It is first of all peace among humankind, i.e., Jews and Gentiles (2:14-15), and only then between God and humanity (2:16-17) (Barth, 1974:262). The same sequence can be noted in relation to the statements about communion and forgiveness in the New Testament (cf. 1 John 1:1-3; Matt. 5:23-24; 6:12,14,15; John 20:23).[5]

Traditionally, theories of atonement have tended to concentrate their attention on the removal of barriers between individuals and God. However, here the concrete barrier which is removed by the death of Christ is the one which separated human groups from each other. Subsequently, both are reconciled to God (Eph. 2:14-16).

Both Peter and Paul refer to the good news as the "gospel of peace" (Acts 10:36; Rom. 10:15; Eph. 2:17; 6:15). In bringing the gospel of peace, Jesus, the evangelist, was also the evangel. Christ in his messianic proclamation and activity reconciled outsiders and insiders. He did, in fact, create peace in the messianic community.[6] In the early church, to be in the messianic community was to be reconciled, to experience the reality of God's peace—*shalom.*

The meaning of peace as Paul uses it has often become obscured due to extraneous influences which have found their ways into the thought and practice of the church. The roots for understanding the meaning of peace as it is used in this passage are to be found in the Old Testament. *Shalom* is a broad concept, essential to the biblical understanding of relationships among people and between people and God. God's covenant with Israel was "a covenant of life and peace" (Mal. 2:5). According to the prophets, true peace reigned when righteousness prevailed, when people were treated with equality and respect, and when salvation flourished according to the social order determined by God in the gracious covenant which he had given his people.

Above all, *shalom* described the messianic kingdom in which God's true intention for his people would be realized. Isaiah writes one of the clearest expressions of this vision:

> How beautiful upon the mountains are the feet of him
> who brings good tidings,
> who publishes peace,
> who brings good tidings of good,
> who publishes salvation,
> who says to Zion, "Your God reigns."
> —Isaiah 52:7

The evangel of peace and righteousness is realized in the realm of God's righteous reign which has come in the person of his Messiah. This helps us to understand why the primitive community identified peace with the person of Messiah.

Another strand of biblical thought which helps us to understand the identification of the Messiah with the peace which he brings is found in the archetypal image of Representative Man, which, as we have already noted, was one of the ways in which the primitive community understood the meaning of the work of Christ. Christ creates "in himself one new man . . . so making peace" (Eph. 2:15). Jesus the Messiah in his life of total obedience to the Father even to the point of death was vindicated by God and glorified in the resurrection. Therefore it can be said that the righteousness of Jesus Christ, the Representative Man, leads to righteousness of life for all (Rom. 5:18).

Jesus Christ, in contrast to the first Adam, is the true human, the real image of God (cf. 1 Cor. 15:20-22,44-47; Rom. 5:12-21).[7] Christ himself is "the new man created after God['s image]" which has to be "put on" by his people (Eph. 4:24; Col. 3:10). This image of Christ, as Representative Man, enables us to see how the phrases "in himself" and "in one body" (Eph. 2:15-16) can be associated concretely with the messianic community, the church (cf. Eph. 1:23; 1 Cor. 12:27). Jesus, who fulfilled the messianic mission of the Father, was representatively what new messianic people are called to be.

The Work of Christ

Ephesians 2:14-18 might well be called a hymn on Christ's death and its effects.[8] The references to the blood of Christ and the cross speak directly to the work of Christ in sacrificial-cultic imagery. But before asking in greater depth what the cultic metaphor meant for Paul in this passage, as applied to the death of the Messiah, and how the blood of Christ is an instrument of reconciliation, we need to recognize that all ten of the New Testament motifs for understanding the work of Christ which we have reviewed are present either directly or by association in this passage.

The expiation motif is present in the sacrifical imagery, and the vicarious suffering and martyr motifs are implied in the references to suffering as a way to make peace. The conflict-victory motif is present in the reference to the hostility which Christ has overcome (Eph. 2:14,16). The parallel passage in Colossians 1:20-22 similarly refers to hostility. In Ephesians 3:3-11, where Paul offers further commentary for understanding this passage, is a reference to "principalities and powers" (3:10), and in Colossians 2:14-15 Christ's victory over them is emphatically declared.

As we have noted, the archetypal image is present in the references to the creation of one new man "in himself" and "in one body" (Eph. 2:15-16; cf. 2:10). The biblical concept of Representative Man helps us to understand an otherwise somewhat obscure identification of Christ and the peace which he creates. The reconciliation motif is specifically mentioned in both its horizontal and vertical dimensions (2:16). In the parallel passage in Colossians this reconciliation is even more inclusive (Col. 1:20-22).

While the redemption-purchase motif is not specifically mentioned in this particular passage, it is implied in the cost of making peace (Eph. 2:15-16). It is specifically mentioned in Ephesians 1:7 and in Colossians 1:13-14. A specific reference to the adoption-family image appears in Ephesians 2:19. As for the justification motif, it is present in the immediate context (2:8-10) and implied in the unconditional obedience to the Father and faithfulness unto death, thereby "abolishing in his flesh the law of commandments and ordinances"—the law legalistically misconceived as a means of perpetuating and justifying divisions from, and enmity with, the Gentiles—and reestablishing God's righteousness (2:15).

If we may take our clue from Ephesians 2:11-22, it is possible to affirm that the New Israel of God, this messianic community of peace, is the point at which all of the principal New Testament images for understanding the work of Christ converge. Peoplehood under God's reign is the organizing center around which all of these images rotate. The early church found this center extremely useful in its varied missionary witness. Extracted from this covenant-community context, the death and resurrection of Christ cannot really be understood in their fullest biblical meaning.

Exactly how the sacrificial death of Christ serves to create a reconciled new humanity is not specifically stated in this text. As we have already noted, Hebrew sacrifice was complex and our attempts to identify its essential elements must be tentative at best. Sacrifice was—among other interpretations—seen as a way of interceding with God.[9] In fact, spilled blood speaks more loudly than the voice alone. Abel's blood cries out to God (Gen. 4:10). This is the image which is picked up in Hebrews. Christ's priestly ministry included intercession for his people offered up in "prayers and supplications with loud cries and tears" (Heb. 5:7) and mediation by "sprinkled blood that speaks more graciously than the blood of Abel" (Heb. 12:24). The power of a life of intercession unto death is apparently augmented by the blood which seals it. The intercessory function of sacrifice is explicitly set forth by the prophets (Isa. 56:7; Jer. 7:10-11). Interestingly, these are precisely the texts which Jesus used in his inclusion of the Gentiles in God's salvific intention. In fact, this apparently contributed to the plot against him which led to his death (Mark 11:17-18).

While the use of the term "blood" to refer to the death of Christ does call attention to him as a sacrificial victim, the verbs employed in the Ephesians 2:13-18 context describe an activity of Christ. Therefore, he is at the same time an interceding priest (cf. Heb. 5:7-8; 7:27-28; 9:22-28). This is made explicit in Ephesians 5:2: "Christ . . . gave himself up for us, a fragrant offering and sacrifice to God."

As we have noted, among the various concepts of vicarious sacrifice which we find in the Old Testament, one interprets it as an act of intercession. This appears to be the understanding of the ministry of the servant which Isaiah 53:12 presents. The servant's death is a sin-offering (53:10) through which intercession is made for transgressors (53:12). A clear Old Testament example of this function of sacrifice is found in Exodus 32:30-32 where Moses seeks to make atonement for the sins of the people and intercede for them. In Isaiah 53 the activity of the servant is described in terms which apply to both the priest and the victim. He "is stricken for the transgression of Israel . . . bears the transgression of many . . . makes himself a sin offering," and then is finally described as making "intercession for the transgressors" (Isa. 53:8,10-12). Moses, in his act of intercession, *offered* his life to God. The high priest *risked* his life by bearing the sin of the people into the holy of holies. The servant of Isaiah 53 actually *gives* his own life in the intercession which he makes.

The peace and reconciliation which result from Christ's sacrificial death (Eph. 2:11-22) really have nothing in common with the pagan understanding of appeasement of gods or people. The purpose of Christ's sacrifice is not propitiatory in the strictly literal sense of the term (i.e., aimed at placating God's anger and thus making him propitious), since its object is expressly declared to be the reconciliation of alienated groups in such a way that "a New Man" is created in order that both together they may be reconciled to God. The function of sacrifice here seems to be that of intercessory prayer. The messianic peace, obtained at the cost of the Messiah's own blood, is not merely a repaired or restored relationship. It is an unheard-of novelty, best described as a new humanity or a new creation.

This understanding of sacrifice—death understood as intercession—is reflected by the seven martyrs described in 2 Maccabees 7:37-38 as giving up "body and soul ... appealing to God to show mercy soon" on the nation. The martyrdom of Stephen is a similar example (Acts 7:60). Romans 8:34 and Hebrews 7:25 and 9:24 speak of Christ's continuing intercession which was once forcefully expressed in his sacrifice. Second Corinthians 5:21 can be interpreted in the same vein. Christ is described as a sin offering which is made in order that God's covenant righteousness might be established. This is, in effect, the *shalom* described in Ephesians 2:15-17.

So Jesus' sacrifice may be viewed as intercession in behalf of hostile people, groups, causes, and conditions, an intercession carried to its highest expression, culminating in the death of the intercessor. Jesus' intercession did not consist merely of words (e.g., the high-priestly prayer of John 17), but was rather a life of intercession magnified by the voice of "his blood" (Heb. 12:24). Jesus' messianic mission consisted of intercession on behalf of alienated peoples to the point of death itself. This is the sacrifice which establishes his ongoing and eternal intercession (Heb. 7:25,27).

The New Community

The obstacle to messianic peace is described as a "dividing wall of hostility" (Eph. 2:14). A wall, in fact, separated the outer Court of the Gentiles from the rest of the temple precincts in Jerusalem. This barrier was a symbol of the most formidable wall in the ancient world. The separation between Israel and the nations was a fact of serious and far-reaching consequences as we have already noted (Eph. 2:11-12). According to Ephesians 2:14-15, this wall was in some way characterized by the Jewish understanding of "the law of commandments and ordinances" which, contrary to God's intention in the Torah, created a divisive barrier between those who were outside and those who saw themselves as insiders. Furthermore, this wall expressed itself concretely in hostility between peoples (2:14,16). Finally, the existence of this barrier was the product of outright enmity of both Jews and Gentiles toward God (2:16,18). So the dividing wall symbolized, without doubt, a complex and demonic phenomenon which was larger than the mere sum of its parts.

According to this text, Christ's death on the cross is viewed as a success. Antagonistic groups have been reconciled into "one new man . . . making peace." Together they "both have access in one Spirit to the Father." And together thy are "built into . . . a dwelling place for God" (2:15,18,22).

The peace achieved by the work of Christ is described as a new act of creation. Paul alternately assigns creative activity to God (3:9; 2:10) and to Christ (Col. 1:16; Eph. 2:15). In this way Paul affirms again that God was effectively "in Christ reconciling the world to himself" (2 Cor. 5:19). The surprising and scandalous element in this act of creation is that it begins on the cross. While the first creation began with nature and culminated in the formation of humankind, here the new creation begins with the formation of a new humanity and the rest of God's creation still awaits its liberation (Rom. 8:18-22).

The concept of newness, especially when used with reference to creation, denotes in the Bible a culmination or final fruition of God's will and work (Barth, 1974:309). Of the two Greek words for denoting newness, this text employs *kainos*, which often means qualitative newness in contrast to mere temporal innovation.[10] *Kainos*, which is used in Ephesians 2:15 to refer to the "one new man," also describes the new covenant in 2 Corinthians 3:6, the new creation in 2 Corinthians 5:17, and the "new man" in Ephesians 4:24.

The fact that this "one new man" is created out of both Jews and Gentiles is underscored in the text (Eph. 2:14-16). However, this "new man" is not the reduction of Jews and Gentiles into a uniform race of a third kind. Rather, the church consists of Jews and Gentiles *reconciled to one another* by Christ who has died for both. The existence of this new humanity is based upon liberation from nationalism, religious pride, individualism, and the fact of being raised to a new kind of social behavior. This work of demolition and construction has happened to both Jews and Gentiles. The implication of this creation of "one new man" out of the two is that neither of the two can enjoy salvation, peace, and life without the other. People need each other if they are to be saved at all (Barth, 1974:311).

However, this new humanity is not composed simply of groups of likeminded and compatible people. The New Testament makes it clear that the reconciliation of erstwhile enemies gives way to "one new man" (Matt. 5:23-24,43-48; Gal. 2:11-14; Rom. 5:6-10). This new humanity is new in a truly revolutionary way. The "one new man" is created to be a social being. But this social existence is totally dependent upon God. It is a community which loves and forgives just as God has done in Christ (Eph. 4:32—5:2).

In a similar way John relates the death of Christ to the creation of the new community. In 1 John the Greek term translated "expiation" *(hilasmos)* appears twice (2:2; 4:10), and in both cases the contexts reflect a vision similar to that of Ephesians 2:11-22. In 1 John 1:1—2:2 the intention of God in the work of Messiah is to create communion (1:3,6,7). This forgiven human community is the context in which we also have communion "with the Father and with his Son Jesus Christ" (1:3). In 1 John 4:7-12 the expiatory work of Christ issues in a new community in which love for others is manifested in the same way in which God loves (cf. 1 John 2:6-11; 3:11-18; 4:7-12,17-21). Both of these realities, a human community in which we experience communion with the Father and the Son and a community in which we love in the same manner in which God loves, are based squarely on the vicarious and expiatory self-offering of Jesus Christ (1 John 2:2; 4:10).

To be "brought near" and to "both have access in one Spirit to the Father" (Eph. 2:13,18) appear to be references to the worship of the new community which arises out of the work of Christ. Jesus, high priest and victim, has joined Jews and Gentiles together through his intercessory act of sacrifice. In fact, according to Ephesians 2:18, Christ's mediation of access to God is an ongoing act of intercession. In the life of the new humanity, worship becomes the tangible result of messianic peace and a sign of its presence. Throughout the New Testament, sacrifice is spiritualized in the life and worship of the messianic community (John 4:24; Rom. 12:1; 1 Pet. 2:5; Heb. 13:15-16). Just as Christ's reconciling of Jews and Gentiles in "one new man" is essential to their continuing access to God, so also every person's worship must be preceded by reconciliation with hostile brothers and sisters. Mutual forgiveness cannot be separated from our prayer for God's forgiveness (Matt. 5:23-24; 6:6,8,14; 25:31-46; Luke 15:25-32).

In Ephesians 2:19-22 peoplehood and family images are employed to underscore the way in which the Gentiles have become an integral element in the new humanity created in Christ. First, the Gentiles are welcomed into God's household (2:19). Then Gentiles and Jews together become the materials from which "a holy temple . . . a dwelling place for God" is constructed (2:21-22).

Three terms in this passage emphasize the communion of Jews and Gentiles in this new creation: "fellow citizens," "joined together," and "built together" (2:19,21,22).[11] To be "fellow citizens with the saints" is to come into a share of salvation history. The history of God's ancient covenant people becomes our history. To be "members of the household of God" is to be no longer outsiders, but to be a part of God's family in which the Father of the Messiah is our Father, and all—Jews and Gentiles—are brothers and sisters.

Jews and Gentiles together become God's holy temple, his spiritual dwelling place. This usage of the temple motif is akin to that which we find in 1 Peter 2:5 where the reference is to "a spiritual house" and "a holy priesthood" which offers "spiritual sacrifices." However, the spirituality of this house built by God of Jews and Gentiles is not to be thought of as something invisible or abstract. It is as concrete and visible as the people who have been reconciled into this new humanity. The life and worship of this new "Israel of God," made up of Gentiles and Jews, offers testimony to the validity of the saving, peacemaking work of Christ.

Earlier we noted the prophetic texts which speak about the coming of the Gentiles to participate in God's saving intention. In these texts Israel's witness consisted fundamentally of becoming that restored city in which God's peace and righteousness prevail (Mic. 4:1-4). The visible power of God at work renewing his people was to prove so attractive to the nations. Jesus shared this same understanding of missionary visibility. Jesus' Beatitudes described the ways in which the sons and daughters of the kingdom are different from others, showing how their lives will fulfill the law and the prophets. These are the messianic people he compared to a mountaintop city which others see and to which they are drawn. This is the power of beatitude—God's *shalom*. Humankind will "see your good works and give glory to your Father who is in heaven" (Matt. 5:16).

This is the same motif which Paul picks up in Ephesians. The saving work of Christ issues in the creation of a new humanity. It is a hitherto unheard-of novelty of erstwhile enemies being reconciled by Christ into one new community characterized by the peace, righteousness, and salvation of God. Through this new creation, the church, "the manifold wisdom of God might be made known to the principalities and powers in the heavenly places." In this new community of peace "the eternal purpose which he [God] has realized in Christ Jesus our Lord" is most visibly present (Eph. 3:10-11).

The peace established by Jesus goes beyond the Hebrew understanding of *shalom* which included righteous relationships among God's people and between the people and God. Messianic peace includes the realization of reconciliation and community totally unattainable by human effort. The peace between Jews and Gentiles is the realm in which the reality of peace with God may be experienced—rather than being a possible secondary and derivative consequence of a solely transcendent peace with God. Traditionally, theories of the atonement have tended to focus on the ways in which barriers have been removed between humanity and God. This Pauline summary, however, focuses on the fact that Christ's death served to remove social barriers and thus to make peace among human enemies, as well as making possible their common access to God (Miller, 1977:1-5).

The creation of human community in which God's peace prevails is not coincidental, nor is it a secondary result of the saving work of Christ. The creation of a new humanity in which personal, social, and economic hostilities are all overcome in reconciliation is a primary and direct result of the death and resurrection of God's Messiah. This is the church which proclaims, with the authority which arises out of authenticity, to all humanity—including the "principalities and powers"—the mystery of God's saving intention in Jesus Christ.

14

The Work of Christ
and Cosmic Restoration

The salvation which arises out of the life, death, and resurrection of Christ is cosmic as well as social and personal in its scope. A Pauline text specifically relates cosmic salvation to the reconciling death of Christ (Col. 1:15-20). However, this vision of cosmic redemption which grows out of the saving work of Christ enjoys much broader support in the New Testament. It is a vision which is already anticipated in the Gospel stories of Jesus' ministry and confessed much more fully in the worship of the early church.

The principal New Testament texts which reflect this cosmic vision are Romans 8:18-25; Ephesians 1:9-10; Philippians 2:5-11; Colossians 1:13-20; 2 Peter 3:13; and Revelation 21:1-5.[1] In the Pauline reflections on the work of Christ and the messianic community we find a remarkable configuration of images for understanding the death and resurrection of Christ which converge in the vision of cosmic restoration.[2]

The biblical conviction that God's intention is to restore all of creation is rooted firmly in the prophetic tradition of the Old Testament. Furthermore, this restoration was viewed as messianic—centered in the saving mission of God's Messiah. According to the paradisaic vision of Isaiah, "The wolf shall dwell with the lamb, and the leopard shall lie down with the kid. . . . The sucking child shall play over the hole of the asp and . . . put his hand on the adder's den. They shall not hurt or destroy in all my holy mountain; for the earth shall be full of the knowledge of the Lord as the waters cover the sea" (Isa. 11:6-10). The harmony which characterized God's intention for relationships in nature and humanity will be restored. The prophets described this restoration in terms of renewed fertility of the soil (Amos 9:13-14; Hos. 2:23-24), of general disarmament

(Isa. 2:4; 9:4; Mic. 4:3-4; 5:9-10; Zech. 9:10), and perpetual peace and justice (Isa. 9:6-7; 11:9; 32:17; 60:17-18; Zeph. 3:13; Joel 4:17; Zech. 3:10). This peace extends to all parts of God's creation, even to the serpent, intrumental in humanity's fall. Paradise restored is the image which points to the eschatological culmination of the saving work of Christ.

The Gospels pick up this thread in their reporting of Jesus' mission. The evangelists' interpretation of Jesus' nature miracles, as well as his healings and exorcisms, points in this direction. Matthew and Mark both report the astonishment of Jesus' disciples at the calming of the sea with the question, "What sort of man is this, that even wind and sea obey him?" (Matt. 8:27; Mark 4:41). A similar rhetorical question reflects the Gospels' interpretation of exorcisms: "What have you to do with us, O Son of God? (Matt. 8:29; cf. Mark 5:7). Exorcisms and the healing of the sick were not merely signs that the kingdom of God has come, although they were certainly that (Luke 10:9; 11:20). They were also pointers in the direction of the ultimate restoration of all things in Christ.

The works of Jesus, his healings and exorcisms, as well as his nature miracles, are powerful signs that the age of restoration to the wholeness of God's intention for creation is beginning to be fulfilled (Matt. 11:5; Isa. 35:5-6; 61:1). The primitive messianic community understood itself to be participant in this process by virtue of the powerful presence of the Spirit of Christ in its midst. Their commission was to proclaim and anticipate in their life and mission the inbreaking of the new creation, including the realm of nature. The version of the Great Commission in Mark emphasizes this cosmic dimension. "Go into all the world and preach the gospel to the whole creation. . . . And these signs will accompany those who believe: in my name they will cast out demons, they will speak in new tongues; they will pick up serpents, and if they drink any deadly thing, it will not harm them; they will lay their hands on the sick, and they will recover" (Mark 16:15-18.)[3] In spite of the fact that this text has been open to abuse in the hands of some fringe groups in the later history of the church, we do well to recognize the kinship between this expression of the early church's vision of its mission and the Pauline vision that cosmic salvation will result in due time from the reconciling death of Christ.

New Testament Reflections
on the Vision of Cosmic Restoration

Romans 8

In Romans 8:18-25 Paul affirms the participation of the natural universe along with the world of humanity in the benefits of Christ's saving work.[4] According to the biblical vision, the cosmos itself has suffered from the consequences of humanity's sin (Gen. 3:17). Human rebellion not only broke the communion relationship with God, it also introduced disorder and violence in creation. The universe, which was created for humanity, shares in humanity's destiny. Cursed, due to humanity's sin, it shares in the violence and disorder which characterize the human race. As human bodies are destined to glory as a result of Christ's death and resurrection, so also the rest of the natural universe is destined to be redeemed.

This restoration is linked together to humanity's restoration in Christ. Redeemed humanity will live together in peace among themselves and with God in a world which has also been transformed by God's Spirit. Because of the death and resurrection of Christ the suffering and pain in which both humanity and creation participate are no longer the unbearable agony of death, but have become the contractions which announce the birth of the new era.

This can be confidently affirmed precisely because we have the guarantee, God's Spirit. Firstfruits was a term used to describe the first portion of the harvest, regarded both as a first installment and as a pledge of the final delivery of the whole. The Spirit of Christ in the midst of God's people is an anticipation of final salvation, not merely of redeemed humanity (including our bodies), but of restored creation. The Spirit is the guarantee which anticipates not only personal and social salvation, but also cosmic restoration (2 Cor. 5:5). The Spirit of Christ, who is the key to the life of God's people here and now (Rom. 8:2,4,5,9,11,13,14,16), is also source and sign of hope for the future salvation of humanity and the cosmos.

Rather than simply serving as scenario for the drama of human redemption, the physical universe will also be a participant. Through the death and resurrection of Christ, both the children of God and the material world will be freed from the disastrous effects of our "last enemy," death.

Ephesians 1

A principal theme in Ephesians is the uniting of all things in Christ (Eph. 1:9-10). This is true of humanity (which here specifically includes Jews and Gentiles, see Eph. 2:11-22). It is also true of the physical world (1:10) as well as the invisible spiritual world (Eph. 1:10, 20-23; Phil. 2:8-11; Col. 1:19-20).

In Ephesians 1:10 the term translated "to unite" (*anakephalaiosasthai*), means literally "recapitulation." This is the term which the ancient Greeks used to describe the practice of adding a column of numbers and placing the sum at the head of the list. In Christ we see the sum of God's intention for the universe. In addition to setting people at peace with themselves, with others, and with God, Christ creates cosmic peace in the universe of things and people. According to the biblical mentality, humanity is intimately related to the universe in which we are placed. The first Adam was commissioned to exercise dominion in the earth (Gen. 1:28). Jesus Christ, the last Adam, is the head of a new humanity and source of restored harmony and unity, not only on earth, but in the entire universe (1 Cor. 15:45).

In this process of cosmic reconciliation the church is both a demonstration and a proclamation of God's reconciling intention. This mystery is already visible in the church where reconciliation has taken place through the saving work of Christ. This is the community charged with the task of passing the good word of reconciliation along to cosmic as well as earthly powers.

Colossians 1

The hymn which appears in Colossians 1:15-20 contains the fullest Pauline statement of the relationship of the saving work of Christ to cosmic salvation. The hymn is used in this context to set forth the supremacy of Christ whom the church confesses to be Lord and Reconciler in both the community and the cosmos. In two parallel stanzas Christ is confessed to be supreme over the created order, "the first-born of all creation" (1:15-17) and Lord of the new creation, the church, "the first-born from the dead" (1:18-20).

This Christological hymn is set in the context of the salvation history of the people of God. Colossians 1:12-14 contains four basic images, all drawn from the Old Testament. "To share in the inheritance of the saints" (1:12) is an apparent allusion to entrance into the land through the gracious providence of God. "He has delivered us from the dominion of darkness" (1:13) is evidently a reference to the Exodus, where God freed Israel from the enslaving powers of Pharaoh. "In whom we have redemption" (1:14) is an image which finds its biblical foundation in Israel's redemption from the Egyptian slave masters. "In whom we have . . . the forgiveness of sins" (1:14) recalls the "mercy seat" where the merciful God met people with offers of forgiveness. The forgiving God also expected that forgiven people would forgive each other's indebtedness. This is the context in which the new community of the Messiah confesses that Christ is reconciler of the universe as well as their own community.

"He is the image of the invisible God" (Col. 1:15), a remarkable statement, tells us as much about God as it does about Jesus. The God of the Bible is a God who makes himself known. He reveals himself in concrete ways which make him fully recognizable. He manifests himself to his people fundamentally in his saving acts. He is essentially a God who acts.

On the other hand, another view, both ancient and modern, presents God as distant and shrouded in mystery and known to the especially initiated through special means at their disposal. In the first century these were known as Gnostics (intellectuals). They tended to reject the concrete human ways of knowing God. According to their view, God was well nigh unknowable to ordinary people.

On the contrary, the primitive Christians confessed that God can be known, just as they had known Jesus of Nazareth, God's Messiah. This was not because Jesus was otherworldly in his nature. (The Gnostics spoke of a spiritual nature in corporeal form who was definitely less human than other people.) Jesus is the image (eikon) of God. In ancient Greece an icon was a portrait. This metaphor must have communicated powerfully to ordinary first-century Colossian Christians.

But Jesus is also the image of humanity as God intended it to be. A vision of humanity, created in God's image and forgotten since the Fall, has come to us afresh in Jesus, God's Messiah. In effect the Colossian hymn invites us to look at Jesus. He not only shows us what God is like. He also gives us a glimpse of what we were intended to be. Here is humanity as God intended. In his utter faithfulness to God, even to the point of death, Jesus has shown us what restored humanity will be.

"The first-born of all creation" (Col. 1:15) can refer to Christ as preexistent Lord (cf. 1:17). But in its biblical usage, "first-born" is a title of honor (cf. Ex. 4:22; Ps. 89:27). Therefore, rather than merely assigning priority in time to Christ, the principal thrust of the term in this confession surely points to supremacy.

"For in him all things were created" undoubtedly expresses the conviction that Christ is the unifying center for restoration of the harmony in which the universe was created. The reference to "all things . . . in heaven and on earth, visible and invisible . . . thrones or dominions or principalities or authorities" points concretely to the cosmic character of the reconciling work of Christ, including physical and spiritual realms of matter and beings, as well as the social order.

"He is before all things, and in him all things hold together" (Col. 1:17). The preexistence of Christ stated here is most certainly not primarily the result of primitive Christological speculation, but a confession of the foundation of the church's life of faith and mission. It is "a dynamic expression of the unrestricted world dominion of Him to whom the church is subject in its mission to the world" (Reicke, 1968:687). This phrase forms the climax of the first stanza which celebrates the cosmic dimensions of Christ's saving work. The confession that in Christ the entire created order finds meaning and coherence provides a powerful overarching motivation for the mission of the church in the world. In the absence of this dynamic context, these words can become mere speculative theology.

The second stanza of the hymn highlights the reality of the new creation. "He is the head of the body, the church; he is the beginning, the first-born from the dead" (Col. 1:18). In Paul's writings "head" appears to carry the idea of source of life and growth as well source of authority. The first sense appears to have been the Greek understanding of the relationship between the head and the human body (Grassi, 1968:337). As "beginning," Christ is the foundation of the new and redeemed humanity, the church, a new beginning or a new creation (cf. Gal. 6:15; 2 Cor. 5:17). The phrase "first-born from the dead" establishes the parallelism with the first stanza ("first-born of all creation," Col. 1:15). The resurrection of Christ is the firstfruits and guarantee of the resurrection of his followers. Furthermore, the risen Christ is supreme both in the church and in the universe.

"For in him all the fulness of God was pleased to dwell" (Col. 1:19). The church confesses that God can be fully known in Jesus Christ, that the completeness of God's presence and character is manifest in Jesus. Jesus is the fullest expression of God's creating and re-creating intention. This climactic expression is reserved for the second stanza which refers to the church. This is even more startling when we recall that the Christian congregation in Colossae was about seven years old and, numerically, was most probably small—a group which could squeeze together into the house of one of the members. In effect, Paul says to this church, "The saving activity of God is most fully in Christ. This he shares with his body, the church, and it will eventually touch the whole universe." More than a mere statement about divine immanance, this is a reference to the cosmic effect of God's saving power at work in Christ and in the church.

". . . And through him to reconcile to himself all things, whether on earth or in heaven, making peace by the blood of his cross" (Col. 1:20). Reconciliation achieved through the death of Christ leads to a whole new creation. "All things, whether in earth or in heaven," are the objects of God's peacemaking mission in Jesus Christ. The goal of Christ's reconciling work is the establishment of God's *shalom* intention for all of creation—natural and spiritual, visible and invisible, on earth and in heaven.

The immediate implication which Paul draws from this great vision of cosmic reconciliation is that estranged and hostile people have been drawn through Christ into the new community of salvation characterized by holiness and blamelessness (Col. 1:21-22).[5] This is the reconciled and reconciling missionary community charged with proclaiming the gospel of hope to all creation (Col. 1:23). God's reconciling and restoring purpose is cosmic as well as personal and social.

Revelation

According to the New Testament vision, all of creation will ultimately be restored as a result of the death and resurrection of Christ. This vision of restored creation was perceived by the prophets (Isa. 65:17; 66:22). It was picked up by Jesus in his compassionate

ministry of healing and exorcisms. The Marcan version of the great
commission envisions the mission of the messianic community in
cosmic terms. Paul, in his attempt to understand the work of the
Holy Spirit in the life of the community, recognized that all creation
will participate in the benefits of the saving work of Christ (Rom.
8:18-25). The two great Christological hymns which appear in the
letters to the Philippians (2:5-11) and the Colossians (1:15-20)
confess the fact that the death and resurrection of Jesus Christ are
the keys to cosmic reconciliation; thus, "at the name of Jesus every
knee should bow, in heaven and on earth and under the earth, and
every tongue confess that Jesus Christ is Lord, to the glory of God
the Father" (Phil. 2:10-11).[6] In the same vein, Peter recalled the
Isaianic vision: "But according to his promise we wait for new
heavens and a new earth in which righteousness dwells" (2 Pet.
3:13).

So it comes as no surprise to find this vision of cosmic salvation
bursting into full flower in the liturgical visions of the book of
Revelation. Although allusions to this reality are scattered
throughout the book (cf. 5:13-14; 7:15-17; 15:2-4; 17:14; 22:1-5), the
vision which appears in Revelation 21:1-5 is representative of the
biblical view of the eventual fulfillment of God's purpose in creation.
The message of the book of Revelation reaches its climax with this
picture of God's new creation.

> Then I saw a new heaven and a new earth; for the first heaven and
> the first earth had passed away, and the sea was no more. And I saw
> the holy city, new Jerusalem, coming down out of heaven from God,
> prepared as a bride adorned for her husband; and I heard a great
> voice from the throne saying, "Behold, the dwelling of God is with
> men. He will dwell with them, and they shall be his people, and God
> himself will be with them; he will wipe away every tear from their
> eyes, and death shall be no more, neither shall there be mourning nor
> crying nor pain any more, for the former things have passed away."
> And he who sat upon the throne said, "Behold, I make all things
> new." Also he said, "Write this, for these words are trustworthy and
> true" (Rev. 21:1-5).

"The holy city . . . [is] coming down out of heaven from God"
(Rev. 21:2). Restored creation is a gift of God's grace. Ever since
human evil overreached itself in ancient Babel God has been offer-

ing an alternative, "the city ... whose builder and maker is God" (Heb. 11:10). God's alternative to the pride and violence and self-centered pretensions of ancient Babel was a people who would bear the name of God (Gen. 11-12). The same motif recurs in the last book of the Bible. Babylon, the city of humanity, the city characterized by terror and exploitation, by deception and violence, has fallen (Rev. 18-20). God has offered a totally new alternative, a holy city, a new heaven and a new earth characterized by harmony, justice, and peace (Rev. 21-22). The city is holy because its life is oriented by God's presence, and that of the Lamb, in its midst.

"The dwelling place of God is with men. He will dwell with them, and they shall be his people" (Rev. 21:3). This new reality responds, of course, to an ancient prophetic vision in Israel which announced God's intimate presence among people in the new era of salvation (Lev. 26:11-13; Jer. 31:33; Ezek. 37:16-28; Zech. 2:10-11; 8:8). The intimate relationships which prevailed in paradise will be restored (cf. Rev. 7:15-17). The peoples of all the earth will become God's people (Rev. 21:3).

God's "dwelling in the midst" of his people occurs concretely, according to this text, by setting up his tabernacle among his people. This expression is strongly reminiscent of the *shekinah*, the glorious presence of God dwelling in his sanctuary in the midst of his people in the Old Testament (Ex. 29:45-46), as well as the presence of God's Word, Jesus Christ, in the messianic era. In fact, the same word which describes God's presence among humanity in restored creation also refers to Christ's dwelling in the messianic community (John 1:14; cf. Col. 1:19).

"Behold, I make all things new" (Rev. 21:5). This is the only place in the book of Revelation where God speaks directly. Significantly, this is God's declaration of the renewal of creation. The apostolic community found it perfectly fitting to refer to cosmic renewal in terms similar to those used with reference to the saving work of Christ as it was being experienced in the messianic era.[7]

"And the sea was no more" (Rev. 21:1) is a graphic way of saying that the terror and violent destruction wrought by humans, as well as the forces of nature, will be notably absent. In this, of course, the conditions which characterize life in the new creation are exactly opposite to those which were characteristic of Babylon, which had fallen (18:21-24). The Lamb occupies a central place in the new city (22:1,3). "The Lamb will conquer them, for he is Lord of lords and King of kings" (17:14).

Implications for the Church

As we have seen, a notable array of New Testament texts link the restoration of fallen creation directly to the death of Christ, seeing in the cross of Jesus the key to cosmic salvation. Although we must surely confess our inability to comprehend the mystery of the full significance of the death of Christ for the restoration of all things, the compassionate, self-sacrificing love of God in Christ is both the means for restoration of creation as well as the determinate force in restored creation. The way of "the Lamb who was slain" (Rev. 5) is literally God's way to cosmic salvation, as well as personal redemption and social reconciliation.

Several implications can be drawn from the vision which these texts project, particularly the Christological hymns. First, the confession that "Jesus Christ is Lord" has a reference which is both present and future and cosmic, as well as personal and social. This inclusive dimension of Christ's lordship has not always been fully appreciated in the life of the church. Sometimes the confession that Jesus is my (or our) Lord carries a primary reference to our own status, i.e., that we are Christ's. While this may be true, and is certainly important, the principal thrust of the biblical confession is other. Sometimes the emphasis seems to have fallen on the hope that Jesus will, in fact, become Lord in the future. This is also true, but it is not the exclusive thrust of this confession. The confession holds that Jesus of Nazareth, the crucified and risen Messiah, is already Lord—a Lord who will be recognized finally and fully in cosmic redemption. In light of the fundamental relationship between the past and future dimensions of Christ's lordship, we may confidently expect that the way, or means, of lordship (servanthood) will also characterize the future.

Second, the affirmations of the second stanza of the Christological hymn in Colossians 1:15-20 are, if anything, even more daring than those of the first. The first stanza confesses that Jesus Christ is supreme in the universe (1:15). The second declares that he is supreme in the church (1:18). This was particularly daring in the light of the humanly precarious situation which characterized the Colossian congregation—a small group of believers meeting in the houses of brothers and sisters with little more than a half-dozen years of experience in Christ. This amounts to a confession that the true meaning of history and human destiny flows through the church with its new life and proclamation of true hope, even though the restored forms of creation are only modestly present, and in an anticipatory way. What a daring vision of reality! Jesus Christ and his body, the church, constitute the nucleus of restored humanity. The restoration of creation has already begun in a seminal but true sense.

Third, only as the church lives and dies by this confession will it really anticipate the future of cosmic restoration. "Peace made by the blood of his cross" can apparently be made in no other way. Only Jesus Christ, the crucified and the risen, is Lord. The church which continues to confess by both life and death that this is true is the sure evidence that Christ's sacrifice has not been in vain. This is the context in which Paul speaks of completing "what is lacking in Christ's afflictions for the sake of his body" (Phil. 1:24). Until the day of cosmic restoration dawns, the mission of the church will be the way of the cross.

15

Missiological Reflections and Implications

In the preceding chapters we have intentionally bypassed the philosophical and speculative issues related to soteriology. We have not appealed to the logical presuppositions which have so fundamentally characterized systematic doctrinal treatments of the work of Christ. Rather, we have sought to focus on the practical and missiological dimensions of the work of Christ. We have taken this approach for two reasons.

First, we missionaries who share a radical evangelical perspective do not live and witness in isolation. We participate with Christians who represent other traditions and perspectives as we share in God's mission in the world. Most of these traditions have historically made peace with Constantinian presuppositions in the areas of ecclesiology, soteriology, and ethics. This includes taking for granted Anselmian or Abelardian perspectives, depending on one's theological inclinations, through which is focused the work of Christ.

In sharing the gospel with peoples outside the Christendom context of the West, whether they are peoples who are still pre-Christendom or those who have become post-Christendom in their orientation, missionaries have intuitively sometimes felt uncomfortable with some of the presuppositions and consequences of those traditional theories of the atonement which have been elaborated in a Constantinian setting. With this basic uneasiness about these Constantinian presuppositions we have tried, insofar as is possible, to discover the meaning of the work of Christ without the aid of the philosophical and dogmatic grids through which Western Christendom has traditionally approached the question.

But even more importantly, this approach calls for a more radical reading of the biblical witness. This implies a more thoroughgoing and rigorous return to the roots. From a strictly rational or logical perspective, it will appear as an intentionally unsophisticated and naive reading of the biblical text. But insofar as is possible, we must attempt to free ourselves from those philosophical and ideological presuppositions which would condition our conclusions.

This calls for us to recognize *all* of the biblical images which are used in the New Testament for understanding the work of Christ. Rather than centering attention on any one or only a few of these images, the entire gamut of New Testament motifs is required in order to understand the meaning of the work of Christ in a genuinely biblical way. To press this multiplicity of motifs into a neat, logically satisfying system of thought may well be difficult, but the use of all of the images will certainly enrich our understanding of the work of Christ. While some of the images may be judged to be more central than others for one reason or another, even these dare not be interpreted in ways which do violence to the so-called minor images.

This pluralism of motifs calls us to embrace the whole Christ as the source of our salvation, and not merely his death. Catholics and Protestants alike have traditionally held that all that is really necessary for the salvation of humankind is the death of a qualified (pure) victim. However, according to the biblical view, the saving work of Christ includes his ministry, his death, and his resurrection as well as the actualizing power of his Spirit through whom his saving work is made immediate in our experience.

Pluralism of Images: Key to Understanding Atonement

The ways in which the meaning of the work of Christ is communicated in the New Testament appear to correspond to the practical exigencies of the missionary activity of the primitive Christian community. Rather than logical, rationally satisfying definitions of the meaning of the work of Christ, we are confronted in the New Testament with a variety of images. In the foregoing chapters we have reviewed ten of these motifs which served to elucidate the meaning of the saving work of Christ as it had been, in fact, experienced.

Someone has suggested that the wide variety of New Testament images which communicate the meaning of the work of Christ probably reflects the variety of contexts in which the primitive church sought to carry out the missionary mandate of its Lord. We probably cannot document this in detail, but in broad outline—at least this appears to be the case.

We have observed, for example, that the use of the *jusification* motif is reserved overwhelmingly for those situations in which the readers were Jews plagued with a fundamental legalistic misunderstanding of Torah, i.e., Romans and Galatians. The justification motif, furthermore, presupposes a background understanding of the nature of covenant law and Yahweh's righteous saving acts. So Paul would understandably find this image particularly useful in his dealings with the Jews of the diaspora.

The images of *vicarious suffering, sacrifice,* and *expiation* also presuppose a Hebrew background. As we note from the book of Acts and the synoptic Gospels, the vicarious-suffering motif was especially useful in the early Palestinian mission. The widespread use of the sacrifice motif throughout the New Testament surely indicates that the early church found in it a useful image to communicate the meaning of the work of Christ. Indirectly it reminds us that Jews were scattered everywhere in the Greco-Roman world and that the synagogue was a strategic point at which to begin the missionary witness, even in predominantly Gentile contexts. However, the expiation motif is relatively limited in its use, and it was employed only by Paul, John, and the writer of the epistle to the Hebrews, apparently with the readers of Jewish descent in mind.

The *martyr motif* was an especially powerful one in Judaism, particularly from the time of the Servant Songs of Isaiah, through the intertestamental period, and on into the first century. This possibly helps us to understand why this particular metaphor is so widespread in the New Testament and is especially prominent in the Apocalypse, a writing which is notably Jewish in its character.

Archetypal images had a special appeal to Jewish audiences, since the Hebrew concept of humankind was essentially corporate. So we find the various archetypal images widely used for Jewish readers. But these images contained a point of contact also with Gentiles, among whom prototype myths were not uncommon. So Paul also used the motif widely in 1 Corinthians, Romans, Ephesians, and Colossians.

The *redemption-purchase motif* and the *adoption-family image* were strongly rooted in the Hebrew covenant tradition. The first found its roots in the Exodus from Egypt. But the manumission of slaves in the ancient world made this a powerful image for communicating the meaning of the work of Christ to audiences in the Greco-Roman world, particularly to those from the lower strata of society. Likewise, the adoption-family image was meaningful to Jewish hearers. But to an even greater degree it communicated to Gentiles who had until then been outsiders. Through the work of Christ they, too, could come to belong to God's family.

The same can be said for the *reconciliation motif*. The context in which this term is used is predominantly that in which Jew-Gentile relationships are treated. Therefore this motif would speak most powerfully to Gentiles who were outsiders. But it also spoke to Jews, showing them that their supposed status of privilege was, in reality, an empty shell to which they clung in their isolation.

The *conflict-victory-liberation motif* is widely used in the New Testament. This may well be due to the fact that its roots are in the Old Testament and to its evident appeal to Jewish audiences. But for Jews and Gentiles alike in the ancient world, the idea of cosmic conflict was a widely held concept. Through this image the meaning of the work of Christ could be effectively communicated to Gentiles and Jews in the mission of the early church.

The plurality of images which we find in the New Testament to communicate the meaning of the work of Christ can be traced to the diversity of contexts in which the apostolic mission was carried out by the primitive community. The center of the gospel proclamation was the fact of the life, death, and resurrection of Messiah and the subsequent coming upon the apostolic community of his Spirit with astonishing power. The meaning of this saving work of Christ was interpreted variously through images chosen according to the demands of particular missionary contexts. This is contextualization as it was experienced in the New Testament community.

In their missionary communication of the saving work of Christ, the apostolic messengers took as their initial point of departure one of these images. The choice of images used undoubtedly depended largely on the nature of the audience. However, the New Testament carefully guards against the temptation to reductionism. No mature community is left with only one—or even with a few, for that matter—of the images, but is encouraged to grow into a full-orbed vision. The fullness of the gospel message holds *all* of the New Testament motifs together. Traditional credalism has moved in the opposite direction and has tended to reduce the biblical vision to an essential core. However, we do well to resist pressures to systematize the manifold imagery of the New Testament. A pluralism of images is essential for communicating the meaning of the work of Christ in its fullness.

Missiological Implications of Atonement

A number of clear consequences for the life and the mission of the church grow out of this vision for understanding the work of Christ.

1. Divine-human communion is God's intention from creation. The restoration of community is the central thrust of God's saving activity throughout salvation history. A visible confessing community is an indispensable structure of reconciliation. It is essential to the moral obedience, worship, life, and piety of God's people. It is the fundamental base for the authentic proclamation of a missionary message to those without, as well as the context for a valid faith experience for persons who are becoming disciples. The saving work of Christ creates community—brothers and sisters, sons and daughters—who become members of the family of God. By definition, atonement, in its biblical sense, cannot be experienced outside a reconciled community. In biblical perspective reconciliation is personal, spiritual, and social.

The church is called to be a reconciled and reconciling community. The essential elements of this ministry of reconciliation are *witness* (word of reconciliation) and *representation* (an ambassadorial community or colony which faithfully reflects God's kingdom interests among the subjects of another realm and which exceeds the "legitimate" ambassadorial function to the point of inviting citizens in the host kingdom to defect and become citizens of the kingdom represented by the ambassador) (2 Cor. 5:18-20). This vision calls for taking the role of the church in God's mission with all the seriousness with which the New Testament invests it.

2. The gospel may be addressed to the entire range of expressions of the human predicament. Missionaries are free to

respond to the needs of people rather than, for example, needing initially to guide every seeker through the guilt-justification cycle as this has been traditionally understood in Protestantism. Queries such as, "How can I become one of you?" or "How can I be freed from my bondage?" or "Who will help me?" or "Who am I?" are surely just as legitimate as "How can I get rid of my feelings of guilt?"

The way in which the juridical image has come to be understood in Western Christendom (i.e., in terms of retributive Roman law with sin being viewed primarily as guilt) has not proved to be useful in many non-Christendom situations. In fact, in shame-oriented cultures such as Japan's, missionaries have reported truly tragic consequences in the lives of people who needed to submit to the predominant Western Protestant way of understanding the work of Christ, i.e., the justification of the guilty.

The real needs of individuals and people can be responded to at the point of their particular problem, be it shame, lostness, alienation, domination by evil powers, slavery to sin, allegiance to other gods, enmity, rootlessness, or guilt. Taking our cue from the missionary experience of the apostolic community reported in the New Testament, we may take as our point of departure in our gospel witness any one of the many motifs which are used to communicate the meaning of the saving work of Christ. Our common experience is that we all must begin at some particular point. The authenticity of our Christian experience and understanding is not determined by where we begin, but by the fullness of biblical vision into which we are finally enabled to grow.

3. Peace and justice are rooted in the atoning work of Christ and are therefore integral to the gospel. Nonresistance to evildoers is not a denominational distinctive, nor an optional doctrine which is espoused by a few minority groups or heroic individuals throughout Christian history but inapplicable to the Christian church as such. In light of the global perspective which emerges from the multiplicity of motifs for understanding the meaning of the work of Christ, kingdom ethics which radically address the questions of economics, prestige, and power are restored to the sphere of the gospel.

The cross of Christ is the essential organizing center from which the kingdom ethics emerge. All of the elements of kingdom ethics are important, but not all the aspects of kingdom living are equally near to the center of Christ's saving work—the cross. The death of Christ is a model for what Christians do about enemies, evil powers, the temptation to dominate. The crucial problems of economic idolatry, desire for prestige, and the thirst for power all receive God's answer at Calvary: generous self-giving sharing, servanthood, and love of enemies.

In light of the meaning of the work of Christ, evangelists must, by the nature of the gospel they proclaim, be peacemakers; peacemakers, in the interests of the authenticity of the peace they seek, should be evangelists.

4. The full-orbed New Testament vision of the work of Christ leads to the integration of justification and sanctification, of evangelism and nurture. Justification involves both setting in right relationship and making righteous. Men and women are called to discipleship as well as being formed into disciples of Christ. Nominal Christianity, which perpetuates the Constantinian premises and subscribes to the Anselmian satisfaction theory of the atonement in one form or another for its self-understanding, does not generally evangelize in the full New Testament sense of the term. Nor does it nurture. The gospel is not generally presented as a call to kingdom living and mission, and as a rule converts do not eventually move on to this as a result of ongoing nurture. Basic value systems tend to remain the same after conversion as they had been before a response to Christ's call. Only the radically covenanted messianic community in which the work of Christ is known experientially and is understood biblically is able to evangelize and nurture as Jesus and the apostles envisioned.

The false dichotomy between justification and sanctification can be overcome in the power of God's Spirit. We are rescued from the need to recur to artifices such as forensic fictions. On the other hand, the alternative need not be the danger of falling into a pharisaic legalism. When the juridical image is understood in terms of God's saving righteousness, rather than from the perspective of human retributive justice, sanctification becomes the outworking of justification. Biblical law may be seen as the social shape which grace takes among God's covenant people. In this context of kingdom ethics questions dealing with economics, prestige, and power become a part of the agenda from the beginning.

We must, of course, realize that in the traditional polarization between justification and sanctification has often been a genuinely valid pastoral concern to reflect God's patience in forgiving us *before* we get things put together in terms of kingdom values, in accepting us as we are *before* we are utterly righteous. Although we should set aside an unbiblical cleavage between justification and sanctification, we must surely grant that this dichotomy in the church's traditional understanding has often responded to felt needs to allow for growth in Christian discipleship. It seeks to recognize that immaturity can be overlooked as long as one is turned in the right direction. Certainly God can be patient with our imperfections.

This stance of patience becomes especially relevant when we recall the historic tendency of missionaries to impose a certain sanctification discipline imported from North America on first-generation churches in a new situation in which missionaries did not even use the best criteria available for determining what this sanctification should include.

While we must refrain from separating obedience from faith, we must affirm clearly the divine acceptance—and our acceptance— of young, fallible, stumbling beginners. Missionary evangelism must not be allowed to become cultural brainwashing or masked colonialism or an occasion to ask more by way of conversion of new believers than we are willing to ask of brothers and sisters in the sending churches.

5. The dynamic role of the Holy Spirit in effectual justification, as well as in the creation and sustenance of the new humanity, can be recognized as absolutely essential to the work of Christ. That those Christian groups which have understood the work of Christ primarily in the rationally logical terms of the traditional theories of the atonement also appear to assign a relatively minor place to the Spirit's role in this work of grace is probably no coincidence. Traditional theories of the atonement have generally tended to view the saving work of Christ primarily in terms of the activity of the Father and the Son.

However, the role of the Holy Spirit in drawing people to—and changing those within—the kingdom is a fundamental presupposition of the New Testament. The spirit by which we live in the kingdom inaugurated by the work of Christ is the product of the transforming power of the Spirit. Our evangelistic invitation to come to Christ means, of course, a change of allegiance. But it also means a fundamental change of energizing power, from the spirit of this age to the Spirit of Christ. This is surely the implication of the apostolic exhortation to "put on Christ" and all those kingdom values which his dynamic presence inspires.

6. The fact that cosmic renewal in the New Testament is anchored in the death and resurrection of Christ calls us to take this dimension of God's saving intention seriously. Salvation is cosmic as well as personal and social. The saving work of Christ, understood in its full-orbed New Testament sense, leads to a vision of salvation which is holistic. This should lead the church to an understanding of its mission which is similarly full-orbed. Like Jesus and the messianic community, the church is called to continue ministries of healing and liberation from the evil spirits which oppress, as well as other activities which anticipate cosmic restoration. The church's so-called service ministries need to be solidly based, not merely in humanitarian concerns, but in Christ's atonement.

The cosmic scope of the saving work of Christ means that the context of the church's mission is universal. No problem is too big for the saving significance of the gospel, and, for that matter, no concern is too small. However, the cosmic dimensions of salvation must not be allowed to dilute our efforts or diffuse our focus. The saving life, death, and resurrection of Jesus Christ in their full-orbed New Testament significance must furnish the center which orients the church's mission. The debate surrounding proclamation (evangelism) and service (social action) is superseded by the urgency of this agenda. Both deeds and words must be evaluated in light of God's concern for cosmic salvation, expressed most clearly in the life and death and resurrection of Jesus Christ and continued by the power of his Spirit in the life and mission of the church. Only those deeds and words which participate concretely in the spirit of Jesus' saving work will be authentic witness.

Whether God will renew creation by making "all new things" or by making "all things new," whether the process will be cataclysmic or otherwise, is probably not the church's most urgent concern. One thing, however, should be clear. The cross of Christ is at the center of this cosmic redemption. The Lamb who was slain is the lamp in the city of God, the light by which the nations shall walk (Rev. 21:23-24). This correspondence between the method of God's saving action in Christ and its culmination in a creation restored to harmony, peace, and justice is of primary importance. Authentic witnesses have no other choice but to proclaim by deed and word the message of the cross in its full-orbed New Testament significance.

7. To evangelize is to become a martyr, in the New Testament sense of this term, a faithful witness according to the likeness of our Pioneer—the original Faithful Witness. The martyr motif tells us that the mission of the messianic community is, of necessity, cruciform. The death of Christ is God's strategy for saving, and it gives meaning to our witness *(marturia)* which includes both witness and suffering. Seen in this light, the many New Testament references to Christians' suffering and cross bearing take on meaning. The meaning of the Christian's cross bears relationship to the meaning of Christ's cross.

Paul responded to the ancient Corinthian desire for instant salvation with the "scandal" and the "folly" of the message of "Christ crucified" (1 Cor. 1:23). This gospel is not merely an objective fact to be believed. It is a way of life to be accepted rather than instant glory to be enjoyed (1 Cor. 4:8). Christian discipleship means identification with our Representative, the crucified Lord. To have faith in God means to have faith in him who raises the dead (2 Cor. 1:9). This is the faith in which Jesus lived and died. To follow the way of the cross set out in Philippians 2:6-8 is to live by faith, literally. It is to rely totally on God's grace. But just as in the case of Jesus, so also the righteous who live by faith must be prepared to share the humiliation and suffering that it brings. This is the path to glory which Christ has opened up to us. (See Hooker, 1981:82-83.)

The cruciform nature of the mission of the messianic community is especially notable in the life and testimony of its foremost exponent, the apostle Paul. He understood his mission, just as Jesus had, in the light of the Servant Songs of Isaiah (Acts 13:47; 26:18; Gal. 1:15-16a). He also understood his suffering as a continuation of Messiah's (Col. 1:24). For Paul to communicate the message of "Jesus Christ . . . crucified" meant to assume the "weakness" of vicarious suffering (1 Cor. 2:2), to share in Christ's sufferings (2 Cor. 1:5a), and literally to carry "in the body the death of Jesus" (2 Cor.

4:9). To bear authentic witness to the gospel of Jesus Christ is to become the victim in behalf of evildoers. In this way alone is it possible for God's Spirit to awaken the consciences of violent and self-centered people and lead them to reconciliation. Eventually Paul, the missionary, literally gave his life for the reconciliation of the most inveterate enemies of the first century, the Gentiles and the Jews.

To be an emissary of the God who reveals himself most fully in Jesus in a world characterized by the idolatry of violent and self-seeking people is to lay one's life on the line in behalf of the enemy. Ultimately, to be an authentic witness of Jesus Christ is to love in the same way in which God has loved us in Christ.

Notes

Chapter 2

1. This indication, as well as those which follow in this section, is a reference to the book and chapter of Anselm's *Cur Deus Homo?* which is being cited.

2. My dependence on John H. Yoder (1981:206-43) throughout this analysis is hereby acknowledged.

Chater 3

1. I am indebted in this chapter to Thomas Finger (1980:273-86).

2. The following paragraphs are based largely on Joachim Jeremias (1971: 85-96).

3. On the theme of the following paragraphs, see H. Berkhof (1962:30ff.).

4. "Surely he has borne our griefs and carried our sorrows" (Isa. 53:4, RSV) is apparently based on the Septuagint translation which, compared to the Masoretic text, shows the results of spiritualization. One suggestion is that Matthew translated this version directly from the Hebrew text (Bonnard, 1975:183).

5. People who were ill came from everywhere to be cured (Luke 5:15; 6:18) and were healed (Matt. 4:24; 14:4; 19:2). Jesus healed all (Matt. 12:15); many (Mark 3:10): the lame, the maimed, the blind, and the dumb (Matt. 15:30; 21:14) (Beyer, 1965:130).

Chapter 4

1. By vicarious suffering we mean suffering in a representative or substitutionary way for the benefit of others. By extension, "vicarious expiatory suffering" refers to the suffering of one person which effects expiation for the transgression of others. In this and the following sections both of these phrases are used in this way. The phrase "expiatory suffering" is sometimes used without reference to the vicarious dimension. It therefore means that by suffering a person expiates his or her own sins. Vicarious punishment means bearing the punishment which was due another.

2. Among the biblical scholars who take this position are Bruce Vawter (1968:425), Joachim Jeremias (1964:339), C. Leslie Mitton (1962:312), Jerusalem Bible notes on Isaiah 53:7 (Jones, 1966:1228-29), Oscar Cullmann (1962), and the Eastern Fathers in general. Leon Morris (1965:174-75) holds that the reference to Jesus as Lamb of God is intentionally vague. Thus the term is able to sum up all that is suggested in the various sacrifices of the Old Testament rather than tying it to one particular sacrifice, be it the Passover, the sin offering, or any other. Alan Richardson (1958:226) also takes

this position, as do many of the Latin Fathers. Charles Kingsley Barrett (1955:147) and many Western Fathers interpret Lamb of God in terms of the Paschal lamb. C. H. Dodd (1954:228-40) suggests that it is an apocalyptic term for Messiah.

3. This is the opinion of Oscar Cullmann (1962:806) and W. Zimmerli and J. Jeremias (1957).

4. The section which follows depends largely on Millard Lind (1980).

5. The Hebrew term can be translated either as *iniquity* or *guilt*. The practice of distinguishing between the reality of sin and the guilt incurred by the sinner so that guilt can be removed while the reality of sin remains existentially unchanged is something foreign to biblical thought. See A. S. Herbert (1975).

6. The Septuagint version translates the term here rendered "offering of sin" as *lutron* (ransom). Cf. Mark 10:45.

7. This radical biblical understanding of the work of Christ, grounded as it was in the prophetic suffering servant vision which proved to be so powerful in the New Testament community, is really fundamentally different from the modern Western liberal view of Jesus as the ideal man and salvation essentially in terms of a universal family of humankind under the parenthood of God.

8. See note 2 above. John probably has in mind the servant of the Lord of Isaiah 53:7-12, where the servant is compared to the lamb (*amnos* in the Septuagint is the same term used by John here). The fact that Jesus is here presented as the one who "takes away the sin of the world" seems to indicate more dependence on the lamb image of Isaiah 53 than the Passover lamb. Although the Passover lamb served to protect Israel from destruction, the iniquity-bearing function is not originally assigned to it. However, this is precisely the function which the servant of Isaiah 53 is to fulfill (Vawter, 1968:425).

Chapter 5

1. Others include Beginning (*arche*, Col. 1:18) and Firstfruits (*aparche*, 1 Cor. 15:20,23).

2. Son of Man appears 25 times in Matthew, 14 times in Mark, 25 times in Luke, 13 times in John, once in Acts, and three times in quotations from the Septuagint. The novelty of Jesus' use of this title rests in the way in which this honorific title, probably taken from Daniel 7:13, is consistently combined with the vision of the suffering servant of Yahweh (Stanley and Brown, 1968:773).

3. This theme is developed in Chapter 13.

4. Compare the use of *arche* in Colossians 1:18.

5. The Greek term which is here translated "likeness" is *homoioma*, which also appears in Romans 8:3 (cf. Rom. 1:22; 5:14; 6:5).

6. This Pauline view is also reflected in passages such as Romans 5:6,8; 6:3-4,8-10; 2 Corinthians 5:21; and in the many texts which refer to solidarity with Christ in his death and resurrection.

7. "The love of Christ" may be seen as a subjective genitive (Christ's love for us) or as an objective genitive (our love of Christ). While in a sense both of these are true, to be controlled by the love of Christ is to love *like* Christ loved, that is, in a qualitative sense (cf. Jn. 13:34; 1 Jn. 4:9-12; Mt. 5:44-48).

8. *Peri hamartias* is regularly used in the Septuagint to translate the Hebrew *hatta't*, or sin offering.

Chapter 6

1. The first is found in Isaiah 42:21-29 and the third in Isaiah 44:18-25.

2. For the preceding analysis I am endebted to Millard Lind (1980:1-8).

3. The foregoing analysis is based largely on H. Strathmann (1967:474-514).

4. The preceding discussion is based largely on William R. Farmer (1982:154-59).

5. For a fuller treatment of this theme, see the chapter on Justification, pages 187-204.

Chapter 7

1. Originally the Paschal lamb was not really a sacrifice in the sense of being brought to the tabernacle or temple. However, by New Testament times the sacrificial aspect began to infiltrate the concept of the Paschal lamb because the priests had arrogated to themselves the task of slaying the lambs. In light of this development, when early Christians compared Jesus to the Paschal lamb, we can understand why they did not hesitate to use sacrificial language (cf. Brown, 1966:I,62).

2. Robert J. Daly lists a number of additional probable and possible references in the New Testament to the sacrifice of Isaac (1978:50-52).

3. Menno Simons, too, pointed out that the Hebrew word for sin may also mean sin offering.

4. However, see Chapter 11, pages 196, 197 for an alternative translation.

Chapter 8

1. In Luke 18:13 *hilaskomai* is translated "be merciful" (RSV and KJV) and "have mercy" (NIV). In Hebrews 2:17 the same verb is translated "to make expiation" (RSV), "to make reconciliation" (KJV), and "to make atonement" (NIV). In Romans 3:25 *hilasterion* is translated "expiation" (RSV), "propitiation" (KJV), and "sacrifice of atonement" (NIV). In Hebrews 9:5 the same word is translated "mercy seat" (RSV) and KJV) and "the place of atonement" (NIV). In 1 John 2:2; 4:10 *hilasmos* is translated "expiation" (RSV), "propitiation" (KJV), and "atoning sacrifice" (NIV).

2. Among those who favor translating *hilasterion* as "mercy seat" in Romans 3:25 are the Greek Fathers (e.g., Origen), Martin Luther, T. W. Manson, S. Lyonnet, A. Nygren, F. F. Bruce, J. N. Darby, E. K. Simpson, W. D. Davies (see Nygren, 1949:156-58; Bruce 1963:104-107). Concerning the choice of this particular translation Bruce observes that in the Septuagint *hilasterion* takes the meaning of "mercy seat." God, not sinful people, takes the initiative. This was also the case in the Old Testament (cf. Lev. 17:11). Therefore, "on the whole it seems best to take *hilasterion* here as a substantive, alluding to the mercy seat as the place where atonement was made in Old Testament days" (Bruce, 1963:106). On the other hand, C. H. Dodd (1932:54-55) suggests translating *hilasterion* as "a means by which sin is forgiven." Leon Morris (1955;125ff.) suggests "propitiation" as the best translation. C. E. B. Cranfield (1975:214-18) translates the term as "propitiation" or, more properly, "a propitiating sacrifice." See Chapter 11, pages 196, 197 for a suggested translation of the entire passage which includes Romans 3:25.

Chapter 9

1. The redemption-purchase word group appears in the New Testament as follows: *lutroo* (to redeem), Luke 24:21; Titus 2:14; 1 Peter 1:18; *lutron* (ransom), Matthew 20:28; Mark 10:45; *antilutron* (ransom), 1 Timothy 2:6; *lutrosis* (redemption), Luke 1:68; 2:38; Hebrews 9:12; *apolutrosis* (redemption), Luke 21:28; Romans 3:24; 8:23; 1 Corinthians 1:30; Ephesians 1:7, 14; 4:30; Colossians 1:14; Hebrews 9:15; 11:35; *lutrotes* (deliverer), Acts 7:35; *agorazo* (to buy), 1 Corinthians 6:20; 7:23; 2 Peter 2:1; Revelation 5:9; 14:3-4; *exagorazo* (to redeem), Galatians 3:13; 4:5.

2. Isaiah 41:14; 43:1,14; 44:6,22ff.; 47:4; 48:17,20; 49:7,26; 51:10; 52:3,9; 54:5,8; 59:20; 60:16; 62:12; 63:4,9,16.

3. On first impression Isaiah 43:3 might appear to contradict this statement. The text undoubtedly points to the fact that Israel has been chosen over the rest of the nations, here represented by Egypt, Ethiopia, and Seba, in order to serve as mediator of God's love toward all. Ransom need not be understood literally here, since God does not need to pay a price to evil in order to save his people.

4. Note the aorist tense of the verb in Luke 1:68f. (Marshall, 1974:154-55).

5. The verb tense (aorist) in Galatians 3:13 indicates that a purchase has already taken place, leading to the release of the slaves.

6. See Chapter 11, pages 196, 197 for an alternative translation.

7. Redemption is "in Christ" (Rom. 3:24; 1 Cor. 1:30; Eph. 1:7; Col. 1:14). This does not permit us to conceive of redemption as a state which indeed has been established by the work of Christ, but somehow has its own intrinsic life and power apart from Christ's living body so that, in some sense, one can be redeemed without being in personal fellowship with him in his community.

To conceive of redemption as objectively autonomous is not biblical. "In Christ," a concept so fundamental for Paul, is not an autonomous state initiated by an encounter once experienced, nor is it merely an amorphous mystical-spiritual relationship. It is concrete communion relationship in Christ's body. It is belonging to Christ and to one another in the sphere of his lordship. So redemption is literally and concretely at-one-ment achieved through grace (Rom. 3:24).

8. See Chapter 5 for further treatment of the theme of archetypal images.

9. The phrase "blood . . . poured out for many" in Jesus' Supper saying in Matthew 26:28 and Mark 14:24 also shares a common dependence on Isaiah 53 (Marshall, 1974:166,169).

Chapter 10

1. *Katallásso* appears (twice) in Romans 5:10 and in 2 Corinthians 5:18-20. *Katallagé* appears in Romans 5:11; 11:15; 2 Corinthians 5:18-19. *Apokatallásso* occurs in Ephesians 2:16 and Colossians 1:20,22. The reference to the restoration of relationships among humans is explicit in Romans 11:15; 2 Corinthians 5:16-21; Colossians 1:19-22 (cf. Col. 3:10-22; Eph. 2:11-22). It is implicit in Romans 5:10-11, which is set in a context which deals with the incorporation of both Jews and Gentiles into Jesus Christ (Rom. 1:5,6,16,17; 3:21-30; 4:16,18; 5:1-2). That "we have peace with God" (Rom. 5:1) and "access to this grace" (5:2) "through our Lord Jesus Christ" (5:1) is a spiritual reality which is both personal and social. This is clear in Ephesians 2:17-19 where the

same terminology is employed in an explicitly social context.

2. The view of God as *Abba*, which the early church learned from Jesus, was also a concept which was apparently foreign to pagans as well as Jews of the first century.

3. In this we observe a situation similar to that of *hilaskomai*, in which the action corresponds exclusively to God (cf. Chapter 8, pages 150, 152).

4. The Hebrew term *hatta't* can mean either sin or sin offering.

5. Among the versions, in addition to *The Living Bible*, which supply "he is" in their translations are KJV, RSV, and NIV.

Chapter 11

1. "Iniquity" is generally used in the New Testament to translate the term *anomia*.

2. I am indebted in this chapter to Thomas Finger (1980, 142-55).

3. The phrase "as if" is used in the Heidelberg Catechism in connection with the explanation of the meaning of justification. More recently, Joachim Jeremias has written, "If we contend that the believer does not cease to be ungodly and if justification consists merely in a change of God's judgment, then we come dangerously near to the misunderstanding that justification is only an 'as if.' This surely was not Paul's intention" (1965:63).

4. For the following section I am largely indebted to Millard Lind (1980).

5. See Luke Timothy Johnson (1982:77-90), Markus Barth (1969:363-70), and Richard N. Longenecker (1974:142-52) for both exposition and additional bibliography.

6. See pages 152, and 154, note 2, of Chapter 8 for discussion of this translation.

7. "Faithfulness," "loyalty," or "steadfastness" are more accurate translations than "faith" for the Hebrew *emunah*. The idea in Habakkuk is that the righteous shall live by their trusting and obedient faithfulness to the God of the covenant (cf. Taylor, 1956:988-89).

8. Richard Longenecker (1974) shows that this concept enjoys wide biblical support, rather than simply being based on a few isolated texts.

9. The Greek verb *pisteuo* may be translated either "to have faith" or "to believe."

10. Other texts where the reference is apparently to "faith in Christ" include Ephesians 1:15; Colossians 1:4; 2:5.

11. Whenever the phrase, *dia pisteos Iesou Christou* or *ek pisteos Christou* is treated as an objective genitive (faith in Jesus Christ), this redundancy is apparent (cf. Rom. 3:22; Gal. 2:16; 3:22; Phil. 3:9). When, however, the expression is understood as a subjective genitive (faith/faithfulness of Jesus Christ, with reference to Jesus Christ's faithfulness in life to the will of God expressed in the Mosaic law), the dual factors of Christ's perfect faithfulness/obedience and humankind's response of faith are set forth (Longenecker, 1974:147, n. 1). Possibly, the phrases in the following passages can be viewed as subjective genitives, referring to the faith or faithfulness, *of* Jesus Christ: Romans 3:22,26; Galatians 2:16,20; 3:22,26; Philippians 3:9; Ephesians 3:12; 4:13. This may well be the meaning in Romans 1:17; 3:25; and 2 Timothy 3:15 as well.

12. "Paul's doctrine of justification is nothing else but Jesus' message of the God who wants to deal graciously with sinners, expressed in theological terms. Jesus said: 'I came not to call the righteous, but the sinners,' and Paul says: 'The ungodly man is justified.' Jesus says: 'Let the dead bury their dead' (a powerful way of saying that

outside the kingdom one finds nothing but death); Paul says: 'He who is justified by faith will have life.' The vocabulary is different but the content is the same. . . . Paul's understanding of justification in reality understands faithfully Jesus' central message condensed in the first beatitude, 'Blessed are you poor, for yours is the kingdom of God' (Luke 6:20)" (Jeremias, 1965:69-70). That this has been so completely misunderstood in Western Christendom has been due to Paul's Constantinian interpreters, rather than to Paul himself.

Chapter 13

1. Conflict-victory motif (Eph. 1:21; 2:14,16; 6:12), vicarious suffering (2:14,17), archetypal imagery (1:10; 2:1,5, 6,10,15,16; 3:16-17; 4:13,20,24; 5:18), martyr motif (2:14; 3:1), sacrificial imagery (1:7; 2:13; 5:3), expiation motif (2:14,18), redemption-purchase motif (1:7; 4:30), reconciliation (2:16), justification (2:10; 4:24; 6:14), adoption-family image (1:5; 2:19; 5:1).

2. Tamar, Rahab, and Bathsheba, the wife of Uriah the Hittite, were also Gentiles (Matt. 1:3, 5, 6).

3. "Made by hand" is the same term which in the Septuagint is used for idols (Isa. 2:18; 10:11) and in the New Testament for the temple which has been superseded in Christ (Mark 14:58; Acts 7:48; 17:24; Heb. 9:11,24).

4. The term appears only here in the Greek Bible. However, it was widely used in religious polemics among pagans to describe dissidents (e.g., Socrates), by Jews and Christians to describe Gentiles, by Gentiles to describe monotheistic Jews and Christians, and by Christians against heterodox Christians (e.g., Ignatius, *Trall.* X).

5. On the other hand, priority is assigned to God's love and forgiveness over human and interhuman love (Matt. 18:21-35; Rom. 12:1-3; Col. 3:13; 1 John 4:7-12,19-21).

6. Witness to this are the factions represented in the disciple community.

7. Chrysostom held that Christ, who became human in order to die for his own people and for the "many," is the prototype of the unity of all people (Barth, 1974:296).

8. The hymnic elements in Ephesians 2:14-18 are generally recognized. See Barth (1974:261) for additional analysis and bibliography.

9. For the discussion which follows I an indebted to Marcus Barth (1974:298-305).

10. However, this distinction between *kainos* and *neos* is not absolute. First Corinthians 5:7 and Colossians 3:10 reveal that the terms can be used synonymously.

11. The Greek terms make this co-participation especially clear: *sumpolitai, sunarmologoumene,* and *sunoikodomeisthe.*

Chapter 14

1. Other allusions include
1 Corinthians 3:22-23; 15:20-28;
Ephesians 3:9-11; 4:11; Philippians
3:21; Colossians 2:9, Hebrews 2:5-8.

2. These include the conflict-victory-
liberation motif (Col. 1:13; Rom. 8:21),
vicarious suffering (Col. 1:20),
archetypal images (Eph. 1:10; Col.
1:15,18), martyr motif (Rom. 3:17-18;
Phil. 1:24) sacrifice motif (Eph. 1:7; Col.
1:20), expiation (Col. 1:14), redemption-
purchase motif (Eph. 1:7; Col. 1:14;
Rom. 8:23), reconciliation (Col. 1:20),
justification (2 Pet. 3:13), and adoption-
family image (Eph. 1:5; Rom.
8:15,16,19,23).

3. While these verses are not included
in the best of the fourth-century
manuscripts, they do appear in a series
of manuscripts dated from the fifth to
the tenth centuries and were apparently
known to early church leaders from the
second century onward.

4. Whether the term translated "creation" *(ktisis)* refers basically to the world
of nature, or to humanity, or to both, is
open to question. The most obvious interpretation of this passage has understood "creation" as referring to the
world of nature. However, Walter
Gutbrod (Foerster, 1965:1029, note 196)
and Juan Mateos (1977, second edition:
1761) prefer to interpret the term as a
primary reference to humanity. In
2 Corinthians 5:17 and Galatians 6:15,
as well as in this passage, humanity
seems to be in focus. Furthermore, the
context of all three of these passages, the
suffering and witness of God's people,
also points toward a primary interest in
the world of humanity. Of course,
humanity is the central element of the
created universe according to the
biblical vision. Therefore, it seems best
to understand "creation" in these texts
in the inclusive sense.

5. See Chapter 10, page 186.

6. Additional allusions to cosmic redemption are scattered throughout
Paul's Epistles (1 Cor. 3:22-23; 15:20-
28; Eph. 4:10; Phil. 3:22; Col. 2:9) and
in Hebrews 2:5-8.

7. The biblical vision of the relationship between the fallen order and the
new creation is not completely homo-
geneous. One current envisions the total
destruction of the fallen creation (Ps.
102:26; Isa. 51:6; Mark 13:31; Acts
3:21; 1 Pet. 3:7, 10-12) which will be
substituted with new heavens and a new
earth (Rev. 21:1). On the other hand,
the New Testament also speaks of the
"setting free" (Rom. 8:21) and the
regeneration *(paliggenesia)* of creation
(Matt. 19:28). We probably do well to
resist the temptation to press the biblical
evidence into a strictly consistent and
logical system. Imaginal language, by its
very nature, communicates realities
which surpass strictly literal or logical
description. It is probably safe to say
that there will be a relationship between
the reconciliation that God has already
accomplished in Christ and the cosmic
reconciliation of all things. God is "making all things new" rather than "making
all new things."

BIBLIOGRAPHY

Chapter 1

Daly, Robert J.
1978 *The Origins of the Christian Doctrine of Sacrifice*, Philadelphia: Fortress Press.

Minear, Paul
1960 *Images of the Church in the New Testament*, Philadelphia: Fortress Press.

Stendahl, Krister
1976 *Paul Among Jews and Gentiles*, Philadelphia: Fortress Press.

Chapter 2

Anselm of Canterbury
1098 *Cur Deus Homo?*

Aulén, Gustaf
1969 *Christus Victor*, New York: Macmillan.

Dunn, James D. G.
1974 "Paul's Understanding of the Death of Christ," *Reconciliation and Hope: New Testament Essays on Atonement and Eschatology Presented to L. L. Morris on His 60th Birthday*, Robert Banks (ed.), Grand Rapids: Eerdmans.

Hodge, Charles
1898 *Systematic Theology*, New York: Charles Scribner's Sons.

MacIntosh, Douglas Clyde
1927 *Theology as an Empirical Science*, New York: Macmillan.

Rauschenbusch, Walter
1917 *A Theology for the Social Gospel*, New York: Macmillan.

Ritschl, Albrecht
1872 *A Critical History of the Christian Doctrine of Justification and Reconciliation*, Edinburgh: Edmonston and Douglas.
1966 *Justification and Reconciliation*, Clifton, N.J.: Reference Book Publishers.

Schlaff, Philip
1877 *The Creeds of Christendom*, New York: Harper and Brothers Publishers.

Schleiermacher, Friedrich
1928 *The Christian Faith*, Edinburgh: T. & T. Clark.

Sheldon, Charles M.
1937 *In His Steps*, New York: Grosset and Dunlap.

Williams, George Hunston
1957 "The Sacramental Presuppositions of Anselm's *Cur Deus Homo?*," *Church History*, J. H. Nichols and F. A. Norwood (eds.), Vol. XXVI.

Yoder, John H.
1981 *Preface to Theology: Christology and Theological Method*, Elkhart, Ind.: Goshen Biblical Seminary.

Chapter 3

Aulén, Gustaf
1969 *Christus Victor*, New York: Macmillan.

Berkhof, H.
1962 *Christ and the Powers*, John Howard Yoder (tran.), Scottdale, Pa.: Herald Press.

Beyer, Hermann Wolfgang
1965 "*Therapeia*, et al.," *Theological Dictionary of the New Testament*, III, Gerhard Kittel (ed.), Grand Rapids: Eerdmans.

Bonnard, Pierre
1975 *Evangelio según San Mateo*, Madrid: Ediciones Christiandad.

Finger, Thomas
1980 "Christian Theology: An Eschatological Approach," typescript, Lombard, Ill.: Northern Baptist Theological Seminary.

Foerster, Werner
1971 "*Sozo*, et al.," *Theological Dictionary of the New Testament*, VII, Gerhard Friedrich (ed.), Grand Rapids: Eerdmans.

Grundmann, Walter
1964 "*Dunamai*, et al.," *Theological Dictionary of the New Testament*, II, Gerhard Kittel (ed.), Grand Rapids: Eerdmans.

Jeremias, Joachim
1971 *New Testament Theology*, London: SCM Press, Ltd.

Oepke, Albrecht
1965 "*Iaomai*, et al.," *Theological Dictionary of the New Testament*, III, Gerhard Kittel (ed.), Grand Rapids: Eerdmans.

Chapter 4

Barrett, Charles Kingsley
1955 *The Gospel According to St. John: An Introduction with Commentary and Notes on the Greek Text*, London: S.P.C.K.

Cullmann, Oscar
1962 "Death of Christ," *The Interpreter's Dictionary of the Bible*, I, New York: Abingdon Press.

Dodd, Charles Harold
1954 *The Interpretation of the Fourth Gospel*, Cambridge: Cambridge University Press.

Hengel, Martin
1981 *The Atonement: The Origins of the Doctrine in the New Testament*, John Bowden (tran.), Philadelphia: Fortress Press.

Herbert, A. S.
1975 *The Book of the Prophet Isaiah: Chapters 40-66*, , Cambridge: Cambridge University Press.

Jeremias, Joachim
1964 "*Amnos*," *Theological Dictionary of the New Testament*, I, Gerhard Kittel (ed.), Grand Rapids: Eerdmans.

Jones, Alexander (gen. ed.)
1966 "Isaiah," *The Jerusalem Bible*, Garden City, N.Y.: Doubleday.

Lind, Millard
1980 "Monotheism, Power and Justice: A Study of Isaiah 40-55," Elkhart, Ind.: unpublished monograph.

Mitton, C. Leslie
1962 "Atonement," *The Interpreter's Dictionary of the Bible*, I, George A. Buttrick, et al, eds., New York: Abingdon Press.

Morris, Leon
1965 *The Cross in the New Testament,* Grand Rapids: Eerdmans.

Richardson, Alan
1958 *An Introduction to the Theology of the New Testament,* New York: Harper & Row.

Stuhlmueller, Carroll
1968 "Deutero Isaiah," *Jerome Biblical Commentary,* I, Raymond E. Brown, Joseph A. Fitzmyer, Roland E. Murphy (eds.), Englewood Cliffs, N.J.: Prentice-Hall, Inc.

Vawter, Bruce
1968 "The Gospel According to John," *Jerome Biblical Commentary,* II, Raymond E. Brown, Joseph A. Fitzmyer, Roland E. Murphy (eds.), Englewood Cliffs, N.J.: Prentice-Hall, Inc.

Zimmerli, W., and J. Jeremias
1957 *The Servant of God,* Naperville, Ill.: Alec R. Allenson, Inc.

Chapter 5

Barrett, Charles Kingsley
1957 *A Commentary on the Epistle to the Romans,* New York: Harper and Row.
1968 *A Commentary on the First Epistle to the Corinthians,* New York: Harper and Row.
1973 *A Commentary on the Second Epistle to the Corinthians,* New York: Harper and Row.

Bauernfeind, Otto
1972 "*Prodromos,* et al.," *Theological Dictionary of the New Testament,* VIII, Gerhard Friedrich (ed.), Grand Rapids: Eerdmans.

Dunn, James D.G.
1974 "Paul's Understanding of the Death of Jesus," *Reconciliation and Hope: New Testament Essays on Atonement and Eschatology Presented to L. L. Morris on His 60th Birthday,* Robert Banks (ed.), Grand Rapids: Eerdmans.

Hooker, Morna D.
1981 "Interchange and Suffering," *Suffering and Martyrdom in the New Testament,* William Horbury and Brian McNeil (eds.), Cambridge: Cambridge University Press.

Jeremias, Joachim
1964 "*Adam,*" *Theological Dictionary of the New Testament,* I, Gerhard Kittel (ed.), Grand Rapids: Eerdmans.

McKenzie, John L.
1968 "Aspects of Old Testament Thought: Israel—God's Covenant People," *The Jerome Biblical Commentary,* II, Raymond E. Brown, Joseph A. Fitzmyer, and Roland E. Murphy (eds.), Englewood Cliffs, N.J.: Prentice-Hall, Inc.

Michaelis, Wilhelm
1968 "*Prototokos,* et al.," *Theological Dictionary of the New Testament,* VI, Gerhard Kittel (ed.), Grand Rapids: Eerdmans.

Stanley, David M., S.J., and Raymond E. Brown, S.S.
1968 "Aspects of New Testament Thought: Titles of Christ," *The Jerome Biblical Commentary,* II, Raymond E. Brown, Joseph A. Fitzmyer, and Roland E. Murphy (eds.), Englewood Cliffs, N.J.: Prentice-Hall, Inc.

Chapter 6

Farmer, William R.
1982 *Jesus and the Gospel: Tradition, Scripture, and Canon,* Philadelphia: Fortress Press.

Jeremias, Joachim
1965 *The Central Message of the New Testament,* New York: Charles Scribner's Sons.

Lind, Millard
1980 "Monotheism, Power, and Justice: A Study in Isaiah 40-55," Elkhart, Ind.: unpublished monograph.

Strathmann, H.
1967 "*Martus,* et al.," *Theological Dictionary of the New Testament,* IV, Gerhard Kittel (ed.), Grand Rapids: Eerdmans.

Zimmerli, W., and J. Jeremias
1957 *The Servant of God,* Naperville, Ill.: Alec R. Allenson, Inc.

Chapter 7

Brown, Raymond E.
1966 *The Gospel According to John,* I, Garden City, N.Y.: Doubleday.

Daly, Robert J., S. J.
1978 *The Origins of the Christian Doctrine of Sacrifice,* Philadelphia: Fortress Press.

Hengel, Martin
1981 *The Atonement, The Origins of the Doctrine in the New Testament,* John Bowden (trans.), Philadelphia: Fortress Press.

Pries, Edmund
1983 "Violence and the Sacred Scapegoat," Elkhart, Ind.: unpublished monograph.

Schwager, Raymund
1978 *Brauchen wir einen Sündenbock? Gewalt und Erlösung in den biblischen Schriften,* München, Kösel-Verlag.

Chapter 8

Bruce, F. F.
1963 *The Epistle of Paul to the Romans: An Introduction and Commentary,* Grand Rapids: Eerdmans.

Büchsel, Friedrich
1965 "*Hileos,* et al.," *Theological Dictionary of the New Testament,* III, Gerhard Kittel (ed.), Grand Rapids: Eerdmans.

Cranfield, C. E. B.
1975 *A Critical and Exegetical Commentary on the Epistle to the Romans,* Edinburgh: T. and T. Clark, Ltd.

Dodd, C. H.
1932 *The Epistle of Paul to the Romans,* New York: Harper and Brothers.

Fichtner, Johannes
1967 "*Orge,* et al.," *Theological Dictionary of the New Testament,* V, Gerhard Friedrich (ed.), Grand Rapids: Eerdmans.

Finger, Thomas N.
1983 "Why Did Christ Come?" unpublished manuscript, Lombard, Ill.: Northern Baptist Theological Seminary.

Hahn, H. C.
1975 "Anger, wrath: *orge,*" *The New Theological Dictionary of New Testament Theology,* I, Colin Brown (ed.), Exeter Devon, U. K.: The Paternoster Press.

Herrmann, Johannes
1965 *"Hileos,* et al.," *Theological Dictionary of the New Testament,* III, Gerhard Kittel (ed.), Grand Rapids: Eerdmans.

Kleinknecht, Hermann
1967 *"Orge,* et al.," *Theological Dictionary of the New Testament,* V, Gerhard Friedrich (ed.), Grand Rapids: Eerdmans.

McKenzie, John L.
1968 "Aspects of Old Testament Thought: Covenant Love," *Jerome Biblical Commentary,* II, Raymond E. Brown, Joseph A. Fitzmyer, and Roland E. Murphy (eds.), Englewood Cliffs, N.J.: Prentice-Hall, Inc.

Morris, Leon
1955 *The Apostolic Preaching of the Cross,* Grand Rapids: Eerdmans.

Nygren, Anders
1949 *Commentary on Romans,* Carl C. Rasmussen (tran.), Philadelphia: Muhlenberg Press.

Stählin, Gustav
1967 *"Orge,* et al.," *Theological Dictionary of the New Testament,* V, Gerhard Friedrich (ed.), Grand Rapids: Eerdmans.

Chapter 9

Barrett, Charles Kingsley
1968 *A Commentary on the First Epistle to the Corinthians,* New York: Harper and Row.

Büchsel, Friedrich
1964 *"Agorazo,* et al.," *Theological Dictionary of the New Testament,* I, Gerhard Kittel (ed.), Grand Rapids: Eerdmans.
1967 *"Lutron,* et al.," *Theological Dictionary of the New Testament,* IV, Gerhard Kittel (ed.), Grand Rapids: Eerdmans.

Jeremias, Joachim
1967 *"Mouses,* et al.," *Theological Dictionary of the New Testament,* IV, Gerhard Kittel (ed.), Grand Rapids: Eerdmans.

Marshall, I. Howard
1974 "The Development of the Concept of Redemption in the New Testament," *Reconciliation and Hope: New Testament Essays on Atonement and Eschatology Presented to L. L. Morris on His 60th Birthday,* Robert Banks (ed.), Grand Rapids: Eerdmans.

Procksch, Otto
1967 *"Luo,* et al.," *Theological Dictionary of the New Testament,* IV, Gerhard Kittel (ed.), Grand Rapids: Eerdmans.

Chapter 10

Büchsel, Friedrich
1964 *"Allasso,* et al." *Theological Dictionary of the New Testament,* I, Gerhard Kittel (ed.), Grand Rapids: Eerdmans.

Yoder, John H.
1980 "The Apostle's Apology Revisited," *The New Way of Jesus: Essays Presented to Howard Charles,* William Klassen (ed.), Newton, Kan.: Faith and Life Press.

Chapter 11

Barth, Markus
1969 "The Faith of the Messiah," *The Heythrop Journal,* vol. 10, no. 4 (October).
1971 *Justification: Pauline Texts Interpreted in the Light of the Old and New Testaments,* A. M. Woodruff (tran.), Grand Rapids: Eerdmans.

Finger, Thomas
1980 "Christian Theology: An
Eschatological Approach," II,
typescript, Lombard, Ill.:
Northern Baptist Theological
Seminary.

Hodge, Charles
1898 *Systematic Theology*, vol. III,
New York: Charles Scribner's
Sons.

Jeremias, Joachim
1965 *The Central Message of the New
Testament*, New York:
Scribners.

Johnson, Luke Timothy
1982 "Rom. 3:21-26 and the Faith of
Jesus," *The Catholic Biblical
Quarterly*, 44.

Lind, Millard
1980 "Transformation of Justice:
From Moses to Jesus," papers
presented at a Lawbreaking and
Peacemaking Workshop, May 3,
1980, at Camp Assiniboia,
Manitoba.

Longenecker, Richard N.
1974 "The Obedience of Christ in the
Theology of the Early Church,"
*Reconciliation and Hope: New
Testament Essays on Atonement
and Eschatology Presented to L.
L. Morris on His 60th Birthday*,
Robert Banks (ed.), Grand
Rapids: Eerdmans.

Sanday, W., and A. C. Headlam
1902 *Romans: International Critical
Commentary*, New York:
Scribners.

Schrenk, Gottlob
1964 "*Dike*, et al.," *Theological
Dictionary of the New
Testament*, II, Gerhard Kittel
(ed.), Grand Rapids: Eerdmans.

Taylor, Jr., Charles L.
1956 "The Book of Habakkuk," *The
Interpreter's Bible*, VI, New
York: Abingdon.

Chapter 12

Moule, C. F. D.
1962 "Adoption," *Interpreters
Dictionary of the Bible*, I,
George A. Buttrick, et al. (eds.),
New York: Abingdon Press.

Schweizer, Edward
1972 "*Huiothesia*," *Theological
Dictionary of the New
Testament*, VIII, Gerhard
Friedrich (ed.), Grand Rapids:
Eerdmans.

Chapter 13

Barth, Markus
1974 *Ephesians: Introduction,
Translation and Commentary on
Chapter 1-3*, Garden City, N.Y.:
Doubleday and Company, Inc.

Miller, Marlin
1977 "The Gospel of Peace," *Mission
Focus*, VI:1, September.

Tacitus, Cornelius
1956 *The Histories*, Vol. 5, English
translation by Clifford H.
Moore, Cambridge, Mass.:
Harvard University Press.

Yoder, John H.
1982 "The Prophet: Isaiah 2:1-4,
Micah 4:1-4," *Church and
Peace*, IV:1, December.

Chapter 14

Foerster, Werner
1965 *"Ktizo,* et al.*," Theological
   Dictionary of the New
   Testament,* III, Gerhard Kittel
   (ed.), Grand Rapids: Eerdmans.

Grassi, Joseph A.
1968 "Colossians," *Jerome Biblical
   Commentary,* II, Raymond E.
   Brown, Joseph A. Fitzmyer,
   Roland E. Murphy (eds.),
   Englewood Cliffs, N.J.:
   Prentice-Hall, Inc.

Mateos, Juan
1977 *Nueva Biblia Española,* Madrid:
   Ediciones Cristiandad.

Reike, Bo
1968 *"Pro" Theological Dictionary of
   the New Testament,* VI,
   Gerhard Kittel (ed.), Grand
   Rapids: Eerdmans.

Chapter 15

Hooker, Morna D.
1981 "Interchange and Suffering,"
   *Suffering and Martyrdom in the
   New Testament,* William
   Horburg and Brian McNeil
   (eds.), Cambridge: Cambridge
   University Press.

Scripture Index

1 Corinthians

2 Corinthians

Galatians

General Index

Abelard, Peter, 38, 44-50, 243
Adoption, 17, 155, 191
Adoption-family image, 28-29, 205-09,
  222, 245-46, 260, 261
  new covenant development of, 207-
  209
  old covenant understanding of, 206-
  207
Agorazo, et al. (to buy, redeem,
  ransom), 99, 167, 209, 258
Amnos (lamb), 94, 256
Anselm of Canterbury, 35, 38, 40, 42,
  43, 44, 45, 46, 47, 48, 49, 50-64,
  137, 175, 243, 249, 255
Antipsuchon (ransom), 93
Apostolic community; *see* Community
Archegos (leader, pioneer, founder), 21,
  109-10
Archetypal images, 20-22, 101-14, 222,
  245, 258, 260, 261
Arnion, 94
Atonement
  images of, 15-29
  missiological implications of, 247-53
  principal theories of, 37-67
  radical evangelical understanding of,
  35-36
Augustine, 43
Aulén, Gustaf, 38, 39, 40, 41, 42, 43
Beginning, 256
Blood, 149, 223, 258
  significance of, 136-37
Calvin, John, 50
Change in order, 177-79
Christian community; *see* Community
Classical view of atonement, 39-44,
  66, 67
Cleanse, 148, 152
Communion, 155
  divine-human, 247

Community
  apostolic, 13
  Christian, 49, 142
  covenant, 35, 83, 184, 193
  disciple, 260
  faithful, 36
  messianic, 74, 82, 94, 127, 213-29,
    231, 232, 238, 239, 249, 251, 252
  missionary, 237
  new, 224-29
Confession, 133
Conflict-victory-liberation motif, 19, 39-
  44, 66, 71-86, 152, 191, 222, 246,
  260, 261
  New Testament understandings of,
  75-78
  Old Testament origins of, 73-75
Constantinian Christendom, 59, 94
Constantinian presuppositions, 13, 243
Constantinianism, 29-31
Contextualization, 246
Conversion, 83, 155, 183
  economic, 215
Corporate personality, 102, 103
Cosmic redemption, 261
Cosmic renewal, 251
Cosmic restoration, 231-41
  New Testament reflections on the
  vision of, 233-40
Covenant, saving, 183
Covenant partnership, 195-96
Covenant community; *see* Community
Covenant sacrifice; *see* Sacrifice
Cover, 148, 152
Day of Atonement, 133, 136, 143, 148,
  151, 154, 172
Dikaiosune, et al. (righteousness,
  justice), 187-88, 189, 196-97, 204
Disciple community; *see* Community
Discipleship, 49, 63-64, 252
Dramatic theory of atonement, 37-38,
  39-44

THE
AUTHOR

John Driver grew up in Hesston, Kansas, where he graduated from Hesston Academy. He received his B.A. degree from Goshen (Ind.) College in 1950, his B.D. degree from Goshen Biblical Seminary in 1960, and his S.T.M. from Perkins Schools of Theology in Dallas, Texas, in 1967. He and his wife, Bonita Landis, are the parents of three children.

The Drivers have been serving under the auspices of the Mennonite Board of Missions (Elkhart, Ind.) since 1951. Prior to this John had served with the Mennonite Central Committee in Puerto Rico from 1945 to 1948 and Bonita from 1947 to 1948. They have served as missionaries in Puerto Rico from 1951 to 1966; in Uruguay from 1967 to 1974; in Spain from 1975 to 1980 and again during 1983 and 1984; and in Argentina during 1981.

During their assignment in Uruguay, John served as professor of Church History and New Testament at the Seminario Evangelico Menonita de Teología in Montevideo. He also served the seminary until its closing in late 1974 as dean of studies. Drivers returned to Montevideo in March 1985 at the invitation of the Centro de Estudios of the Mennonite Church in Uruguay where John divides his time between teaching and writing.

John Driver is the author of a number of books which have appeared in both Spanish and English. Among these are *Community and Commitment* (Herald Press, 1976) which first appeared as *Comunidad y Compromiso* (Certeza, Buenos Aires, 1974); *Kingdom Citizens* (Herald Press, 1980), published earlier under the title *Militantes para un Mundo Nuevo* (Ediciones Evangélicas Europeas, Barcelona, 1978); *Becoming God's Community* (The Foundation Series for Adults, 1981); *El Evangelio: Mensaje de Paz* (Mostaza, Zaragoza, Spain, 1984).